AN ECONOMIC AND SOCIAL
HISTORY OF EUROPE, 1890–1939

Related Macmillan titles for students:

Michel Beard, *A History of Capitalism 1500–1980*
Paul Dukes, *A History of Europe, 1648–1948: The Arrival, The Rise, The Fall*

Studies in Economic and Social History

B. W. E. Alford, *Depression and Recovery? British Economic Growth, 1918–1939*
Alan S. Milward, *The Economic Effects of the Two World Wars on Britain*
John Lovell, *British Trade Unions, 1875–1933*
J. R. Hay, *The Origins of the Liberal Welfare Reforms, 1906–1914*
R. J. Overy, *The Nazi Economic Recovery, 1932–1938*
P. Fearon, *The Origins and Nature of the Great Slump 1929–1932*
Ian M. Drummond, *The Gold Standard and the International Monetary System, 1900–1939*

An Economic and Social History of Europe, 1890–1939

FRANK B. TIPTON AND ROBERT ALDRICH

University of Sydney

MACMILLAN
EDUCATION

First published 1987

Published by
MACMILLAN EDUCATION LTD
Houndmills, Basingstoke, Hampshire RG21 2XS
and London
Companies and representatives
throughout the world

Typeset by Wessex Typesetters
(Division of The Eastern Press Ltd)
Frome, Somerset

Printed in Hong Kong

British Library Cataloguing in Publication Data
Tipton, Frank B.
An economic and social history of Europe,
1890–1939
1. Europe — History — 1871–1918
2. Europe — History — 20th century
I. Title   II. Aldrich, Robert
940.2'8   D395
ISBN 0–333–36806–1
ISBN 0–333–36807–X Pbk

2002400 2

CONTENTS

ACKNOWLEDGEMENTS

We would like to thank our research assistants, Janell Mills and Ayling Rubin, for their invaluable assistance in finding information, giving suggestions and providing a critical reading of our work; they have been involved in this project from the outset. We would also like to thank Mark Hayne for reading the manuscript and John Roberts of the Department of Geography at the University of Sydney for preparing the maps.

Note: throughout, the number 'billion' is used in the sense of 'thousand million'.

To Lee and Christine, my daughters

FBT

To Rudolph Binion, my teacher and friend

RA

INTRODUCTION

EUROPE 1890–1939

We identify historical epochs both by their successes and by their failures. During the half-century from 1890 to 1939 the accelerating pace of economic and social change led Europe both to the most brilliant of successes and to the most abysmal of failures. A series of events centring on 1890 signalled the beginning of movements which revolutionised the life of Europe and of the world. The Berlin Congress of 1885 opened the age of the 'new imperialism', the apogee of Europe's dominion over the rest of the world. The construction of the all-steel Eiffel Tower in Paris in 1889, the provision of high voltage electrical current over an entire region of western Germany in 1891 and the creation of the modern automobile in Britain in 1895 announced the 'second industrial revolution' and unprecedented economic growth. However, along with political and economic expansion came international insecurity and domestic conflict. In 1891 Russia imposed protective tariffs to create a 'national industry' for self-defence, Germany desperately sought both European allies and overseas acquisitions, and in 1898 Britain and France very nearly went to war over disputed territory in Africa. In 1890 Bismarck's fall allowed German socialists to campaign openly, and they won 35 seats in the Reichstag; in 1894 German landlords and peasants founded the Agrarian League to defend traditional rural values against urban, industrial radicalism. The pattern repeated itself across Europe. In France the struggle between left and right crystallised in 1894 in the debate over the fate of Alfred Dreyfus, an army captain accused of being a spy, which pitted socialists, intellectuals and the cultural avant-garde against the conservative military establishment, the Catholic church and

1

a new extreme right wing including those who condemned Dreyfus simply because he was a Jew.

Once set, the lines of development remained fixed: Europe became more industrial and urban, the working class expanded, the artisan and agricultural classes contracted, all classes organised to press their cases, and all nations struggled to maintain or improve their positions in the world. Economic development continued and Europe still ruled the world, but the tensions of the 1890s remained, and worsened. Europe's successes posed problems with which existing social and political systems could not cope; in 1939 Europe had already suffered one world war and depression, and war threatened again. However, most contemporaries failed to see the underlying continuities of the age through which they lived. For them, a tragic divide separated the 'good years' before 1914 from the upheavals of the 1920s and 1930s. The First World War stood like a barrier between two generations, two societies, two worlds. Before the war each area of activity had seemed to possess an accepted set of rules; diplomacy, politics, economics, society and the family all moved according to laws whose operation appeared both natural and beneficial. After the war the old rules failed to function, the old truths were disputed and in place of the old certainty and unity were only division and chaos. Many agreed with the British foreign minister who said that in 1914 'the lights went out in Europe', and in the darkness it seemed appropriate that Sigmund Freud should stumble upon a previously hidden 'death instinct' which had arisen to overwhelm civilisation.

The trauma of the First World War and the division and despair of the following twenty years were real enough; yet the war was not simply an inexplicable accident, and the problems which emerged in its aftermath had a long history in the prewar years. Beneath the apparently placid surface of prewar society economic and social developments had opened deep divisions. Europeans were divided into national states, and an increasing tension between rival states and alliances marked the entire prewar generation. Closely connected to diplomatic rivalries were glaring disparities in economic development; as the wealthy and powerful states of northwestern Europe jockeyed for pre-eminence, the developing economies along Europe's northern, eastern and southern perimeters began more seriously to compete with them. Emerging social groups demanded in increasingly strident terms that their interests be satisfied. Their common complaint was inadequate political representation, and their protests made domestic harmony as difficult to achieve as international understanding.

In 1914 the entire range of problems with which European society had not dealt came together in the explosion of the First World War. Not surprisingly, when the exhausted survivors emerged four years later, their first concern was to re-establish the prewar order. Their perceptions of the rules they thought had previously governed political, economic and social behaviour led to attempts to reimpose those rules, as in the restoration of the gold standard. Meanwhile governments which did not abide by the rules were quarantined, as in the isolation of the Soviet Union. Nevertheless the problems remained and re-emerged in new and even less tractable forms.

The failure of the leaders of the 1920s and 1930s to solve the problems inherited from the previous generation is implicit in the term by which they are known; they are the 'interwar' generation. Far from solving the problem of national rivalries, the outcome of the First World War left an immense residue of disappointment and bitterness. The related problems of economic development were only further exacerbated by the policies of the 1920s, and then culminated in the crash and worldwide depression of the 1930s. Dissatisfied social groups became increasingly violent in their discontent.

In the absence of solutions to the problems of political, economic and social life, the nations of Europe slipped towards war once again. Those who had appeared on the fringe of European politics became influential and powerful, supported by masses of dissatisfied individuals who demanded change. National competition became vicious racial chauvinism, and anti-Semitism became a programme of extermination. Calls for economic development became demands for mobilisation and conquest, and social discontent expressed itself in assassination and mob violence. The demand for political change was exploited in country after country by unscrupulous leaders aiming for dictatorial power. A substantial unity therefore characterises the period from 1890 to 1939. In diplomacy, economics, social development and political conflict, the thrust of change and the resistance to change remained constant. National competition in Europe and overseas, the need both to foster and to come to terms with the new pace and direction of economic development, social conflict and demands for changes in political systems dominated debate. New solutions were tried, some of which, such as communism and varieties of authoritarianism, differed radically from old approaches. At the end of the 1930s, the clash of ideologies turned into war.

ECONOMIC AND SOCIAL HISTORY

There are many sorts of history. The chronology of kings and presidents, parliaments and elections, battles, wars and treaties – political history – is the best known. But most historians, including political historians, hope to produce something more than mere chronology. Historians aim to explain events as well as describe them, and the urge to explain has resulted in the creation of an expanding array of specialised branches of historical study. Historians are intrigued by problems, and the sudden appearance of a problem often stimulates historical study. The tragedy of the First World War, for instance, created a veritable boom in the field of diplomatic history during the 1920s, as scholars attempted to assess the policies of individuals and nations which led up to the outbreak of the war.

Thus we have economic and social history, two closely allied fields in a broad spectrum of historical research. Both are problem-oriented, stimulated by the desire to understand the process of economic development and to understand the ways in which societies function. Economic history is the history of the production and exchange of goods and services and the relations among the producers and consumers of them. Economic history may be the history of technology, transportation, money and finance, but it is also the history of the entrepreneurs who invent, market and profit from goods and services, the workers in farms, factories and offices who produce them and the consumers who buy and use them. Economic historians are interested in the development and adoption of new ways of making and distributing goods and services, and in the cycles of economic activity connected with new investments. They are also concerned with the operation of the institutions which regulate the markets, from governments to individual enterprises, and with the changing theories which have attempted to explain the operation of the economy.

For economic historians the period from 1890 to 1939 is one of particular interest. In 1890 the European and world economies still lay under the domination of the wealthy industrial centre of northwestern Europe – actually a few small regions in Britain, the Low Countries, western Germany and northern France which exchanged manufactured products for food and raw materials produced elsewhere. The 'second industrial revolution' in steel, machine tools, chemicals and electricity shifted the balance among the old leaders and spread industrial development among the 'periphery' of nations to the north, east and south. The First World War, despite its destructive impact, accelerated this development; at the same time the Russian Revolution isolated the Soviet Union and set the Soviet economy on a distinctive path. The war did nothing to alleviate the problems of economic development, and the failure of the leaders and institutions inherited from before 1914 to cope effectively with those problems resulted in the collapse of 1929 and the depression of the 1930s. At the same time, the expansion of European empires meant that the 'European' economy now embraced much of Africa, Asia and Latin America, and the development of industrial centres outside Europe meant that Europe's well-being depended in part on conditions in the two emerging industrial giants, the United States and Japan. An understanding of European development therefore increasingly demanded an appreciation of changes along the European perimeter, and of Europe's relations with the rest of the world.

Social history has much the same domain as economic

history, but focuses on the people rather than the things. Social history is concerned with humans in all their activities – from birth to death, at work and at play, individually and collectively. Social historians investigate movements of population, the development of social classes and the relations among them, and the way in which material culture affects these relationships. The struggles of various social groups to obtain economic and political rights – workers, women, ethnic groups and cultural minorities – have also interested social historians. The institutions governing social relationships, from churches and national labour unions to individual families, make up another field of social historical research, as does the history of social theory.

For social historians the period from 1890 to 1939 is a rich one. In 1890 most Europeans still identified themselves as belonging to the social class into which they had been born; 50 years later this was no longer true. The increasing proportion of the population living in an urban environment, the rising numbers of industrial, office and clerical workers, and the concomitant decline of the artisan and peasant classes, had created a society in which recruitment into a social group was determined more by individual choice and formal training than by birth. Workers organised themselves to demand improvements in their economic conditions, but in addition they created a broad range of institutions catering to their social and cultural aspirations. Previously quiescent groups, such as female suffragettes in western Europe and national minorities in southeastern Europe, began to demand recognition. The war accelerated social change by uprooting peasants from their traditional environments, pressing increased numbers of women into the labour market and forcing governments to intervene in economic and social relations. The Russian Revolution eventually resulted in the complete restructuring of the society of Europe's largest state. In western and central Europe the struggle between competing social groups paved the way for such events as the Fascist seizure of power in Italy in 1922 and the general strike in Britain in 1926. The onset of the depression increased the tensions arising from continued social development, and the groups who had suffered most provided critical support for the rise of authoritarian regimes.

The relationship between economic and social history is obvious; social relations are, to a great extent, dependent on economic relations, and in return social groups organise themselves to improve their economic positions. Neither sphere is divorced from other areas – science, culture and collective attitudes not only influence but can create new economic and social relations. In particular, economic and social history cannot be understood without reference to the political structures existing in a particular place and time. One of the most important developments of the period from 1890 to 1939 was the increasingly close connections among economic, social and political events. Though at times politicians seemed prisoners of economic and social developments beyond their comprehension, European governments gradually groped their way towards more extensive and effective intervention in economic and social life. Politics became the sphere where social and economic issues overlapped.

In 1890 throughout Europe political power remained firmly in the hands of members of an elite who considered it their hereditary right to rule. By 1939 all governments claimed to rule in the name of and with the participation of the majority of the population, and even where the claim was patently false this new basis of legitimacy limited the new rulers' options. Before the First World War the position of the political elite was challenged by workers, women and national minorities, and in northern and western Europe substantial progress was made in broadening political participation. Here again the war accelerated change, for the extraordinary powers assumed by governments required the consent and collaboration of their subjects. During the interwar years the franchise further broadened; however, though labour governments came to power in Scandinavia, Britain, France and Spain, a broad spectrum of public opinion still considered them essentially illegitimate, and this was important in the manipulation of parliamentary politics by authoritarian movements in their rise to power. The attempts by all governments to alleviate the economic and social distress of the depression recalled the economic development programmes of the 1890s and the experiences of the First World War but the fundamental division between political systems which accepted the modern world and those which rejected it remained. By the 1930s, it was obvious that the attempt to restore the pre-1914 order had failed, but the questions at issue were what new order should be instituted and how far each nation was prepared to go to defend its choice.

ECONOMIC DEVELOPMENT IN EUROPE BEFORE THE FIRST WORLD WAR

THE SECOND INDUSTRIAL REVOLUTION

In economics as elsewhere, to refer to the 'good years' before the First World War is to conjure up a nostalgic picture of a time when things were somehow better and simpler. The generation living before the war did see themselves as especially fortunate compared to those who had gone before. Optimism might be tinged with foreboding; even the most sanguine were well aware that not everyone benefited equally from economic advance. In retrospect both optimism and foreboding proved justified, for the complex promises and problems of twentieth-century development had clearly emerged well before the war appeared to drop a curtain on one world and raise it on another.

Prices rose throughout the period from 1896 to 1914, and more rapidly at the end than at the beginning. Two factors were at work. Firstly, production of such basic agricultural commodities as wheat, wool and cotton rose somewhat less rapidly than previously, and their prices therefore tended to rise. In addition large numbers of Europeans were shifting towards higher quality foods such as meat, dairy products, fruits and vegetables, adding a further upward pressure to prices. Secondly, the supply of money increased relatively rapidly. Gold began to flow from the new fields in South Africa and Alaska, expanding the base of the world's money supply. Additionally, central banks in all countries expanded the supplies of both currency and bank credit more rapidly than they had in the previous generation.

Increases in prices and credit made large-scale, long-term investment seem particularly attractive, and urban construction and heavy industry accordingly benefited. The international construction boom responded not only to the need for housing of the millions who flowed from the countryside to the cities, but also to the need to supply the enlarged cities with power, lighting, water and transportation. Industrial investment was distinguished by the introduction of new technologies and their rapid spread, particularly in underdeveloped regions of Europe. In western Europe, old leading sectors such as textiles and railway construction slowed, but were overtaken by new leaders, notably steel, machinery, chemicals and electricity.

Investment in steel especially marked the years of the second industrial revolution. Perhaps the best example of the new uses to which steel could be put was the Eiffel Tower in Paris, built for the World Exposition of 1889. Three hundred metres tall, twice as high as the pyramid of Cheops, the tower was constructed of 8.5 million kilograms of steel. Although it was not immediately popular, it quickly became the symbol of Paris, and a symbol, too, of this new age of steel. Hard and strong, yet elastic and plastic, steel combined the best features of pure wrought iron and high-carbon pig iron. It could therefore be used to make lighter, smaller, more rigid, and therefore faster and more precise machines, and also to construct structures – ships, buildings, bridges – of previously inconceivable size. Steel's high cost had always precluded such uses, but in the 1880s the Bessemer converter and the Siemens-Martin furnace reduced prices dramatically. Developments during the 1890s increased the scale of the furnaces and mechanised the loading and handling processes. The lower price and higher quality of the output of the new integrated steel plants, given high and increasing demand, led to startling increases in output. Between 1890 and 1910 British output doubled, but French and German production rose nearly sixfold, and that of Belgium and Luxembourg nearly eightfold. The countries of the old industrial core continued to dominate production in absolute terms, but the countries of the perimeter increased their output rapidly as well: threefold in Sweden, fourfold in Austria-Hungary, sixfold in Spain, sevenfold in Italy, and tenfold in Russia.

Steel's toughness and durability, while making it desirable, also made it correspondingly difficult to work. At the same time, surging demand for accurately-made machine parts – for high-velocity firearms, sewing machines, cash registers, typewriters, complex farm machinery, bicycles and motors, resulted in a matching surge in demand for more rapid and accurate machine tools, and in revolutions in both measurement and techniques of metal working. The development in the 1880s and 1890s of more precise measurement and new techniques allowed more accurate work, permitting greater uniformity of parts. Machine tools could operate more easily, yet at greater speeds. Steel parts produced by the new generation of machine tools made possible the creation of the internal combustion engine, the automobile and the aeroplane.

The development of the internal combustion engine and the automobile dramatically illustrate the process of technological innovation during this period. The internal combustion engine required a precise balancing of the fuel (petrol was not favoured at first because most experts considered it too dangerous), fuel-air mix, compression, ignition and exhaust. Daimler's enclosed crankcase and flywheels, automatically timed fuel inlet and exhaust valves, and water jacket for cooling had by 1889 produced the outlines of an engine which would run at high speeds and could therefore be much smaller and lighter than earlier versions with no loss of power. A new carburettor, invented by Maybach in 1893, delivered a regulated fuel-air mix to the cylinder automatically, eliminating one of the weaknesses of Daimler's design. Meanwhile in 1885 Benz had introduced ignition via an electric spark rather than an open flame or hot tube, improving the safety and reliability of ignition, and Bosch's high-tension magneto generator of 1902 provided the spark rapidly enough to take advantage of the higher speeds at which the new engines could run.

Daimler, Benz and others, including those favouring steam or electric motors, were looking for a light but powerful engine specifically to provide the motive force for a self-propelled vehicle. Both the Frenchman Levassor (1891) and the Englishman Lanchester (1895) had produced automobile designs free of 'carriage' features, and the German Mercedes of 1901 was a 'car' in the pattern which became standard – the beginning of the automobile age. By 1913 yearly automobile production in Britain, Germany and France ranged from 25,000 to nearly 50,000. However, in the meantime the United States had overtaken Europe. Ford alone produced nearly 200,000 model T's in 1913, and already 1.3 million automobiles were registered in the United States, three times the European total. Europe equalled America in design and enthusiasm for the new machine, but lacked America's mass market. American income per capita was some 50 per cent greater than British and probably twice French or German income, and was more equally distributed. Ford and the other large firms which survived the American industry's drastic winnowing process primarily produced low-priced automobiles intended for that mass market, in particular by introducing moving production lines to speed production and cut costs. European prices remained higher than American, and most European automobiles were designed to be driven by a chauffeur rather than by the owner – a luxury product, certainly, and one whose direct social impact was as yet severely limited. Yet the automobile's impact on Europe's consciousness was profound. The first Futurist manifesto appeared after a late-night, impromptu automobile race, and the image of the automobile assembly line crystallised as the vision of man's technological, urban-industrial future even before the first European assembly lines came into being.

The aeroplane grew out of the automobile. The Wright brothers had piloted a prototype aeroplane in America in 1903, and the first European powered flight took place in 1906; in 1909 the Frenchman Blériot flew across the English Channel, becoming the first of the heroic aviators. Rapid improvement in aeroplane design followed, especially in France, and European design was well ahead of the United States by the outbreak of the war. Regular air flights would come only much later, but these early developments inaugurated another means of mobility and heralded a further integration of nations and economies.

At the same time, the chemical industry also progressed.

Among the heavy chemicals, the shift in the production of soda from the Leblanc to the Solvay process reduced fuel costs by half, benefiting a wide range of industries and textile manufacturing in particular. Within the light chemical industries, medicine received an important impetus from the creation of synthetic anaesthetics, antiseptics, disinfectants and drugs. Novocaine, a synthetic local anaesthetic, was first produced in 1897, and the carbolic acid extracted from coal tar soon became ubiquitous in doctor's offices and hospitals. Similarly the rare natural substances which had traditionally served as the raw materials for essential oils and perfumes began to give way to synthetic replacements, placing still another luxury product within reach of the mass of potential consumers. New and improved processes also appeared in the petro-chemical and coal tar derivative industries. The advent of the automobile greatly increased demand for the distillate petrol. Crude coal tar formed the surface of the roads which the new automobiles began to travel; distilled, coal tar yielded more than a dozen basic compounds and hundreds of final products, the most notable of which were synthetic dyes.

Most spectacularly, the chemical industry began to create products which had no equivalent in nature. The polymer compounds or plastics were a well-established branch of industrial chemistry by the turn of the century. Cellulose nitrate had been used since the 1870s in the development of a wide range of consumer products ranging from shirt collars to billiard balls, and its use as photographic film in the 1890s provided the technological basis for the motion picture industry. Films and fibres were formed from cellulose acetates beginning in 1894, and were applied to aircraft wings and formed into textile fibres such as acetate rayon.

The theory and techniques of the heavy electrical industry were also largely complete by the late 1890s. The high-speed steam turbine and the matching high-speed dynamo dated from 1884, and the distribution of current over long distances from a central power source demonstrated its practicality in 1891, when a 30,000-volt current was delivered from a power station at Lauffen, on the upper Neckar, to Frankfurt-am-Main, 179 kilometres away. Electric streetcars replaced horse-drawn omnibuses, and the first steps were taken to electrify the railway as well. The gaslight era ended, and streets, houses and factories were lit with electric lamps and buildings cooled with electric fans. By 1900, not only could electricity illuminate the factory, but separate electric (or internal combustion) motors had been supplied for each machine, increasing the flexibility of planning, efficiency and safety. Some new machines, such as mobile overhead cranes, would have been difficult to realise in the absence of electricity. Without cheap electric power, moreover, a number of crucial electrochemical processes would have remained only theoretical possibilities.

The new technologies making up the second industrial revolution worked to increase the size of industrial firms and therefore of their financial requirements. Only large firms could afford the research laboratories which became increasingly necessary. The new technologies all required relatively large capital investments and long-term planning, and specialised skills such as finance and accounting began to emerge within the hierarchy of management alongside production and research. They were joined by advertising and market research in the final years before the war, as firms began to seek ways of ensuring the profitable disposal of the products of their research and production decisions.

Ownership of large joint-stock corporations was necessarily diffuse, compared to the owner-managed firms of previous generations. Control of the firm thus passed from the formal owners, the holders of the firm's stock, to salaried managers – the 'managerial revolution'. As management skills became specialised, large firms came to be controlled through specialised divisions, often themselves of substantial size and operated as independent firms. The need for control and coordination among the branches of such firms led to the employment of increasing numbers of supervisors and record-keepers, an entirely new class of salaried 'white collar' workers recruited on the basis of formal education rather than experience. These developments changed not only the pattern of authority relations within firms but also the career patterns and expectations of individuals and had a profound impact on middle-class family life as well.

The increased size of industrial firms and the dominance of joint-stock organisation also affected the banking system. Whereas bankers had traditionally relied on their own family capital and catered to a solid, select class of customers, the new banks were themselves large impersonal corporations issuing stock to anonymous investors, absorbing deposits through extensive branch networks and investing both their own capital and their deposits. The old family banking firms had kept the bulk of their business in commercial operations which turned over every three to six months and therefore involved little risk, or in government bonds backed by the security of the state's powers of taxation. Now banks moved to invest directly in new industrial undertakings. Some observers saw this alliance of banking and industry as a new stage in economic development – 'finance capitalism'.

Large firms with heavy fixed capital investment required stability above all else, and firms throughout Europe therefore sought stable sources of labour and raw materials, as well as assured access to markets at profitable prices. Often the search took the form of attempts to influence government policy regarding labour organisations, tariffs and colonial expansion. Equally common was the tendency for large firms to collude with one another to monopolise and divide existing markets among themselves. The formation of national and international trusts and cartels became one of the most characteristic features of industrial organisation during this generation, though combination took different forms, depending on the institutional environment in each country. To the extent that their market dominance and protective tariffs permitted, cartels charged monopoly prices and earned excess profits on their domestic sales. In addition, cartels often dumped excess production in foreign markets at low prices, but many viewed such cutthroat competition as wasteful and potentially dangerous because of the danger of retaliation. Accordingly international cartels were formed to protect members' domestic markets and give them exclusive rights in certain export markets. As many as 80 such agreements may have been operating in 1914.

PROBLEMS OF LARGE-SCALE INDUSTRIAL DEVELOPMENT IN WESTERN EUROPE

Both the promises and the problems of the second industrial revolution displayed themselves most obviously in the countries of the western European industrial core. The old leading sectors slowed. Domestic markets for textiles approached saturation and exports suffered from tariffs and increased competition. The railway system neared completion, increasing by only 10 per cent from 1900 to 1910. Coal's position as the world's chief source of energy began to erode, as shipowners and navies substituted fuel oil for coal and the electrification of the railways began. Yet new sectors arose to replace the old – output and employment in the metals and machinery industries outdistanced textiles, clothing and food processing.

Rapid change strained the economic and social fabric of even the most 'advanced' and 'modern' countries and regions. Because of their wide applicability, the new techniques threatened all existing firms, both large and small, with new competition. Old industrial districts, dependent on declining resource bases, outmoded technologies and stagnant industries, found their prospects suddenly blighted. The explosive growth of new industries drew massive numbers of workers from increasingly distant sources, straining social services in the expanding urban and industrial districts, but also draining resources and reducing the possibilities for development in rural areas. The resulting social conflict and political protest dominated public life. Not only social groups and regions, but also entire nations could feel themselves threatened by new competition, and economic development therefore contributed to the increasing polarisation and bitterness which marked international relations.

Britain

Britain was the traditional leader in both industrial development and international trade. Agriculture employed only a small fraction of the population, and Britain relied on imported foodstuffs. But now British industry lost ground to new competitors. Though industrial production, national product and per capita product all increased, all increased more slowly after 1896 than they had during the previous generation. In the cotton industry and coal mining, the classic fields of the first industrial revolution, Britain retained a large lead in absolute terms but found that other countries' output was growing faster. In steel, chemicals and electricity, the key areas of the second industrial revolution, British output rose very rapidly, but again significantly less rapidly than in other countries. Two sets of factors lay behind this shift in economic leadership away from Britain and towards new competitors. Firstly, the natural resources available to British industry were relatively unfavourable to the newer and more rapidly expanding branches of industry. Secondly, however, in the late nineteenth century traditional British energy and inventiveness seemed to suffer a decline.

The supply of natural resources affected productivity directly, and in addition had important indirect effects through its influence on the choice of techniques. In the case of coal, though British supplies were abundant, they were relatively expensive to mine and relatively inefficient for smelting metal ores. As for iron ore, British supplies were being exhausted, forcing iron and steel producers to rely on more expensive imports. Britain also lacked adequate supplies of many of the key raw materials of the new chemical industry. Britain controlled by far the largest mass of capital of any nation at the end of the nineteenth century, the result of an early lead in industrialisation and a unique commercial position. However, precisely because of that early lead, much of Britain's capital was sunk in old industries such as textiles, and in outmoded plants in unfavourable locations. The high cost of land in the crowded industrial centres limited the ability of British firms in expanding industries to extend their plants. In addition, capital may have been relatively less easy to obtain than formerly. The share of investment in the national product was declining, while the share of foreign investment in total capital formation was very high. Britain's domestic capital stock therefore grew slowly. This meant that the British economy had little opportunity to update itself.

British banking had grown up in the late eighteenth and

early nineteenth centuries and remained bound by the habits of earlier periods. London had been and remained the world's most important centre for international finance; however, British industry depended on regional capital markets in Manchester, Birmingham, Newcastle and elsewhere. British industry in general could not tap the London capital market because the large London bankers preferred overseas commerce, public utilities and government securities. The typical British banker's passive waiting for clients and suspicion of new fields also probably affected the pattern of industrial concentration and expansion. With their domestic market unprotected from foreign competition and by Continental standards only loosely connected to the banking system, British firms pursued market dominance through creation of monopolies and also exploited their privileged position in the country's possessions overseas.

Population movements may have contributed to the deceleration of British growth. The birth rate had been declining for some time, but to worried observers it seemed to be dropping more rapidly than before. Emigration meanwhile had been increasing. The reduction in the potential labour force increased costs directly by reducing the supply of labour, and indirectly by raising the average age of the available workers. The loss of young adults through emigration, at the age when they would be establishing households and bearing children, also reduced the size of the British domestic market, and British manufacturers were therefore correspondingly less willing and able to introduce new techniques of mass production. The quality of the British labour force also slowed technological change. Alienated by recurrent unemployment and static or declining real wages, workers resisted attempts to increase their traditional pace of work or introduce new techniques. The relatively strong unions, divided along lines of craft rather than by firm or industry, likewise rigidly insisted on maintaining existing jobs and labour practices. Many potentially promising technologies either could not be adopted, or if adopted were less profitable than expected.

Manufacturers therefore were justifiably hesitant to press for a rapid changeover to the latest innovation. Nevertheless, the British domestic market was wide and deep, the Empire provided further opportunities, and the British worker was worth his wage, being more productive than any European competitor. Yet Britain remained slow to move into new fields and slow to adopt new techniques in older areas. The reorganisation of enterprises to integrate production processes often seemed beyond British manufacturers. Government and industry both failed to support scientific and technical research, and British inventions tended to be exploited more fully elsewhere, as in the cases of coal tar derivatives and steel production.

Germany

While Britain seemed to be resting on its laurels, there was no shortage of new and increasingly formidable competitors. The rise of Germany seemed the most spectacular and the most threatening to British observers. The unification of Germany in 1871 created a potential economic giant. German industrial production, national product and per capita product all rose more rapidly beginning in the 1890s than before, and all rose substantially faster than the British indices. The German textile and coal industries grew more rapidly than their British counterparts, and in the new steel, electrical, and chemical industries German growth was spectacular.

Explanations for Germany's surge toward industrial leadership parallel those for Britain's relative decline. Germany benefited from an excellent resource endowment. German output of iron ore increased rapidly and imports only rose to significant levels after 1905. In addition, Germany's domestic supplies of iron ore, especially in the Lorraine district taken from France in 1871, had proved ideally suited to the new steel-smelting techniques. The German chemical industry also profited from the unique potash deposits centred around Stassfurt, in Hannover and in Alsace, a region also taken from France in 1871. Abundant supplies of salt, sulphur and brown coal completed the list of critical raw materials for both the heavy and light chemical industries.

Germany took advantage of these natural resources. Scientific and technical research enjoyed extensive government support, and in addition large industrial firms began to establish independent research departments. By 1900 the largest of these employed as many as 200 workers, and in several new fields this system had given Germany a virtual monopoly of new knowledge in the years before the First World War. The AEG and Siemens-Schuckert combines dominated world trade in heavy electrical machinery; of the world's nine largest plants producing chemical dyes in 1914, six were German.

Population movements also favoured German economic development. Though the average birth rate was declining, it remained higher than in Britain and much higher than in France. German emigration overseas, having peaked in the 1880s, virtually ceased after 1895. In the growing urban and industrial districts, the demand for housing and services worked to reinforce the boom. Workers' organisations, though bitterly opposed to the existing social and political order, made little headway against large firms. Employers in large-scale industry relied on subsidised housing and other paternalistic welfare measures on the one hand, and the state's coercive powers on the other, to prevent any interference by workers.

Capital was readily available to German industry. As German national income rose so did the proportion devoted to investment. Germany also devoted a large share of total investment to domestic capital formation. German foreign investment, though rising in absolute terms, declined relative to total capital formation. The rapid growth of the German capital stock meant that a high percentage of plants in operation employed the most advanced technology available, and in the relatively open spaces to the north of the Ruhr into which industry was expanding, large-scale, efficient layout and integration of technical processes could be relatively easily achieved.

In addition, German banking institutions were well suited to mobilise capital. German banks had grown up with German industry since the mid-nineteenth century, investing both their deposits and their own capital, and were known for their active search for investment opportunities. The large size of the German banks and their willingness to form syndicates minimised the risk of large investments. German bankers took justifiable pride in their accomplishments. An official of the Dresdener Bank boasted in 1908: 'In Germany our banks are largely responsible for the development of the empire. To them, more than to any other agency, may be credited the splendid results thus far achieved'. Banks placed representatives on the boards of directors of firms with which they were involved – the Deutsche Bank held seats on 161 corporate boards in 1913 – and encouraged the formation of cartels, with their emphasis on the preservation of existing market shares and elimination of competition. A court decision of 1897 held cartel contracts to be legally binding, and Germany accordingly became the home of formal agreements among independent firms fixing production quotas, prices, market shares and planned expansion. From some 200 in 1890, German cartels increased to nearly 400 in 1906 and 600 in 1911. Protected by higher tariffs adopted in 1894 and 1902, they charged high and sometimes discriminatory prices to their domestic customers and attempted to dump excess production on the world market.

Rapid economic development imposed strains on German society which would later cause its collapse in the crisis of war and defeat. Large segments of industry had been left behind in an essentially artisan state, pressed severely but not yet destroyed by factory competition. Further, though the industrial and commercial sector as a whole had grown rapidly, agriculture was still relatively large, employing 35 per cent of the labour force in 1907. Industry was concentrated in a few favoured regions, especially Berlin and the Ruhr, into which large numbers of persons had migrated. Rural agricultural regions suffered from the loss of population, relatively low income and increased international competition. The regions suffering the most, and those loudest in their complaints, were the eastern provinces of Prussia, dominated by the same class of landowning aristocrats, the Junkers, who controlled the imperial government. The threat to their traditional economic position led them to demand tariffs and other forms of protection, and led them to adopt an ideology based on rejection of industrialisation, urbanisation, democratic government and the modern world as such.

France

The economic development of France often appeared paradoxical, but in retrospect can be seen to have been in important respects typical of the age of the second industrial revolution. Aggregate figures moved at the deliberate pace established decades earlier, but beneath the surface a rapid structural transformation was in progress, one which produced serious social and political strains. Total national income rose slowly, in part because the French birth rate, already the lowest in Europe, continued to decline and total population increased by only one million in the generation preceding 1914. France had been severely injured by the losses of Alsace and Lorraine in the Franco-Prussian War. The Alsatian cotton industry had been the most modern segment of the French textile industry. When the techniques for smelting Lorraine's phosphoric iron ore appeared in the 1880s, the ore belonged to Germany and not to France. Agricultural output grew relatively slowly, and agriculture still employed some 40 per cent of the labour force. The phylloxera epidemic which ravaged French vineyards in the 1870s had reduced wine production by a half. The expensive cure of grafting new vines on root stock from California and spraying with copper sulphate eventually overcame the crisis, but in the 1910s production still averaged only 85 per cent of the 1860s level.

The transformation of agriculture in France as elsewhere was a difficult process, requiring much knowledge and capital. Partly because of the centralising impact of the railway network focused on Paris, provincial industry grew slowly, posing problems parallel to those in rural Germany. As in Germany, the political result of the pressures felt by French farmers was a campaign for protective tariffs which portrayed agriculture as the natural and proper employment for the nation's labour and the production of bread grains as the basis of the nation's health. The 1889 general election revolved around Jules Méline's campaign for agricultural tariffs, and in 1892 France introduced the tariff which bore his name. Grains and meats received high levels of protection, but the new tariffs failed in their stated purpose. Agriculture continued to decline, and the changes within the sector continued, though certain groups of farmers profited as prices to urban consumers increased by as much as 50 per cent.

Nevertheless, France enjoyed a 22 per cent increase in per capita production from 1901 to 1911. French industry proved able to move into several of the areas making up the leading edge of development. Steel, electricity and heavy chemicals developed rapidly. In these fields France dropped behind Germany, but more than held even with Britain. In addition, France became the largest European producer of automobiles, some 14,000 in 1905 and 45,000 in 1913. These successes were achieved within the traditional structure of French industry. Though large metallurgical firms such as Le Creusot had recourse to credit provided by the growing banks more often than in the past, they did not alter their basic pattern of family ownership. Similarly, though the growth of the largest firms increased industrial concentration, the large firms tacitly divided the protected domestic market with their smaller brethren.

The Low Countries, Switzerland and Northern Europe

Industry in the Low Countries expanded rapidly after 1896. In contrast to Britain, producers did not fall behind in the introduction of new technologies after 1880. The number of firms in the iron industry had already declined by nearly half, and the remaining firms went over to the new steel production methods as soon as they became available and therefore were well placed to exploit increasing world demand. Steel output in Belgium and Luxembourg rose from 318,000 tons in 1890 to 2.5 million tons in 1910. This seems small compared to Germany's 13.1 million tons, but Luxembourg alone produced nearly as much steel as Italy, and the increase in the share of Belgium and Luxembourg in total European production almost exactly matched the decline in Britain's share. Moreover, over half their output was exported. In the textile industry, direct exports of Belgian cotton cloth to Britain rose from 1,600 tonnes in 1890 to 2,800 tonnes in 1913.

Agriculture in the Low Countries had virtually completed its modern transformation before the First World War. Farmers emphasised the production of high-quality food products for sale in the urban industrial centres, a specialisation made easier than elsewhere by the dense and inexpensive rail system which had created a relatively dispersed urban pattern. Increased use of machinery and chemical fertilisers by farmers raised demand in the metal and chemical industries, and in the case of superphosphate fertiliser eventually created an important export industry. Where the share of agriculture in the economy remained high, notably in parts of the Netherlands, the expanding industrial sector focused on food processing, primarily for export markets.

If the Low Countries seemed obvious candidates for economic development, Switzerland looked unpromising in the extreme. Switzerland possessed no coal and had a mountainous terrain, which reduced agricultural productivity and increased the cost of internal communications. Nevertheless a machinery industry had grown up to serve traditional manufacturing export branches such as clocks and watches, and the railway system provided further impetus. The Swiss dyestuffs industry, concentrated in Basel, emphasised high-quality products using raw and intermediate materials imported from Germany, and featured advanced technical advice to customers as part of an aggressive marketing strategy. Coal became less crucial as a power source as electricity became available; Switzerland produced four-fifths as much electrical power as France in 1920. Industrial employment rose 63 per cent from 1890 to 1910. The Swiss birth rate declined to low levels, but the necessary workers could be imported from neighbouring areas of Italy and Germany when needed. Agricultural employment, meanwhile, declined absolutely after 1890. Though still making up 38 per cent of total employment in 1910, Swiss farmers specialised almost completely in high-quality food products, usually as suppliers of raw materials for processed products intended for export. Condensed milk, prepared children's foods and dehydrated soups appeared alongside old favourites such as chocolate and cheese. Switzerland depended on exports, but needed imports as well, covering a trade deficit with invisibles, particularly the earnings of the banking industry and tourism. Employment in services rose fourfold from 1890 to 1910. As the total of personal servants and domestics declined, the staffs of the new hotels multiplied, making the hotel industry one of the most dynamic elements in the economy.

Certain areas of northern Europe had already developed profitable and sophisticated economies. The farmers of Denmark seized the opportunity offered by rising world income after 1895. An efficient fishing industry and farms employing relatively high levels of technology provided the raw materials for an expanding food processing industry, important segments of which were organized on a cooperative basis. Agriculture, in fact, was most profitable; fully 90 per cent of Danish exports were from this sector and Denmark had the fourth highest per capita income in Europe. However, Denmark did not remain a purely agricultural producer. Industry increased its share of employment and national income, and the advance accelerated after 1900. Local machinery builders emerged to serve the food processing industry, laying the basis for further development. Denmark began to produce machinery and finished consumer goods from imported raw materials and semi-manufactured products, and industry moved to a high technological level despite the absence of coal and iron resources.

Sweden since the middle of the nineteenth century at least had enjoyed a high literacy rate, a relatively high degree of social mobility, a government which actively encouraged economic change and an energetic entrepreneurial class. However, Swedish development continued to depend on foreign markets and capital. Western Europe provided some 16 per cent of all Swedish domestic investment from 1900 to 1910. Funds for the acceleration of railway construction beginning in the 1890s came largely from France. The railway north to Narvik was opened in 1905, and the output of the new iron mines it served flowed primarily to Germany. Timber exports still accounted for 25 per cent of the Swedish total in 1914. Overall Swedish industry grew only moderately and continued to rely on tariffs introduced in 1888. In addition, the expansion of wheat exports in the middle decades of the nineteenth century had led to the creation of an interest group which also demanded protection. Consumer goods were manufactured to replace imports, but in general could not be exported. The capital goods industry remained limited to satisfying the demands of the export sectors. The traditional timber industry, which faced increased international competition, reduced employment 20 per cent but increased horsepower per worker 75 per cent from 1900 to 1912. Industry failed to absorb the increasing population. Emigration continued and employment in agriculture continued to increase until 1920.

The remaining areas of northern Europe found their possibilities for development affected by political dependence as well as by social and ethnic conflicts. Norway only became fully independent from Sweden in 1905. Finland, in theory enjoying a certain degree of autonomy within the Russian empire, suffered under an aggressive Russification campaign begun in 1899, and large agricultural estates continued to dominate the economy. In Estonia, Latvia and Lithuania, all Russian possessions, the large agricultural estates, active commercial life and beginning industrialisation were controlled by a minority of ethnic Germans who often did not speak the language of the majority of the population, a situation which had significant effects when the three states achieved independence following the First World War.

MEDITERRANEAN EUROPE

In the south, Spain in the late nineteenth century possessed a relatively poor social and political base for economic development. Regional differences in culture and language bred an atmosphere of distrust, and the long history of civil wars and changes in government during the earlier decades of the century had further undermined chances for a firm social and political consensus. The agricultural sector continued under the domination of large estates. Landowners relied on cheap labour and on the tariffs of 1891 and 1906 to remain competitive with foreign imports. Grain output had expanded, but primarily by the extension of cultivation into marginal lands. Productivity may actually have declined, but landowners found it inconvenient to introduce expensive new techniques. Despite emigration, population growth held wages low and led to heavy pressure on the land available for peasant cultivation, creating a social environment where violence became endemic. The famine of 1904–6 gave graphic and painful evidence of Spanish backwardness, with the mass of the population dependent on each year's harvest. Spain's wine industry, virtually the only bright spot in the agricultural picture, had profited from the decline in French production during the 1880s, but suffered in its turn as the phylloxera epidemic spread southward in the 1890s.

The Spanish industrial sector remained dominated by textiles, though these never became significant on the world market. Low income reduced the potential size of the domestic market, making it difficult to introduce large-scale production techniques. Because the technologies employed in textiles and other industries remained backward, the machine industry did not profit from the linkage effects of their demand as was beginning to be the case in northern Europe. Spain possessed valuable mineral deposits, but the expanding mining industry was dominated by foreign firms and had little impact on other sectors of the economy before 1914. Beginning in the 1880s an iron and steel industry began to develop around the iron mines of Bilbao in northern Spain. The major firms were not competitive with foreign manufacturers, however, and depended heavily on government orders for the construction of naval warships.

In 1908 the government contracted with the British Vickers group to construct battleships at Ferrol and Cartagena, with the provision that the British would introduce their own best practice into the Spanish naval shipyards and into civilian industry as well, but this conscious attempt to create the conditions for a 'spin-off' from military spending had achieved little by the outbreak of the war. Foreigners were also granted very favourable concessions for the construction of Spain's railways, but these too had failed to exercise the desired influence on Spanish industry.

The economy of Portugal was much like that of Spain. The majority of the population worked in agriculture, and primary products were the key export items. Wine was the major export commodity, particularly the wine of the Porto region; wine accounted for three times as many sales as any other product, and for a short while after the phylloxera epidemic hit France, Portugal dominated the world market. Other major exports were cork, sardines and fruits. Meanwhile, Portugal relied on imports of wheat, and the 'bread question' prompted the imposition of tariffs to protect local farmers beginning in 1889. Industrially, Portugal was little developed; textiles remained the main branch of industry, employing one-third of factory workers. The 110,000 steam horsepower employed in Portugal in the early 1900s represented a rapid advance, but Belgium, only half the size of Portugal, used seven times as much steam power.

After the unification of Italy in 1861, the new national government had introduced a policy of free trade calculated to force Italian industry to become more competitive with foreign producers. However, the owners of the large grain-producing estates of the south began to demand protective tariffs as foreign competition became severe in the 1870s, and had achieved their aim in alliance with industrial groups in the tariffs of 1878 and 1887. Agriculture could have become more competitive in international markets by specialising in fruits, vegetables and dairy products suitable to the Italian climate. Such a shift would have required a change in social structure in the grain-growing areas, away from the traditional forms of sharecropping, which predominated in southern Italy, and towards more capital intensive smaller farms. The local elites in those districts resisted such a change, preferring to continue growing grain behind the tariff wall, using the labour of the numerous landless peasants and a low level of technology.

In conjunction with the new policy of tariff protection, the central government had moved to stimulate industrial development directly. Various forms of subsidies were employed, in particular the requirement that government departments and contractors place a certain fraction of their orders with Italian suppliers. The government nationalised the railways in 1905 and embarked on a large program of expansion and modernisation, earmarking most of the purchases for Italian firms. The shipbuilding industry received large subsidies, and munitions manufacturers benefited from large government orders. As in Spain, foreign armaments manufacturers had been encouraged to establish plants to supply military orders, with the additional hope that they would stimulate technical advance in civilian industry as well. The government also hoped to increase industrial efficiency by stimulating the formation of large banking combines and cartels on the German model. However, industry in general used the tariff as a crutch to avoid technical improvements. The government budget suffered from a chronic deficit and government borrowing drove all domestic interest rates up, injuring those industries not receiving subsidies. Producers of consumer goods found themselves especially disadvantaged by the government's preference for heavy industry and the military, while at the same time tariffs on machinery raised their costs and tariffs on foodstuffs decreased the potential size of their market. The limited opportunities for private investment seemed to indicate the need for yet more government subsidies and direct investment to stimulate development, further hampering the very investment government policy hoped to stimulate.

Italy was divided into two economies: a highly developed north, with many features similar to the industrialised countries like Britain and France, and a much poorer, agrarian south. The development of the concentrated northern 'industrial triangle', bounded by the cities of Genoa, Turin and Milan, was real and substantial, particularly in the transportation, heavy industry and military sectors favoured by government policy. One example of Italian entre-preneurship was the Fabbrica Italiana degli Automobili di Torino, Fiat, founded in Turin in 1899. By 1904, the factory had tripled in size and Fiat was the leading Italian exporter of motorcars. The textile industry, which monopolised the domestic market behind the tariff wall, began to develop toward international competitiveness. Raw cotton consumption increased from 102,000 tons in 1890 to 175,000 in 1910, and had passed that of France. The Italian textile industry benefited from low wages compared to those of western Europe, and from extensive contacts with Latin American markets, where Italian migrants had moved into positions of economic leadership.

However, the increase in measured per capita income, and much of the capital for this burst of industrialisation, depended on the massive migration of Italians to foreign countries – and on the money they sent back to Italy. Collectively the emigrants sent some six billion lire to their families in Italy between 1901 and 1913, enough to turn a large negative trade balance into a positive overall balance of payments and to provide the capital for much of the industrial expansion of these decades.

In Greece during the late nineteenth century the development of mining and transportation, and large military expenditures, depended upon loans from western Europe negotiated at high rates of interest. The French tariff of 1892 closed the largest market for currants, Greece's most important export product, and the resulting 70 per cent decline in price caused a crisis in Greece's international payments. The government's negotiations with its western creditors in turn were wrecked by defeat in the war with Turkey in 1897, and the powers imposed an international commission to collect certain taxes to ensure repayment of the foreign loans. The slow growth of the economy led to the beginnings of large-scale emigration. The political demoralisation following defeat and loss of fiscal independence paved the way for the military revolt of 1909 and the creation of a new government committed to political and administrative reform and the development of both industry and agriculture. Beginning in 1910 a surge in government-sponsored railway construction led to a burst of investment in heavy industry. Industrial growth was further stimulated by the Balkan Wars and by the First World War, but as late as 1917 only 282 Greek industrial plants employed more than 25 workers, and their total labour force had risen to only 23,700. Much of the capital for the new ventures had come from the remittances sent home by the emigrants, and Greece remained precariously dependent upon much larger trading partners both for markets for cash crops and for supplies of food.

THE STATE AND ECONOMIC DEVELOPMENT IN THE EAST

Along Europe's eastern perimeter central governments pursued active policies intended to promote economic development, and especially the growth of modern large-scale industry. The full range of supportive measures had appeared by the 1890s – tariffs and quotas on imports, direct investment by state agencies, tax reductions, government grants of money to would-be priviate industrialists, land set aside for factories, preferential transportation rates, access to raw materials and commitments by the state to purchase all or part of the output of subsidised firms. Eastern European governments achieved some undeniable successes in stimulating the growth of their modern economic sectors. The output of heavy industry in particular tended to grow at an extremely high rate. However, from the perspective of overall economic development, the results were much less impressive. The most advanced areas of the east remained well behind even laggard districts of the west. Heavy industrial development remained concentrated in a few favoured urban and industrial centres, and textiles, clothing and food processing remained substantially larger than the metals and machinery branches favoured by the governments. The overwhelming majority of the population remained agricultural, and eastern agriculture remained backward compared to that of the west.

The development of eastern Europe depended on the needs of western Europe. As in the north and south, the countries of the eastern perimeter relied on exports of primary products to the west. Some were industrial raw materials such as oil, but much more than in the north and south, eastern exports were unprocessed agricultural goods. In return the eastern countries imported manufactured goods which they could not produce themselves, or which the west produced cheaply enough to export despite eastern tariffs. In addition domestic savings proved inadequate for eastern Europe's needs, but the capital borrowed from the west often went for purposes which contributed less than they should have to domestic development, and foreign loans always brought with them a greater or lesser degree of political and economic dependence.

Eastern development was also hampered by an inherent conflict between the economic policies of the central governments and their social and political goals. Most governments were clear enough in their desire for western-style economic development, and especially for the sort of heavy industries on which military power depended. However, governments in the east also wanted to maintain the existing social and political structure, in particular the privileged position of the landholding aristocracy and the unrestrained powers of an autocratic ruler and an irresponsible bureaucracy. Where they arose, the new large-scale industries created new social groups, but the governments typically refused to allow a significant voice to the bourgeois leaders of domestic industry and commerce, much less to the rapidly expanding industrial proletariat. Connected by family ties to the aristocracy, most central government bureaucrats refused to contemplate significant changes in agriculture which might have led to truly widespread economic development, and the overall pace of change therefore remained slow.

Austria-Hungary

Austria-Hungary was a 'dual monarchy', a state in which the Habsburg emperor was also king of Hungary, a realm whose dual politics paralleled its economic divisions. Industrial development concentrated in the north and west. The Austrian capital of Vienna and the Hungarian capital of Budapest, like Berlin, Paris and Madrid, profited by being the central points in radial railway networks, and both expanded dramatically. In addition, industry in Bohemia and Slovakia developed extensively, based on traditions reaching back into the eighteenth century and earlier. In Bohemia, by the turn of the century industrial plants with more than 20 workers already employed nearly 800,000 persons, and the share of agriculture in the province's employment had shrunk to 32 per cent. In Slovakia, under Hungarian rule, industry had not been encouraged until the 1890s, when the Hungarian government decided to attempt to create a counterweight to economic growth in the Austrian portion of the empire. Total industrial employment rose by half in the next twenty years, and by 1910 the 620 large industrial plants in Slovakia employed over 85,000 workers. Outside these favoured regions and the capital cities, however, industrial development was limited indeed. The competition of the northwestern industrial districts injured industry in other areas of the empire. The Hungarian government in particular intended that Slovakia, Transylvania and Croatia would provide raw materials and semi-manufactured goods to be processed by the textile, machinery and chemical industries of the Magyar districts and especially Budapest. Austro-Hungarian industry as a whole remained inefficient compared to western Europe, relying on protective tariffs and cartels to monopolise existing domestic markets.

Even within the protected domestic market, industry found itself hampered by the low levels of income and high share of agriculture in many provinces, which reduced the overall size of the market and left industry highly dependent on yearly harvest fluctuations. In the north and west, agricultural patterns approximated those found in the adjacent areas of western Europe. Even in these more advanced areas, however, levels of productivity tended to be lower than in their western neighbours. In Hungary, the immense Magyar estates produced at low levels compared to the large Junker holdings of eastern Germany. In the regions along the empire's southern and northeastern borders conditions resembled those found in the less fortunate areas of Russia and southeastern Europe. Local artisan manufacture declined, but the expansion of urban and industrial centres in the northwestern portion of the empire could not absorb the rapid increases in the population of these outlying provinces. Overseas emigration had barely begun to provide an outlet in the final decade before the war. The continuing pressure of rising population led to further division of peasant holdings, decreasing the already small chance for improvements in agricultural techniques.

The government in Vienna did make sporadic attempts to stimulate industrial growth, but the policies of the German-dominated central bureaucracy were regularly hamstrung by the Hungarian government. Government investment in railways and public works aided the moderate industrial boom after 1900, but such efforts were hampered by the absence of a clear policy and by a long-standing shortage of funds. The wars of the 1850s and 1860s had virtually bankrupted the government, and the refusal of privileged groups – notably the Hungarian nobility – to permit any increase in their taxes had hampered attempts to restore order to the budget ever since. In addition, though the emperor did grace the annual ball given by Vienna's industrialists with his presence, many among the influential landowning nobility continued to oppose industrial expansion on principle.

In the meantime the Hungarian government's attempts to build up an independent 'national' industrial structure under Magyar control achieved some undeniable successes. The comprehensive programme of favours to industrial firms developed during the 1880s in fact became the model for other eastern European states, notably Rumania and Bulgaria. Nevertheless, the results remained limited in terms of overall development and were achieved only at relatively high cost. In 1910 only 16 per cent of the population of the Hungarian portion of the empire was employed in industrial production of any sort. Perhaps even more than in the Austrian portion of the empire, in Hungary aristocratic elites opposed any attempt to restructure the agricultural sector and therefore precluded policies which could have laid the foundations for broadly based development.

The Balkans

The economic development of Serbia lagged until 1906, largely because of a highly unfavourable trade agreement with Austria-Hungary dating from the 1880s. The empire purchased over four-fifths of Serbian exports, virtually all unprocessed grains and live animals, and supplied over half of Serbian imports, virtually all manufactured goods. Under the agreement Serbia could not impose tariffs on imports from Austria-Hungary, and as a result, while Serbia's indigenous handicraft industry disappeared, no modern mechanised factories emerged to take its place. In 1914 perhaps 85 per cent of the population was still employed in agriculture and only 7 per cent in industry. The heavy government debt resulting from military spending, industrial subsidies and transportation investment had forced the creation of a Monopolies Commission whose revenue from tobacco, salt, petroleum and liquor sales was administered in part by representatives of Serbia's western creditors.

Serbia indeed remained backward even compared to the South Slav provinces of Austria-Hungary, despite the active discrimination of the Hungarian government against industrial development in Croatia, and the imperial government's refusal to interfere with the property rights of the Muslim landlords in Bosnia-Herzegovina after the provinces' annexation in 1908. Though the rail system was oriented northward to the empire, the South Slav provinces did enjoy some 7,500 kilometres of railways in 1919, compared with Serbia's mere 1,500. Slovenia, the small northernmost district of the South Slav region, actually contained more than twice the number of large industrial establishments found in Serbia in 1910. The South Slav provinces benefited from efficient government administration and relatively easy access to capital through the banking systems of Vienna and Budapest. On the other hand, severe social conflict and Hungary's aggressive Magyarisation policies resulted in increasing discontent, unrest and violence.

Rumania had pursued a systematic industrialisation policy modelled on that of the Hungarian government since the 1880s. Protective tariffs were imposed and large industrial enterprises were offered extensive subsidies. Industry remained small, however; domestic capital was scarce, and foreign investment remained confined to primary exports, particularly timber and petroleum. These, and the grain produced on the large agricultural estates, gave Rumania a positive balance of payments and a correspondingly good credit rating in western capital markets. Rumania obtained loans for military hardware and railway construction on relatively easy terms, and escaped the imposition of foreign control over government finances. Approximately 5,000 huge estates occupied half the arable land, and 85 per cent of the peasants either possessed no land or too little to support their families. When the peasants revolted in 1907, the uprising was brutally repressed. The agrarian reform laws passed by the government in the aftermath of the revolt had little impact, as their implementation depended on the cooperation of the landlords. In the meantime the government's institutionalised anti-Semitism drove some 70,000 Jews to emigrate from Rumania, even as the Hungarian government's Magyarisation policies were driving a similar number of ethnic Rumanians from Transylvania.

During the 1890s Bulgaria also developed a system of protection and subsidies intended to stimulate industry. As elsewhere, the results were modest; the 345 large industrial plants in the country in 1910 employed fewer than 16,000 workers, and in 1902 the heavy burden of government debt had resulted in the imposition of a foreign commission to oversee the revenue from a special tobacco tax pledged to the nation's creditors. Four-fifths of the population remained agricultural. Alone among eastern European countries, Bulgaria had become a land of independent small farmers. Compensation paid to the old Turkish landlords had left a heavy burden of debt, however, and population increase and the equal distribution of inheritances had resulted in extreme fragmentation. A 1908 survey estimated that nearly half of all holdings were too small to support a family.

Poland

Poland had been divided among the eastern powers in the late eighteenth century, and the more virulent nationalism of the late nineteenth century added active discrimination to the facts of division and dependence to hamper economic advance. In Austrian Poland, the province of Galicia, local artisans had been driven out of business by competition from other regions and no encouragement was given to local industrialists. In 1900 industry and handicrafts together employed only some 10 per cent of the population, and modern development remained confined to a few plants supplying raw materials and semi-manufactured goods to the more favoured industrial districts or for export, as in the case of petroleum. Hundreds of thousands of Galician Poles worked as seasonal agricultural labourers in neighbouring provinces of Germany, and equally large numbers emigrated overseas.

German Poland, the Prussian provinces of West Prussia, Posen and Silesia, included one major industrial region in Upper Silesia, but the remaining districts were the most backward in Germany, with some two-thirds of the labour force employed in agriculture in 1907. Though coal and steel output grew rapidly after 1895, Upper Silesian industry lost ground relative to other German industrial regions. This in part reflected poor location with respect to German markets and sources of raw materials, but certain branches such as pig iron also suffered from decisions by national cartels to restrict their development. Outside of Upper Silesia most industry remained small-scale, and the central government refused to support new large-scale manufacturing in the eastern provinces in part because 'the great mass of the workers' would be Polish. Poles suffered official discrimination in borrowing capital and purchasing land, and after 1900 were subjected to an intensive Germanisation campaign focused on the schools.

In Russian Poland, officially the Kingdom of Poland, industrial development actually proceeded more rapidly than elsewhere in eastern Europe except for Upper Silesia, but this was despite rather than because of Russian government policy. The tariffs imposed after 1891 drastically increased the prices of imported raw materials, forcing many firms to relocate closer to domestic supplies in the interior of Russia. The state railways charged higher prices to ship coal from Polish mines to Polish industrial centres than to more distant Russian markets. Nevertheless, in 1910 large industrial plants in Russian Poland numbered 11,000 and employed 400,000 persons, a disproportionate share of the Russian total.

Russia

Seen in comparison with the other nations of eastern Europe, Russia appears a large variation on several common themes. Though industry grew rapidly, it remained very small compared to agriculture. Government policy, though generally favouring industrial development after 1890, remained ambivalent, especially when industry seemed to threaten existing ethnic, social and political interests. As elsewhere in the east development in Russia remained dependent on capital and machinery supplied by western Europe and was paid for with exports of primary products. Agriculture, the major sector of the economy and the ultimate basis of any plan for development, remained extremely backward. The emancipation of the Russian serfs in 1861 burdened the peasants with redemption payments far higher than would have been justified by the market value of the land they received. Furthermore, emancipation was not intended to stimulate economic development and in many ways worked against it. Most land had been granted not to individual peasants but to the peasant commune or *mir*. Collective responsibility for taxes and redemption payments, collective decision-making and periodic redistribution of land among families belonging to the *mir* limited individual mobility and the possibility of introducing new techniques.

Many government officials remained hostile towards industry, traditionally regarded as an unwanted 'western' intrusion into Russian life. They worried about the political danger presented by a concentrated proletariat and remained paternalistically concerned about the possible negative effects of industrial labour on the health and morals of the workers. Because of the immense distances involved, however, they had come to see the necessity of railways in Russia's development. The main grain-producing areas had been linked to the Baltic and Black Seas in the 1870s, in 1883 the Baku-Batum line linked the Caspian and Black Seas to facilitate petroleum exports and in 1885 the Ekaterine Railway linked the coal resources of the Donetz basin with the iron ore of Krivoi Rog, making possible rapid industrial development in southern Russia in the 1890s.

Beginning in the 1880s the government became more actively involved in industrial development, both to produce exports to cover the balance of payments deficit resulting from foreign loans for the railway system and to overcome Russia's military backwardness relative to the other European powers. Tariffs had been raised in 1877, and further increases during the 1880s culminated in the 'monster' tariff of 1891. Many foreign firms opened plants in Russia to avoid the new duties, though tariffs on raw materials kept Russian production costs high and injured industry in Poland and the Baltic provinces. The government gradually took over the construction of new railway lines during the 1880s, and under Minister of Finance Sergei Witte began a crash programme of industrialisation in the 1890s. The 'Witte system' rested on an attempt to maintain monetary stability. Russia shifted from an inconvertible paper currency to the gold standard in 1897 in order to stimulate international confidence in the ruble and make foreign borrowing easier. High tariff protection was combined with government investment in strategic industries, particularly railways and those heavy industrial sectors crucial to the military power of the state. The necessary foreign loans were paid for by exports of grain and petroleum products and by heavy taxes levied on the peasantry, and Russian maintained a consistently positive balance of payments.

The government's programme achieved impressive results during the 1890s, with rapid increases in industrial output and employment. However, the boom suddenly slowed around 1900, and industrial production stagnated until 1908. The economic crises of 1901 and 1907 both affected Russian output, as did the war with Japan in 1904–5 and the subsequent revolution. The boom of the 1890s had depended heavily on the government's willingness and ability to purchase the output of the new factories with money derived from tax revenues. Nothing had been done to improve agricultural productivity, however, and now the ability of the peasants to pay was nearing its limits. Severe famines struck agricultural regions in 1891 and 1897, and by 1900 some districts were as much as four years behind in their tax payments.

The land reform begun in 1907 in response to the revolution was intended to modernise agriculture and peasant society and provide a long-term basis for social stability in the countryside. The new system permitted individual peasants to leave the communes to establish their own farms. Ideally, this would eliminate the *mir*, lead to the consolidation and expansion of the holdings of the most efficient farmers, raise agricultural productivity, and provide the labour force, internal market, and tax base required to resume the drive towards industrialisation. The response was rapid; by 1915 over half of all peasant households held their land in hereditary tenure, and even Lenin was concerned that the reform would remove all revolutionary potential from Russian society. Agricultural output rose rapidly, and internal grain shipments rose 50 per cent from 1900 to 1913, as the urban industrial centres expanded to increase the size of the domestic market.

Industry recovered rapidly after 1908, expanding at a rate comparable to that of the 1890s. Government stimulation remained important, as spending on railways and the military resumed, but demand was now more broadly based than before. Rising grain prices and the relatively high wages paid to an expanding industrial labour force increased the size of the domestic market. However, if there were positive signs to be read in the Russian situation before 1914, there were negative signs as well. In terms of per capita product Russia had failed to gain on the nations of western Europe, and industry remained small compared to total population. Though industry was larger than shown in the official statistics, it was also less advanced, for the enumerators largely ignored textiles, clothing and food processing in rural areas, most of which relied on traditional techniques. Despite the land reform, there had been no decline in the absolute number of peasant households still in the *mir*, because population had continued to increase. Despite some improvement, agricultural productivity remained very low, particularly because withdrawal from the *mir* did not automatically mean consolidation of holdings; nearly 90 per cent of all peasant land was still held in strips in open fields in 1917. Good weather rather than improved productivity had increased output of grains. In the countryside, the reforms had contributed to continued unrest, and in the urban industrial centres there was a sudden upsurge of unrest beginning in 1912 to match that of the countryside.

As the case of Russia illustrates, even during the 'good years' all was not well in Europe. Though industrial development was spreading, it remained restricted; though it was possible, it remained difficult. The new technologies opened new prospects, but their introduction imposed demands which seriously strained economic, social and political structures. Capital could come from foreign sources, but the necessary loans could lead to political dependence. Capital could be raised from domestic sources, but the resulting taxes could press on backward agricultural systems. Privileged aristocrats rejected increases in their taxes, but the burden imposed on the peasantry led to unrest, violence and occasionally revolution. On the other hand, industrial growth was proceeding at unprecedented rates, and disputes over the distribution of its benefits added to older social and political conflicts. In no country were the rights of the new working class adequately represented, or their representatives considered legitimate participants in the contest for power. Even in the most 'advanced' nations development created problems whose solution required fundamental changes in governing systems.

2

EUROPEAN EXPANSION: THE GOLD STANDARD AND IMPERIALISM

International economic relations during the generation before the First World War have remained a field of contention. On the one hand, nostalgia for the gold standard comprises an important part of the yearning for the lost 'good years' before 1914. On the other hand, the period also witnessed the outburst of a 'new' European imperialism, systematic exploitation of those unable to defend themselves and increasing international conflict leading to the final catastrophe of world war. The same statesmen who harvested the peaceable fruits of the gold standard also sowed the seeds of imperialistic discord and violence. Both the gold standard and imperialism have been defined, analysed and interpreted in widely varying ways. A substantial number of economists, for instance, still regard the international gold standard as both simple and 'natural', a system of universal application which functioned automatically to promote both economic growth and social stability before the First World War, and which would do so again if only governments would submit themselves to its discipline. Other economists and most historians, though admitting the elegance of the theory of the gold standard, argue that since the international economy never operated as the theory predicts, some other explanation of what actually occurred will have to be developed. In the case of the 'new' imperialism, European expansion may have been the logical and automatic result of capitalist economic development, the conscious policy of specific individuals and groups within Europe, or merely the accidental outcome of the unique historical circumstances of the late nineteenth century.

At the centre of the dispute is the question of the relationship between the economic system and political expansionism. Contemporaries recognised that the system distributed its benefits narrowly, and increasingly so the further from the centre one had the misfortune to be. It was best to be a European, better to be a western European, and best of all to be a member of western Europe's privileged upper class. At the same time the system was expanding, not only in the amounts of goods and services exchanged, but also in penetrating previously isolated and inaccessible regions of the world. For upper-class western Europeans, the profits accruing to the owners of property not only appeared morally unexceptionable, but also seemed to provide the crucial motor of expansion which would benefit not only the rich but also the poor both in Europe and overseas. Those who spoke for Europe's poor and for the peoples overseas, however, argued that profit resulted simply from the illegitimate use of force, and that expansion benefited no one but the users of illegitimate force.

THE GOLD STANDARD: MYTH AND REALITY

The myth of the gold standard was and remains precisely that, but it remains persuasive because the international economic system did in fact function remarkably smoothly before the war. Because the fact is often forgotten it is worth emphasising that the international gold standard operated for only an extremely short period of time. Its effective operation cannot be placed before 1880, and important areas of the world were still excluded until 1900; it came to an abrupt end in 1914 and has never been revived. The system which in retrospect appears so natural and stable therefore operated for at most 34 years, and perhaps for as few as 14.

The extremely stringent requirements imposed by the gold standard slowed its adoption and limited its operation. Adherence to the gold standard required that a nation's currency be tied to a certain weight of gold, that banknotes be convertible into gold on demand, that there be no restrictions on the melting down of gold coins and that there be no restrictions on the export of gold. Wealthy Britain was the only nation in the world adhering to a gold standard until the 1870s, and it had taken nearly half a century to establish the gold standard even in Britain. The new German empire adopted the gold standard in 1875, using the indemnity levied on the defeated French to purchase gold reserves. Other western and northern European countries and the United States ceased to coin silver in the 1870s, but only adopted the full convertibility of notes into gold during the 1880s. Austria-Hungary declared for the gold standard in 1892, and Russia and Japan in 1897. Most Asian and Latin American countries moved to the gold standard after 1900, but there and in eastern Europe currencies remained subject to sudden and extensive political interference. Some countries, such as China, remained outside the system.

For the gold standard to provide its full benefits, contemporaries argued that restrictions on the free flow of goods should be eliminated, and that authorities in all countries should be prepared to intervene according to widely recognised 'rules of the game'. A negative balance of payments was the signal for the central bank to raise interest rates. Such a policy might cause a depression, but lower prices and the enforced movement of resources into their most efficient employment would eventually raise exports and eliminate the balance of payments deficit. Increased efficiency and export earnings would end the depression and raise income, according to the theory. In fact, the gold standard system did not function in the manner predicted by its theorists. Free trade, the policy which was supposed to ensure adjustments to increase economic efficiency, disappeared even as the gold standard was being adopted. By 1900, except for Britain, every country which could had adopted high protective tariffs. In addition, most nations ostensibly adhering to the gold standard did not in fact permit the 'rules of the game' to determine their economic policies. Governments in general were not willing to risk a depression in order to correct a deficit in the balance of payments. Nonetheless, total world trade expanded dramatically, and trade relations became far more complex and sophisticated than previously. Immense numbers of workers moved over immense distances in the hope of a better life. Immense amounts of capital flowed among nations, encouraging a rapidly spreading economic development.

The efficient operation of the international economy depended not on the gold standard, but on the unique role played by Britain. Despite the growth of other national economies, the sheer size of the British market and Britain's continued commitment to free trade maintained Britain's position as a crucial outlet for both primary and manufactured products. The size of the British market had led to the early growth of a huge re-export trade and the development of shipping, insurance and credit facilities. Large merchant houses emerged which were willing to accept bills of exchange and guarantee payment, thereby making their credit available to small firms and foreign correspondents by means of the 'bill on London'. Gradually, these firms had moved from short-term commercial credits to long-term investment overseas. The British balance of trade was traditionally positive with producers of primary goods outside of Europe, most of which belonged to the British empire. They financed their negative trade balances with loans raised in London. British loans worked in turn to increase their purchases of goods and services from Britain and therefore reinforced Britain's position.

The fact that London remained the largest international capital market worked to stabilise the system in a number of ways. Countries in debt to Britain paid interest on their loans in London, making large movements of gold unnecessary. In addition, payments by British firms to foreigners, and payments among foreigners as well, often remained in London, either to finance additional trade or to be placed in loans being marketed in London. Since all such payments remained in sterling, relatively little money moved among different currencies. The pound sterling was a stable and easily convertible medium of exchange, better in fact than gold for it drew interest when on deposit, and sterling became in effect the international currency. Because of its stability there was no opportunity to speculate against the pound sterling; similarly, because of the highly centralised exchange market and the role of sterling, opportunities to speculate against other currencies were also relatively limited. Therefore little capital moved from one centre and currency to another in response to actual or threatened changes in exchange rates.

THE 'NEW' IMPERIALISM

The outburst of imperialist expansion which accompanied the growth of the international economy and movements of people, goods and money differed from previous epochs of expansionism, but the differences were of degree rather than kind. Certainly the mere fact of expansionism was not new. European nations had won and lost empires in the Americas by the beginning of the nineteenth century. Nonetheless, the speed and extent of the conquests were astonishing. In three decades after 1870 European nations divided up the remainder of the unconquered world; by 1900, Europe controlled almost all of Africa and Southeast Asia and had made significant encroachments on the independence of China. Britain had taken over 345 million non-Britons in Africa, India and the Pacific region; Queen Victoria's realm was so vast that Englishmen proudly proclaimed that the sun never set on the British flag. France had raised its tricolour flag over 56 million people outside Europe, the Netherlands controlled 35 million, Germany almost 15 million.

The 'new' imperialism of the late nineteenth century involved the employment of superior technologies and also involved a complex mix of competition among the major European powers, economics, politics, culture and ideology. Europeans genuinely thought their ventures had an altruistic motivation, for they believed that they were bringing civilisation to the savages. For the French, this was a 'civilising mission' to the rest of the world, and for the British (in the words of Rudyard Kipling), it was the 'white man's burden' to take European government and culture to the Asians and Africans. For these reasons, religious missionaries, educators and doctors led the soldiers, traders and governors. A French archbishop named Lavigerie founded an order of monks, the 'White Fathers' (after their white cassocks) to spread the faith among the Africans, joining the older British London Missionary Society and numerous others. Europeans' commitment to this mission ought not to be downplayed, although it reflected ethnocentric and racist biases. Europe was at the height of its political and economic power, and with unhidden prejudice, Europeans imagined Arabs and Africans, Indians and Asians alike to be quite bereft of culture. For them, non-European art was but folklore and non-European religions were misguided blasphemies; tribal chieftains, maharajahs and other leaders needed the benefits of western parliamentary rule, albeit in the form of statutes passed in the legislatures of London, Paris or Berlin.

Along with these collective motives for imperialism went the ambitions of individual men. European explorers and businessmen saw fame and fortune in the jungles of Africa and Asia, and explorers and adventurers such as Carl Peters and Henry Stanley paved the way for businessmen like Cecil Rhodes. Rhodes was the most famous imperialist, a man with unbounded ambition; 'I would annex the planets if I could', he is reputed to have said. In South African diamond mines he found the domain for his work and eventually established an economic and political stranglehold on the southern tip of Africa. He wielded immense power in London and used his government connections to further his investments and marketing in Africa. Similar men from other countries did the same thing, establishing virtual fiefs for themselves and their partners with the informal accord of their home governments.

No European power dared be left behind. Britain, despite the already immense extent of the Empire, added still new territories. Germany, newly unified in 1871, sought a place in the colonial sun. France, the loser in the war with Prussia in 1870, saw in overseas possessions an opportunity to recoup some of those losses. The Netherlands had long-standing interests abroad, and the Dutch now moved to extend those holdings. Latecomers Italy and Belgium were determined not to be left out of the game. Russia contended in northern India with Britain, in the Balkans with Austria-Hungary and in the Far East with a new non-European imperialist power, Japan. The last third of the nineteenth century saw increasing political tension in Europe, spurred on by the creation of new alliances and ententes, and these political conflicts were transferred to the colonial sphere. Land abroad was a political advantage, a source of economic profits, prestige and strategic bases, and empire was also a good card to play in the domestic political game.

At the base of this political struggle was the question of nationalism. Nationalism extolled 'racial' virtues, demanded the enlargement of national territories and insisted on the conquest of territory abroad. Colonial areas were ideal spots in which to flex the national muscle and preach the nationalist gospel. Nationalism and politics inevitably implied military might and strategy, which also played a role in imperialism. Britain's prize possession was the Indian Empire, and some British expansion in the late 1800s can be explained as an attempt to protect the flanks of the Indian subcontinent. In Africa, England acquired a controlling interest in Egypt and in South Africa, with the grand scheme of linking the two regions with a Cape-to-Cairo railway as the main axis. Similarly, the French had been involved in Algeria since the 1830s and later began to establish an empire on the west coast of Africa, whereupon they became interested in linking their two areas of interest.

Economics also played a role in imperialism. Indeed, two contemporary writers, one British, one Russian, argued that economic motives were paramount in the European conquest of Africa and Asia. J. A. Hobson, a journalist and economist, wrote *Imperialism: A Study* in 1902, based on his academic research and also on his personal observations gathered while a reporter in South Africa during the Boer War. Hobson was far from being an economic determinist; indeed, his book is a comprehensive examination of the multitude of factors involved in imperialism. But he was particularly interested in understanding the economic necessity of imperialism. Imperialism was not a limitless source of profits, he said; after all, the nation had to pay for the military and administration necessary to conquer and maintain a colony. However, imperial conquests were good for capitalist businessmen, who found in foreign parts markets for their manufactured goods, sources of raw materials for their factories and placements for their investments. Production costs abroad were lower than at home, and even a small colonial profit might spell the difference between red and black ink at the bottom of the balance sheet. Hobson's statistics made his point clear: Englishmen had earned 3.5 million pounds from the Indian public revenue in 1900, 4.7 million from the Indian railway, 18.4 million from colonial and foreign public securities, 14 million from railways outside the United Kingdom and 19.5 million from foreign and colonial investments. These profits lined the pockets of the middle-class businessmen who had the political power to determine the course of British foreign policy. All of this led Hobson to speak of the 'economic taproot of imperialism'.

Writing in Zurich in 1916, Lenin said he had made use of Hobson's work in writing his own *Imperialism: The Highest Stage of Capitalism*. Although the Russian revolutionary did not deny the non-economic factors in imperialism, he was much more rigorous than Hobson in seeing economics as the cause of imperialism. For Lenin, the capitalist system necessarily became imperialist. New technologies lowered the rate of profit; the European market had become saturated; to survive, capitalism had to move abroad. Imperialism was simply finance capitalism in an internationalist stage, at the point when the monopolies which concentrated production in the hands of large units looked outward. Imperialism was not just the extension of European influence abroad or merely an attempt by businessmen to improve their individual fortunes; rather, it was a necessary and inevitable stage in the history of capitalism.

The political activities and the profits made by European colonialists pointed to the economic origins of the imperialist impulse. On the other hand, controversy surrounded imperial expansion in all European countries. In addition, the chronology of imperialism suggests that the theory followed the fact; colonial areas were first reconnoitred by explorers and missionaries and only then by businessmen and politicians. Many different people, as individuals or groups, could reap advantages from the exploitation of colonial areas, and for their own reasons they pressed the home governments to take over foreign areas. Also, the process of expansion appears relatively easy and inexpensive. Never before (and never again) was the technological gap between societies so large and the application of sufficient force so uncomplicated. The steamboat permitted Europeans to penetrate the interiors of Asia and Africa with unprecedented ease, advances in medical knowledge made it possible for Europeans to survive once they reached the interior and overwhelmingly superior firepower permitted Europeans to overcome the resistance their presence inevitably called forth. From the position of an African or an Asian, all of this was readily apparent. As an Ethiopian emperor remarked with bitter, perceptive irony before he committed suicide in 1868 after suffering defeat by the British: 'First, the traders and the missionaries; then the ambassadors; then the cannon. It's better to go straight to the cannon'.

Britain and India

India was a special example in the domain of imperialism. In 1757 the victory of the British over the French at Plassy secured British dominance in Bengal. By the beginning of the 1800s, the British controlled the eastern coast of India, as well as the island of Ceylon, substantial territory in the north and scattered parcels in the west. Through the nineteenth century, the British used armies raised in these areas to extend their control. In 1877 Queen Victoria was proclaimed Empress of India. The Raj was the jewel of Britain's imperial crown; in 1903, the viceroy, Lord Curzon, stated: 'As long as we rule India we are the greatest power in the world. If we lose it we shall drop straight away to a third-rate power'. Britain considered India's strategic importance so great that British armies needed to move into peripheral areas (such as Afghanistan and Burma) to protect Britain's interests against the French, Russians and others.

India was a source of raw material for the British, and Indian farms interested the British more than did Indian factories. The cotton mills of Lancashire, the heart of Britain's industrial revolution, needed the raw cotton from Indian fields, and textile merchants in Britain saw India as a perfect market for sales of the finished textile products. The converse was the decline of Indian manufacturing. In the eighteenth century, India had an extensive manufacturing sector. However, competition from British goods, and discriminatory tariffs, drove many unemployed Indians back to the land, where overpopulation and poverty were omnipresent. The late nineteenth century saw an increasing number of famines. The British levied high land taxes – 'no native Prince demands the rent which we do' concluded a British bishop visiting India. Such taxation prevented savings and investment in improved techniques and forced landowners to produce crops for sale and neglect domestic food supplies. Indian opium exported to China covered the large negative balance incurred by the British in purchasing Chinese goods.

The British did invest major sums of money in India to build railways, roads, irrigation systems, postal services and other public works. But such projects, though the loans were paid for with Indian tax revenues, were designed to meet the needs of the British, not intended to foster a progressive development of the Indian economy. British rule sparked resentment and the seeds of nationalism; the first meeting of the Indian National Congress in 1885, which demanded reform of legislative councils and the inclusion of more Indians in the public service, marked the birth of nationalist sentiment. Yet the path to independence would be a long one, and the period until the First World War remained one of solid British hegemony in the subcontinent.

Latin America

South America provides the major example of European 'business imperialism' during this period, not territorial acquisition but a major incursion into a non-European economy through trade and investment. By 1824, the last Spanish bastion in South America had fallen, and Britain emerged as the major European power in South America's economy, a role consolidated during the nineteenth century. London's bankers had already issued large loans to pay debts incurred during the South American wars of independence. Now new joint-stock companies in the City began to finance various ventures in mining and land settlement schemes. But the major British interests were projects to create a new economic infrastructure, particularly the construction of railway networks. In 1913 British investment in Latin America was fully a fifth of total British investment abroad. Railroads accounted for 21 per cent of British capital in Latin America; in Argentina, the most attractive area for British capital, British interests in the railway represented 61 per cent of British investment. Britain supplemented the revenues from railways with increasing trade with Latin America; the railway in fact was a major aid to this, for example, by opening up the Argentinian *pampas* to intensive exploitation. British trade increased dramatically; the value of British imports from South America increased fourfold from 1880 to 1913. From Argentina, Britain bought beef, transported in the newly invented refrigerated cargo ships; from Brazil, Britain took rubber, cotton, coffee and cocoa; from Chile, nitrates, copper, wool and tin; from Mexico, metals (gold, silver, copper, zinc and tin) and petroleum; from Peru, cotton, sugar and rubber. In return, Britain exported coal, transportation equipment, machinery, textiles and other manufactured goods.

Great Britain was not the only European nation active in South America. France had established colonies in the Caribbean to grow such products as sugar cane and rice; because of climate and the fertile soil, Haiti, Martinique and Guadaloupe became treasure-troves for French planters. France had also taken over Guiana in South America proper, establishing the notorious penal colony Devil's Island there in 1854. French trade in Latin America rose from 80 million dollars in 1855 to 144 million dollars in 1896 and 187 million dollars in 1907. Germany, for its part, lacked a territorial foothold in the New World, but did pursue trade with great initiative, surpassing French totals and rivalling British interests. In 1900, Germany had 500 million dollars in investments in South America (primarily in state loans, railways and plantations) and yearly trade worth 146 million dollars. By 1913, German investment had risen to 2 billion dollars and trade to 470 million dollars. In addition to investment and trade Europe also sent migrants. British and German businessmen and workers lived scattered in

Argentina, Mexico and Central America, Venezuela, Brazil and Chile. Southern Europeans constituted a major current of migration from the old world to the new, particularly to Argentina, which actively encouraged immigration.

Europeans did not seize Latin American territory in the late 1800s. Nevertheless, the pattern of trade was similar to that in other areas: the importation of primary products from South America to Europe, in return for manufactured goods. Returning to Europe, too, were the profits made by the investments in Latin America. South American governments maintained great powers of decision in restricting or encouraging investment, trade and immigration, but profits reaped by South Americans generally accrued to a very small proportion of the population. Europeans were not above using force to protect their nationals or preserve an 'open door' for trade. In 1902, for example, Great Britain, Germany and Italy set up a blockade of ports in Venezuela to secure payments for losses incurred during revolutionary disturbances several years earlier, and in 1908, the Dutch mounted a blockade after a controversy involving political refugees and the dismissal of a Dutch envoy. South America foreshadowed later relations between Europe and the 'developing world' and gives evidence of the long-term effects of European economic incursions into foreign areas.

Africa

Africa was the domain par excellence of nineteenth-century European imperialism. Africa was still a vast, uncharted region – the 'Dark Continent' – and thus a perfect foraging ground for Europe's missionaries, adventurers, soldiers and administrators. Relations between Europe and Africa were built on the heritage of the slave trade; from the 1440s when slaving began to the 1800s when it ended, almost nine million Africans had been forcibly taken to the western hemisphere. Slave-trading disorganised coastal societies, but larger states had risen in the interior which exchanged slaves for manufactured goods, particularly firearms, and which discouraged European penetration inland. Europeans indeed could not survive in areas where malaria was prevalent until the accidental discovery that a sufficient amount of quinine in the bloodstream protects against infection. From 1848 quinine prophylaxis was official British policy and the gin and tonic became a permanent feature of colonial life. Europeans still required greater firepower than their opponents, however. The machine gun invented by Maxim in 1884 and the smokeless powder developed by Vieille in 1885, as well as the new, cheaper processes for manufacturing steel, gave Europeans a decisive advantage. African artisans could produce iron muzzle-loading muskets, but could not imitate the new steel breech-loading repeating rifles and machine guns.

Protected by quinine, armed with repeating weapons and travelling in small steamboats, Europeans penetrated the African interior along any convenient river – and some not so convenient. Leopold II, king of Belgium, hired Henry Stanley in 1878 to secure an empire in the Congo Basin. Stanley's nine-ton steamboat was dismantled and carried piece by piece over a road cleared through the jungle around the falls below present-day Leopoldville, an undertaking requiring a full year, but by 1884 Stanley had established a viable land and water route extending along the Congo over some 1,500 kilometres. In the meantime, Leopold managed to convince the European powers that the Congo Basin should become a 'free trade area' under an 'international' regime rather than falling under the domination of any single great power. Leopold actually intended to set up a monopoly over the entire vast area for his own personal benefit, but his campaign reinforced the mutual suspicions of the powers and increased the determination of all European states not to be excluded. The French immediately dispatched the explorer Savorgnan de Brazza to secure their claim to at least the area north of the Congo. The French also extended their empire in north Africa and showed interest in western Africa. Britain occupied Egypt in 1882. In 1884 and 1885 Germany announced the establishment of 'protectorates' over regions of east and west Africa on the basis of some rather tenuous claims of exploration and settlement.

The Berlin Congress of 1884–85, held ostensibly to sort out colonial disputes in Africa, had the effect of further stimulating colonial rivalries. Along with resolutions calling for 'effective' occupation before claiming African territory, free trade in Africa and the abolition of the slave trade, the congress recognised the Belgian claims in the Congo, which Leopold ruled as his private domain until 1908. The delegates returned home and began poring over maps of Africa. Soon the Portuguese were extending their area of 'effective' occupation in Angola and Moçambique, Spain and Italy were pressing into north Africa and the British were moving northward from Cape Colony and southward from Egypt, bringing them into conflict with the Boers in the south and the French in the north. The French meanwhile, in part merely to frustrate the British, extended their claims throughout western Africa to cut off Britain's west African coastal possessions. By 1890 the main lines of occupation had already been drawn, and in 1914 only two territories remained independent: the tiny west African state of Liberia, founded in the mid-nineteenth century as a refuge for freed slaves from America, and the east African empire of Ethiopia, which the Italians had tried and failed to conquer in 1896.

But what did Europe do with its new-found continent? Until the final years before the First World War, very little. Except in the extreme north and south, Africa provided no region for settlement by Europeans. Only the French in Algeria and the Boers and the British in South Africa made up European colonies of any size. Elsewhere a thin sprinkling of adventurers and administrators strove to realise Africa's vast economic potential while attempting to 'pacify' the natives and rule the new colonies as economically as possible. Minerals still attracted the most interest, especially the gold and diamonds of South Africa. Such companies as the DeBeers Consolidated and entrepreneurs like Rhodes made huge profits. Other sorts of development, such as the cotton, tobacco and coffee of eastern Africa, had to wait for railways to penetrate the interior. Before 1914 Africa never accounted for the bulk of Europe's profits – but it did provide a healthy chunk of them. Hobson and Lenin might or might not be right that the marginal profits from the exploitation of Africa told the difference between red and black at the bottom of the balance sheets or that the dynamics of capitalism impelled the movement – but certain it is that great profits were reaped by individuals, firms and governments. The success of their African venture encouraged Europeans to expand still further afield, to risk wars to consolidate and extend their holdings in Africa and elsewhere and to think of themselves as a race apart, destined to wield imperial power forever.

Southeast Asia

In Southeast Asia, Europeans encountered a baffling variety of civilisations and cultures. Southeast Asia in the nineteenth century was a region of agriculture and of peasant societies, a poor and unhealthy part of the world, a particular victim of a cruel list of diseases. Yet these tropical climates yielded a variety of products of interest to the Europeans. Sugar was a crop of some significance already at the beginning of the nineteenth century in the Philippines, Java and Thailand, and its importance grew. Coconuts, which had been important in the subsistence economy of Asian peasants, acquired a new significance as a source of oil for the manufacture of soap and margarine. Rice, of course, was the staple foodstuff of Asia, but in the 1800s, the growing urban population of Europe created a demand for larger supplies of rice. Rubber also became a major product of Southeast Asia, especially after the invention of the pneumatic tyre by Dunlop in 1888. In addition, Europeans were attracted to the mineral wealth of Southeast Asia, especially tin.

Europeans had traded with Southeast Asia since the days of the spice trade, and governments in Europe set up companies to handle the commerce. The most famous was the Dutch East India Company, chartered in 1602, but most of the other nations had an interest – even Denmark established an East India Company in 1616. The difference between this early trade and the imperialism of the nineteenth century was the extension of political control. In 1886 Britain completed the subjugation of the Burmese kingdom and, moving north from Singapore, extended further in the area of Malaya. Meanwhile, the French became involved in Indochina, establishing a protectorate over Vietnam in 1883 and over Laos a decade later. The Dutch consolidated their interests in the islands, subjugating Bali in 1906 and taking over all of Sumatra in 1907. The only losers among the Europeans were the Spanish, whose defeat in the Spanish-American War in 1898 left the Philippines in the hands of the United States. Thus, by the beginning of the twentieth century, Southeast Asia was divided up much like Africa. Only Thailand remained independent, and although it managed to keep its political sovereignty, economically, it too had been tied to the western powers. In 1941 fully 70 per cent of Thai trade was with the British, and Britain held the public debt and controlled the bulk of Thailand's financial undertakings, with room left only for some small operations by the Germans, Danes and Belgians.

Technology was particularly important in Europe's relations with Southeast Asia. The opening of the Suez Canal in 1869 shortened the route from Europe to Asia. The replacement of sailing vessels by steamships made it practicable to export perishable and bulky Southeast Asian commodities, such as rice and tin, to European markets. The building of railways and highways during and after the takeover connected agricultural areas with ports, and the construction of telegraph lines improved communications. Once established, the Europeans used their technological prowess to increase possibilities for exploiting local resources. The introduction of steam pumps and the chain-bucket dredge by large European firms in the Malay peninsula, for instance, made it easier to extract tin and also squeezed small Asian-owned firms out of the industry.

East Asia

When Europeans first came into contact with China, they encountered a mature and very sophisticated civilisation. Throughout much of history, the Chinese were technically superior to Westerners; gunpowder and the printing press, for instance, were Chinese inventions. The Chinese had a precise ideology and belief system centred on Confucianism and focused on attaining proper relationships between members of a family, between friends and between the ruler and his subjects. The Chinese emperor exercised authority through a centralised bureaucracy, entry to which was based on examinations in the Confucian classics. In the Chinese world view, the civilisation of the Celestial Kingdom was far superior to that of the 'barbarians'.

Yet, Europeans had always been curious about this exotic oriental empire. When Marco Polo returned to Venice in 1296 with stories of his sojourn in China, Europe marvelled at the news. Trade routes developed during the next centuries to import Chinese silks and spices, yet Europeans made little direct contact. Both Westerners and the Chinese were satisfied with the 'Canton system' during the 1700s and early 1800s. Under this arrangement, western traders were allowed to go to China, although they were confined to certain designated areas of cities and allowed to trade only with a *cohong*, a licenced group of merchants. The British were particularly keen on contact with the Empire and integrated Chinese trade into their expansion in India. The triangular trade was based on the export of opium from India to China by the East India Company, which also had a monopoly on opium growing. British consumers desired Chinese tea, silks and porcelain, but Britain produced nothing desired by the Chinese; the silver earned in the opium trade covered Britain's resulting negative trade balance with China. The Chinese, however, were trying to stamp out opium trading, and the result was the Opium War and the Treaty of Nanking in 1842 which opened China to European penetration.

From the Opium War dates the incursion of Britain and other nations into China. Merchants from all countries arrived to buy Chinese products and traders became powerful influences on the emperor's government. Foreigners were still resented and resentment of them played a part in internal Chinese politics, notably the Taiping Rebellion of the 1850s. Meanwhile, China's economy was developing rapidly; the Nanking Arsenal was opened in 1867, new shipyards were built four years later, the Chinese Merchants Steam Navigation Company opened in 1872 and a railway was built in 1881. Thus, not only western trade penetrated

China, but also western technology and western ideas. The cultured elite was becoming divided on the relative merits of westernisation of the Celestial Empire. The dynasty in Peking was proving less able to resist the challenge of foreign merchants and also of dissenters demanding reforms from inside.

European attitudes toward China now bordered on naked aggression; in the 1880s, France fought a war with China over Indochina, and Britain extracted even more favourable trade concessions. By the 1890s, competition was intense, for now there were Germans, Americans and Russians contending with the English and French for a share of China. For a moment, it looked as if the great empire would suffer the same fate as black Africa. Already the foreigners were inching their way onto Chinese soil; in 1897 the Germans obtained a leased area, the port of Kiaochow, and in 1898, Russia obtained a 25-year lease on Kwantung.

Then in 1900, the Chinese revolted against this western incursion. The Boxers were a group of anti-foreign, anti-Christian rebels headquartered in Shantung. Formally known as the Society of Righteous and Harmonious Fists, the Boxers had begun their propaganda in the 1890s to diminish western influence and protest the displacement of the handicraft industry by foreign trade and the advances of the Germans. By late 1899, however, their position was openly xenophobic and they were being encouraged by the dowager empress, who was the power behind the Chinese throne. Empress and rebels declared war on the westerners, but the Europeans proved too strong to be dislodged; the Boxer rebel leaders were executed, and China agreed to a monetary indemnity to the foreigners of 333 million dollars. The failure of the Boxer rebellion marked the beginning of the end for imperial China. The decade from 1901 to the nationalist revolution of 1911 which overthrew the Ching dynasty and established a republic under Sun Yat-sen was marked by a weakening of the old government and the strong-arm influence of westerners. The Europeans never divided up China – their mutual suspicion led them to a more or less willing acceptance of the American suggestion of an 'open door' – but they never really needed to do so to achieve their aims. Westerners were able to trade freely, to exert pressure on the government, and when things went badly, to intervene militarily.

In Japan, conditions differed significantly from those in China. The ruling elite, the samurai, though in fact a salaried bureaucracy, possessed a tradition of military service and a keen eye for technological inventions which could be of military use. Despite the formal closure of the country to foreigners in force since the seventeenth century, western scientific knowledge and weapons had penetrated in significant amounts, and Japanese leaders were acutely conscious of China's defeat in the Opium Wars and of the necessity to meet the western threat by force if necessary. Japan enjoyed a much more cohesive social structure than China, whose mutually incomprehensible dialects and vast distances made direct rule by the central authorities extremely difficult. The Meiji Restoration of 1868, a revolt led by discontented elements among the samurai, in theory 'restored' the Japanese emperor to direct rule over the country, but in fact imposed a dictatorship of a small group of men dedicated to strengthening the nation militarily. Their reforms, particularly the introduction of universal military service and the elimination of the privileged legal position of the old samurai, went far towards completing Japan's evolution as a nation-state very similar to the European model.

Tea, silk and increasing quantities of cotton textile exports provided Japan's foreign exchange earnings. In 1901 the opening of a government-owned ironworks marked a significant shift towards heavy industrial development. The government had also invested heavily in roads, harbour facilities and irrigation projects, not only in the major urban centres, but in smaller cities and towns as well. Shipping and shipbuilding benefited from government regulation and subsidies, and in 1905 the government took over the previously private railway system. Japan had enjoyed an exceptionally high literacy rate before 1868; the Meiji government made primary education compulsory, and after 1906 also eliminated fees.

Japan alone succeeded in meeting the challenge posed by the imperialist powers, by arming itself effectively. Japan contracted very few foreign loans. Foreign trade paid for part of the government's investment programme, but by far the largest share came from heavy taxes levied on the peasantry. Serious peasant uprisings marked the late 1870s and early 1880s. At the same time, however, the spread of improved techniques of production was raising agricultural productivity, and the tax burden therefore did not depress living standards. Japan, in contrast to the countries of eastern and southern Europe, all of whom pursued similar policies of government-sponsored industrialisation, therefore enjoyed a high degree of social stability for the quarter century before 1914. Living standards, though low, did improve slightly and were high enough to provide a firm base in the home market for industries which gradually moved into foreign trade.

TRADE AND FINANCE IN AN IMPERIAL SYSTEM

Within the expanding worldwide system (and despite rising tariffs) the amount of trade rose to new heights, and the pattern of trade became far more complex than previously. Total world trade rose 156 per cent from 1880 to 1913. Britain had taken the lion's share of world trade in the late nineteenth century but the British share was diminishing. In 1880 most international trade had been bilateral, between pairs of neighbouring nations and between each nation and Britain. By 1913 nearly every nation possessed three or even four major trading partners, and though trade with all partners was rising rapidly, trade with 'new' partners was rising faster than average. In addition, Europe as a whole had to contend with the increasingly formidable competition of both the United States and Japan, which became substantial exporters of both manufactured goods and primary products.

In its trade with the rest of the world, Europe continued to import primary products and to export manufactured goods. However, Europe itself supplied nearly one half of world exports of primary products, notably in the trade of the northern, southern and eastern perimeters with western Europe. Further, the European nations themselves constitued the market for a large and increasing share of manufactured imports. Not only did the countries of western Europe supply manufactured goods to the perimeter; they were in fact their own best customers. Britain was France's most important partner and Germany's second most important partner. Germany's most important partner was France, and Britain, France and Germany together were overwhelmingly the most important partners of Belgium, the Netherlands and Switzerland.

Until the 1870s and 1880s most international payments had moved within a few simple triangular networks, with Britain serving as one corner of the triangle. For instance, Britain had covered the usual deficit in trade with the United States by earning a surplus with Latin America, and the chronic British deficit with China was balanced by the large surplus of trade with India. Thereafter a new pattern emerged in which Britain was only one element in a payments network which embraced most of the world. In a 'typical' year the United States might offset a deficit with tropical countries with a surplus in trade with Canada and Argentina, while Germany offset a deficit with overseas primary producers with surpluses derived from exports of manufactured goods to other European nations. Canada, Argentina and Australia all ran deficits in their trade with Britain and the United States, offset by surpluses with Germany and other Continental European nations. These European nations in turn offset their deficit with Germany and overseas primary producers with a consistent surplus in their trade with Britain.

The size and distribution of capital flows also changed dramatically as the international economy developed. In 1870 London had been the only international money market and Britain the only international lender of any magnitude. A tremendous expansion of foreign lending followed. Total foreign lending rose from 1.3 billion pounds in 1870 to 4.8 billion in 1900, and by 1914 had reached 9.5 billion pounds. At the same time Britain had been joined by other lenders. Britain still controlled 44 per cent of all international loans, but France controlled 20 per cent, Germany 13 per cent, the United States 8 per cent and Belgium, the Netherlands and Switzerland together some 12 per cent. Of the borrowers of these funds, 27 per cent were in Europe, notably Russia,

Turkey and Austria-Hungary. Some 24 per cent of the loans went to North America, about two-thirds to the United States and some one-third to Canada. Latin America received some 19 per cent, with Argentina, Brazil and Mexico together accounting for four-fifths of the total. Asia took 16 per cent, with India, Ceylon, China and Japan receiving the bulk of the funds, while Africa's 9 per cent went almost entirely to South Africa and Egypt and Oceania's 5 per cent almost exclusively to Australia.

As international investment had grown, the direction of investment had changed, especially the direction taken by British capital. Around 1850, over half of British foreign investment had gone to Europe. By 1870 the total of British investments had trebled, but only a quarter went to Europe, while another quarter went to the United States, over a fifth to India, and something over a tenth each to Latin America and the other British dominions. By 1914 Britain's total foreign investments had more than quadrupled from the 1870 level, but only five per cent went to Europe. The United States and Latin America each took a fifth, but India took only a tenth while the rest of the British empire absorbed nearly two-fifths of British investment. Though maintaining an interest in early non-European areas such as Argentina and the United States, Britain had substantially withdrawn from investment in Europe, while increasing investment in the overseas dominions outside of India. One could say that Britain had financed European economic development, then turned to other areas to finance their economic development. Alternatively, one could argue that Britain consistently invested in those areas subject to British political control or pressure, and when forced out, moved into other dependent areas. From this second perspective, the size of British foreign investment was not based on Britain's 'willingness to lend', but on the political fact that Britain possessed the largest overseas empire of any European nation.

The pattern of investment by other lenders also suggests that in the final decades before the First World War international lending tended to become competitive rather than cooperative or complementary. By 1914, the major lending nations were committing their funds overwhelmingly to their political allies or to regions they controlled. French loans to Russia and German loans to Austria-Hungary clearly reflected diplomatic alliances. From 1880 to 1914 French lending more than trebled, but increasingly France's money was invested in Russia, as well as France's colonies, rather than in France's Mediterranean neighbours. German foreign investment rose rapidly before 1914, but fully half of German loans went to Austria-Hungary, while the rest dispersed throughout the world. The European nations placed large loans in their overseas colonies, while the United States lent funds to weak and dependent neighbours in the western hemisphere, but none of the major lenders placed significant funds in the others' colonies. There were some exceptions, such as the remnants of the original French investment in the Suez Canal in Egypt, United States investment in Canada, the loans of all four to Latin America, and smaller international lending operations elsewhere, such as the Balkans, north Africa and the Far East. However, France was effectively shut out of Egyptian loans after the 1880s, and United States investment in Canada was only a small fraction of British loans. Latin America was clearly divided into zones of influence, with the United States dominant in Mexico and Cuba, and Britain in Argentina. The international loans to Morocco, Tunisia and China, finally, were accompanied by serious diplomatic disputes among the powers which threatened on occasion to lead to war. Though long-term investment flowed in unprecedented amounts, the world seemed to be increasingly divided into rival economic empires, each dominated by one of the great financial powers.

Britain's role continued to be crucial. London remained the largest source of long-term investment in overseas regions, and Britain remained the only major world market for both primary products and manufactured goods not restricted by high and increasing tariffs. The system therefore depended on the competitiveness of the British economy. Britain could and did accumulate a continual deficit in trade relations, but the deficit could not become consistently larger than Britain's traditional surplus in the 'invisible' elements in the balance of payments – freight and insurance fees, and especially interest on foreign loans – for continued British long-term lending depended on continued surpluses in the overall British balance of payments. Given Britain's importance in the international economic system, it was a matter of international concern as well as injured British patriotism that the British economy steadily lost ground to foreign competitors in the generation before the First World War. As British industry became less competitive, Britain's trade deficit increased, from an average of 117 million pounds per year in 1875–84, to an average of 147 million pounds per year in 1904–13, an increase of 25 per cent.

Until the war Britain proved able to 'afford' the trade deficit. British national product rose some 66 per cent in the three decades before 1914, and therefore the trade deficit declined from 8.5 to 6.5 per cent of national product, while at the same time Britain continued to enjoy large and increasing earnings from shipping, insurance and interest charges. Nonetheless even in the absence of war the British payments position would have continued to deteriorate as international competition continued to increase. In the event, the shock administered by the war to the old system proved irreparable. The war not only accelerated Britain's decline relative to the United States and Japan, but also forced Britain to liquidate a large portion of the debt owed to British lenders by other nations to pay for the conflict, lowering the amount received in interest payments and increasing the difficulty of covering the negative trade balance. Britain entered the postwar world weakened both relatively and absolutely, and the attempt to continue in the traditional international role, though understandable, was doomed from the outset.

RESULTS OF IMPERIALISM

Imperialism changed the colonial areas irrevocably. Cartographers and politicians in the capitals of Europe arbitrarily divided the continents of Asia and Africa without regard for traditional boundaries. Rivers were often chosen as convenient borders between administrative areas, although many African peoples lived on both banks of rivers – after the map-makers had wielded their pens, they found themselves divided into two different territories. Similarly, the straight lines which divide many African states today were convenient lines of longitude or latitude agreed upon by European statesmen. European imperialism disrupted the culture of the colonial areas, imposing western notions of religion, art, education and government on local populations, and attempting to destroy local cultures. Socially, the immigration of Europeans into colonial areas established new elites of farmers and businessmen, administrators and soldiers; the native populations were forced into an economically and socially inferior role as workmen on their farms and servants in their houses. Meanwhile, Europeans recruited a certain number of local people to collaborate with them in the imperialist enterprise; this so-called 'comprador class' became Europeanised and indebted to their white patrons. In their turn, they forced the masses of the population to serve them; in many cases they replaced the whites as the dominant class in the independent Asian and African nations in the mid-twentieth century.

Economically, imperialism turned the colonial areas into vast regions for the production of primary products for the industries of Europe. Capital loaned by the countries of western Europe and the United States unquestionably made possible economic development which otherwise would not have occurred. Nevertheless, the kinds of investment favoured by the lending countries served their own interests first and the interests of the recipient countries only second. From the standpoint of the majority the benefits were nebulous. Few of the Rumanians who revolted in 1907, for instance, had profited from western European investments. The construction of the railway required to by-pass the falls on the lower Congo between 1888 and 1898 took the lives of so many thousands of workers that the entire surrounding region was depopulated. Payment of interest and principal imposed direct burdens on the majority in the form of high prices charged by government-supported monopolies and taxes levied to repay state loans. French investors in the Russian coal and iron industries attempted to ensure a high level of profits by forming cartel organisations. Throughout eastern

Europe the burden of state loans threatened to bankrupt governments. In 1914, 30 per cent of Bulgarian government revenues went to service the state debt, and in all the Balkan states except Rumania foreign bondholders administered special taxes earmarked for repayment of the government debt. In Africa and Asia colonial administrations insisted that their new subjects pay for improvements in transportation and government services which benefited European entrepreneurs.

The effects of imperialism on Europe were the converse. Europe benefited economically from the raw materials, and socially the colonial areas provided a domain for fortune-seekers and officials. There was a darker side to colonial conquest, not only for the conquered, but for the conquerors as well. By 1914, many Europeans had become used to treating masses of other men as less than human. In addition, the very fact of Europeans dividing up, to them, distant areas of the world was bound to produce conflict over territorial boundaries and spheres of influence. In the years from 1898 to 1912, a constant succession of colonial crises pitted one imperialist power against the other, though always at the expense of the local populations. Any one of them could have become a major conflagration, indeed a world war. The first of the crises occurred in the Sudan in 1898. Britain and France were rivals for this territory, and armed parties representing the two powers were marching towards each other, the French from the west and the British from the north. They met at Fashoda; politicians in London and Paris realised that a military encounter would be highly dangerous and that only Germany and Italy would benefit from an Anglo-French confrontation. So, in 1899, they signed a convention partitioning Africa into spheres of influence; France would have an informal hegemony over the northwest and Britain would have the upper hand in Egypt. This act rounded off the partition of Africa, but it did not put an end to conflicts in the continent.

Imperial rivalries actually exploded into war in 1898 when the American battleship *Maine* blew up in the Harbour of Havana, capital of the Spanish colony of Cuba. Blaming the Spanish for the explosion, the United States declared war and defeated the Spanish in a series of naval engagements and land sorties. Cuba, where a revolt against Spanish rule had been in progress for some time, became independent, though some in the United States favoured annexation. However, the American president McKinley, after a night of prayer, decided that it was the 'duty' of the United States to take possession of the Philippine Islands, to 'civilise' the inhabitants and also, as he said later, to guarantee American access to the markets of Asia.

Also in 1898, there began a war in South Africa, the Boer War, which Hobson (and another young correspondent, Winston Churchill) saw at first hand. Southern Africa was a prize for the imperialists with its store of natural resources. Competing interests came to a head and the result was a war between the British and the Boers, cattle-raising descendants of seventeenth-century Dutch settlers. Frustrated by the Boers' guerilla tactics, the British resorted to concentration camps, hostages and reprisals. The war, and the necessary large numbers of British troops, created opposition in Britain. No other power intervened, however, and the Boers were forced to come to terms in 1902.

In 1905 there was another international crisis, this one in Morocco, caused by German meddling in an area of French interest. France had begun to twist the arm of the sultan of Morocco, whereupon the German chancellor persuaded the kaiser to sail to Tangier, the capital of Morocco, and tell the sultan that the Germans would aid him against the French. This was a bluff, as the Germans had no intention of going to war, but they did want to irritate the French. The crisis was defused, and the major result was a strengthening of the bond between France and Britain and the aggravation of anti-German sentiment in Paris.

Just as the Moroccan crisis was being resolved, another war was winding up on the other side of the world. Russia was also an imperialist power – throughout the late 1800s, the tsar had extended his influence in the Balkans and annexed territory in central Asia. Then Russia had become interested in the Far East, particularly Korea. But the Japanese were also interested in Korea. Japan secured an alliance with Britain in 1902, and made good use of Britain's benevolent neutrality during the drift towards war in 1904. The Japanese had the advantage of proximity, while the Russians had to transfer men and ships from the west to Asia, though the Trans-Siberian railway had not been completed and Britain refused use of the Suez Canal or British harbours ana coaling stations along the sea route around Africa. The destruction of the Russian fleet at Tsushima and the storming of Port Arthur gave notice that another new imperialist power had emerged upon the world scene. Russia's defeat, coupled with the dislocation of food supplies to the cities during the war, led to the 1905 revolution. The tsarist government survived, though forced to establish a representative assembly. Russian military prestige suffered a severe blow; more importantly the war was a major defeat inflicted on a major European power by an island nation in Asia. Significant too was the fact that the treaty which ended the war was negotiated by the Americans, the other newly emergent non-European power.

In 1911, attention shifted back to North Africa once again with a second Moroccan crisis. It was a contrived crisis, engineered by the Germans and directed at France. The Germans sent a gunboat to the Moroccan port of Agadir, ostensibly to protect German interests, but really to threaten the French. Just as in 1905, the kaiser threatened to use force if necessary. The British, who felt left out, in their turn began to rattle sabres. In a replay of 1905, the tensions eased; Germany agreed to give France a free hand in Morocco and France rewarded Germany with territorial concessions in the Congo. The animosity between the two nations, however, did not lessen.

These crises were not all determined by economic grievances, but political control obviously determined the ability to exploit a colonial area efficiently. What had happened was a transferal of European war-making from the Continent to the far-flung possessions of empire. The conflicts in Africa and the Pacific heightened tensions in Europe and underlined the role of the colonial areas in European foreign policy and economic strategy. In some ways, they were dress rehearsals for a bigger conflict; after Lenin many Marxist authors would later interpret the First

World War precisely as an imperialist war, pitting the imperialist powers in a death struggle. And certainly in 1914, the economic competition between England and Germany, and the political antipathy between France and Germany, had been aggravated by the tensions in the colonial world.

3

EUROPEAN SOCIETY IN THE BELLE EPOQUE

SOCIAL CLEAVAGES

Antoine Sylvère was a peasant boy in the French region of Auvergne at the turn of the twentieth century; his memoirs describe the wrenching poverty of the countryside. Malnutrition, unemployment, accidents, sickness and illiteracy plagued the landless farmers of central France. Some managed to eke out a bare existence on miserable plots of land, but others were less fortunate and had to resort to begging. Toinou, as the author was called, remembers one particular couple. The woman had fallen prey to leprosy at the age of 45, and the disease rotted away her nose, pockmarked her face with black holes and pulled her lips back from toothless gums. Her husband had become blind with an eye disease which caused him so much pain that he screamed for hours on end. The couple could no longer farm their land and resorted to going from house to house asking for alms. When they received charity, they offered a prayer for their benefactors in return: 'We have only that to give for the bread that we eat'. Toinou comments:

At that time, France was the richest country in the world. She produced too much wine, too much wheat. The banks pumped billions of francs, their surplus of resources, into all of Europe and even across the oceans. She financed the construction of American ports and various foreign enterprises. A part of the profits returned to the country to be invested in luxury, in retribution for venal loves and scandals. The *demi-monde* shone from the fire of its pearls and diamonds and the city man fantasised about the

gommeuse in her black stockings. It was the happy year
1900, the 'Belle Epoque'. A half-century later I, Toinou,
would be most surprised to learn about it.

Toinou's anecdote reveals the two sides of social life: the
poverty of the majority of the population and the wealth and
brilliance of a tiny elite, the contrast between beggars and
party-goers. Society filled the spectrum from capitalists in
Paris to mendicants in the Auvergne. The economic changes
of the nineteenth century had brought wealth to a few and
maintained others in poverty, whether the poverty of the
agricultural countryside or the industrial ghetto. A few
fortunate individuals tussled for political and economic
domination in centres of power while peasants and
proletarians struggled just to put bread on the tables of their
shacks. In the wide gap between lived the artisans and the
petit bourgeois, perhaps not poverty stricken, but living
precariously in the maw of the new economic system.

Demographically, Europe was a continent with a large
population unequally divided among nations and also
unequally distributed between city and countryside. Though
the absolute size of a country's or a city's population in part
simply reflected the accidents of its previous history, size
itself could powerfully affect the course of economic, political
and social developments. Russia had over 126 million
inhabitants in 1900 and was counted a great power despite
its poverty. London, with nearly seven million inhabitants,
was larger than some nations on the Continent. Meanwhile,
there were 2.7 million Parisians and 1.9 million Berliners, 1.7
million Viennese and 1.3 million residents of St Petersburg,
making the political capitals of Europe its demographic capitals as well. There were many other large cities: Moscow had
just under a million residents, Budapest, Glasgow, Hamburg
and Liverpool each had over 700,000 inhabitants, Manchester
and Warsaw over 600,000 and Amsterdam, Barcelona,
Birmingham, Brussels and Naples over 500,000. If there was
a certain correlation between industry and large cities, it was
not perfect; neither Barcelona nor Naples was a factory city.
These main cities centralised political administration,

economic activities and national culture. Most had seen accelerating population increase since 1890; nevertheless, except for Britain a majority of Europe's population still lived outside the major cities. Most western European regions had a dense network of small towns and villages; in eastern Europe towns were fewer and metropolises were the exceptions which proved the rule of a rural society. In west and east villages often grouped together only several hundred inhabitants in a small settlement around a main street, a church, a few shops and perhaps a school or an artisan's workshop. The economies and ways of life in such hamlets were, both literally and figuratively, miles away from the glitter of city lights.

Not only residence, but other cleavage lines as well, divided Europe's population. One such was religion, even in an increasingly secular age. Most Europeans were nominally Christian, but they were divided in their loyalties; France, southern Europe, Ireland and parts of eastern Europe remained bastions of Roman Catholicism, but a large part of the Balkans and almost all of European Russia were Eastern Orthodox. Northern Europe was dominated by varieties of Protestantism: Anglicanism in England, Presbyterianism in Scotland, Lutheranism in the Scandinavian countries and northern Germany. Other Protestant groups – such as Methodists and Calvinists – formed minority religions around the Continent. The Ottoman Empire was Europe's Islamic state, and a substantial number of Muslims practised their religion in Russia. Throughout Europe there lived colonies of Jews, and certain cities, such as Berlin and Thessaloniki, were centres of Jewish civilisation. Each of these religious groups provided a certain ideology for its adherents and an ethical code. Furthermore, each religion provided both an international loyalty – the body of all believers – and a centre to daily life. The village church was a meeting place and social centre, as well as the place of worship. Religious tensions occasionally flared up, particularly in areas with mixed populations. Especially threatening was the wave of anti-Semitism directed against the Jews; racist social theories and anti-Semitic propaganda spread throughout

Europe, anti-Semitic political parties emerged in western and central Europe, and in eastern Europe persecution occasionally culminated in pogroms of destruction and death.

Another source of division, which sometimes overlapped with religion, was ethnicity and language. Few European nations were culturally homogeneous, and even the standard 'national' culture was often a local dialect and folklore that had been adopted officially by the nation-state. Large countries like Germany or Italy had a multiplicity of dialects, often so different that people from different provinces could communicate with each other only with difficulty. In the Habsburg empire there was a baffling intermixture of languages, including German, Hungarian, Czech, Polish, Croatian and Rumanian. Even a country like France, with a centralised culture in Paris, had a variety of dialects and regional variations in speech, and along the borders there were totally different linguistic groups. In the north were Flemish speakers along the Belgian border and German speakers along the borders of Alsace and Lorraine (whose French speakers in turn had constituted a linguistic minority in Germany since 1870, when the provinces had been annexed by the new German empire); in the west there were Bretons, in the southwest lived Basque speakers and in the southeast Catalans; the island of Corsica preserved its own language, a mixture of French and Italian. Often the speakers of these languages formed cohesive groups with their own particular identity. Such was the case of the Basques in France and Spain; their language was totally different from the Romance languages spoken around them and their culture varied markedly from either French or Spanish civilisation. In addition to these localised ethnic groups, other minorities were widely dispersed. The gypsies with their caravans and violins were common travellers from Spain to the Balkans. Marginally more fortunate than the poor gypsies were the Greeks, Armenians and Jews. The last two lacked an independent homeland and were ruthlessly persecuted by other groups; the Greeks had possessed a nation-state since the early 1800s, but many Greeks still lived in Istanbul, Smyrna, Cyprus, Alexandria and elsewhere. These groups carried with them their own languages and religions and formed communities in alien environments, usually in cities where they worked in commerce.

A further dividing line across European society was legal or governmental. This again related to ethnicity and religion, as many minority groups were restricted in their liberty to speak their language, practise their religion or even live in certain regions. Schoolchildren in France were punished for speaking in dialect, and the programmes of 'Germanisation', 'Russification', 'Magyarisation' and the like increased the level of discrimination against ethnic minorities in central and eastern Europe. Throughout Europe, women were particularly the object of legal discrimination: they were almost nowhere allowed to vote, and seldom allowed even to own their own property or manage their own affairs. In most Catholic countries, divorce was prohibited; where permitted, it was always easier for men to obtain than for women. But if the law oppressed some, it favoured others. Artisan guilds still existed in many countries. Members of the British universities elected their own representatives to parliament until after the Second World War. Government employees enjoyed many perquisites and rewards, as did the clergy in most countries. Throughout Europe, the aristocracy enjoyed numerous rights denied to the non-nobility. Sometimes the rights were symbolic, as the right of English noblemen to be hanged with a silken cord if convicted of a capital offence. In other cases, noble status conferred more tangible advantages: exemption from taxes, the right to sit in certain parliamentary chambers (as in the English House of Lords), the right to discipline employees and former serfs.

All Europeans therefore saw themselves and others as members of particular groups – residential, religious, ethnic, legal – and that corporate identity restricted or enlarged the possibilities for an individual's economic and political activities. But the main division among Europeans had to do more directly with economics – the divisions between those in different occupations and thus of different status and income. Professional training for a doctor or barrister took years, yet many a manual labourer had neither training nor specific skills. Hordes of chambermaids cleaned the homes of Europe's wealthy, while armies of factory workers produced the materials traded by agents of major stock exchanges. Here the link with economics was obvious; you were what you earned. Status was increasingly determined by wealth and the ability to accumulate it rather than by other criteria common in earlier centuries. Every European was locked into a certain position by his or her occupation; although possibilities for social mobility existed, the chances for a pauper to become a prince were highly unfavourable. Even the examples of the 'self-made men' who rose from simple inventors or foremen to become heads of major companies through their entrepreneurial ability had become rare. So, each European had an occupational identity as a cobbler or bookbinder, a factory hand or a farmer; in fact, each might join a mutual aid society, religious fraternity or trade union composed of members of the same profession united for social or political purposes.

SOCIAL CLASSES

Elites and middle classes

Europe's nobility may have been a declining class at the beginning of the twentieth century, but it was far from negligible in public life. Even in republican France, many titled citizens served in the army, the diplomatic service or the church – three areas where they could work without loss of prestige, it was thought – and an aristocratic name could add a cachet to a board of directors of a company or the life of a Parisian salon. In England, the aristocracy held a great deal of power; not until the reform of 1911 was the House of Lords' power diminished, when the chamber was reduced to being able to impose only a suspensory veto on legislation approved by the House of Commons. The 'old' nobility were not averse to exploiting new economic opportunities, and 'new' industrial magnates were increasingly coopted into the upper class with patents of nobility. In England, there were 'beer barons' such as Guinness, 'press barons' such as Northcliffe and also Lord Ashton, known as 'Lord Linoleum' from the source of his wealth. In central and eastern Europe, 'new' nobles were more likely to be those who had served the state as bureaucrats or army officers. Determining the wealth of such men in statistical terms is impossible; what is certain, however, is that they continued to exercise great economic and political power. In Prussia in 1913, three-quarters of the members of the upper house of the parliament and a fourth of those in the lower house were noblemen. The nobility throughout Europe was still an expanding class; from 1871–1918, the German emperor created over a thousand new nobles, and between 1886 and 1914, the English monarch created two hundred new peers. Indeed, the advantages of noble status led many to claim it, not always legitimately. The Italian government felt compelled to legislate heavy penalties for such frauds as late as 1896. Though perhaps 'diluted', a legally segregated class still existed at the pinnacle of society.

Slightly lower in the hierarchy, though not difficult to differentiate, were the members of the upper middle class, bankers and investors, manufacturers and merchants. These were people who had 'made it' in the new industrial world. A theory making the rounds of France in the early twentieth century held that two hundred families ran the country, a cliché based on the fact that only the two hundred largest shareholders in the Bank of France were entitled to vote for the bank's board of directors. In France, as everywhere in Europe, an oligarchy of the rich and powerful did exist. They maintained their power through diversification of their economic interests and interlocking directorships of corporations, and they kept their social power through easy access to cultural institutions (such as elite secondary schools) and intermarriage. Politically, they often supported conservative parties in western Europe and formed the inner councils for autocratic monarchs in eastern Europe. In this period of finance capitalism and imperialism, the upper middle class found it easy to consolidate its fortunes, and the First World War would see the further enrichment of such businessmen as arms manufacturers.

In addition to this economic *crème de la crème* of European society, there was a large middle class and lower middle class. The more prosperous of these were the lawyers, doctors, teachers, engineers and various other professionals whose qualifications were certified by diplomas and who worked in offices. Some were conservative, some liberal; some had pulled themselves up from peasant or proletarian origins, but many, and perhaps most, had been born into their class. The middle classes thus tended to be a self-perpetuating group, not so prestigious as the haute bourgeoisie and the aristocracy but clearly differentiated from the working class. The middle classes were marked by a propensity to save a proportion of their earnings, while the workers and peasants did not – but then rarely did their earnings leave them enough to save. The middle classes tended to have progressively fewer children, a trend that ultimately spread to the working class as well. They tended to live in certain sections of the city, the West End of London, for example, or the middle storeys of apartment buildings in Paris (where before the electric elevator social segregation was more a question of the floor of a building on which one lived than of neighbourhood). The middle classes sent their children to schools and then on to universities; they patronised cultural institutions; they upheld many of the beliefs of the church and state. They were not a monolithic group; neither were they all exemplars of the political conservatism, cultural philistinism and moral prudery with which they are often charged. In western Europe, their numbers were great; in eastern and southern Europe, they were fewer. Many lived in cities, but large numbers lived in the countryside; here they dominated the peasant population and formed a link between the urban world and the peasant world, between the powers of the central state and its subjects. Such middle-class people were often the mayors, schoolteachers and priests in the rural community.

The bottom of the middle class was composed of a large number of white collar workers. A 'service revolution' had taken place in Europe's economy, swelling the number of people occupied in low-level white collar jobs: secretaries, accountants, shop assistants and clerks. Their work separated them from the manual labour of proletarians, yet their incomes and origins often made them more like workers than the bourgeois whom they emulated. That precariousness made them particularly vulnerable to periods of economic difficulty; the closure of a bank or a stock exchange crisis could ruin hundreds of small investors and result in unemployment for equal numbers of clerks and accountants. Such vulnerability also made them prey to political demagoguery, and from the ranks of the dissatisfied lower middle classes political reactionaries would recruit their supporters in later years. It was they who would be most afraid of Bolshevism politically, and, socially, afraid that their hard-won middle-class status could be lost and that they would join the proletarian masses. Here, in fact, lay a tension just as strong as the one between the lords of finance and their proletarian menials – the tension between the lower middle class and the working class. The lower middle class might sometimes ally itself with the workers to overthrow a government or support a dissident politician, but at other times it would ally with its social superiors to fight off the proletarians whom it despised and feared.

Workers

The 'working class' of Europe was a large and heterogeneous group ranging from the proletarians in giant steel manufacturing plants to individual artisans working at home or in small shops. In many regions, particularly in western Europe, the former predominated by the turn of the twentieth century, but by no means was a European 'worker' synonymous with 'factory hand'. In eastern and southern Europe, with the exceptions of factory cities like Milan or Breslau, most of the working class was still composed of artisans, each of whom worked with at most a few assistants (often family members) in a system little changed by the industrial revolution. Nevertheless, these artisans and workers, together with the peasantry, formed the overwhelming mass of the population. Over three-quarters of the population of Europe (and up to 90 per cent in some regions) could be classified as either peasant or proletarian in this period, and these 'lower orders' lived in poverty and hardship.

In Great Britain in 1901, there were over 4 million workers in manufacturing, almost a million more in mining, and 1.2

million in construction. As the earliest industraliser, Britain had the highest percentage of factory workers. Germany, which had passed Britain as the major industrial power in Europe by the year 1907, had 6 million workers in manufacturing, almost 2 million in construction and over 1 million in mining; in France, there were about 3 million workers in manufacturing, 500,000 in construction and 250,000 in mining – an indication of the somewhat slower nature of French industrialisation. On the peripheral areas of the continent, areas of lesser industrialisation, the number of factory workers was correspondingly smaller; in Italy, for example, of a population roughly three-fifths as large as Germany's, there were only 2.5 million industrial workers. The Netherlands and Ireland each had roughly 5 million residents in 1900, but the number of manufacturing workers in the Netherlands was more than twice that of Ireland. Russia had 90 million more people than England and Wales, but the tsar's empire counted only 3 million factory workers and 155,000 miners, though these concentrated in exceptionally large plants. Disparities of economic development, therefore, also meant disparities in the distribution of the workforce.

Although working conditions could be harsh anywhere in Europe, they were best in the west. Higher wages, better housing, more effective labour organisations and new laws which limited hours and provided for compensation in cases of accident or illness – and the first old-age pensions – made life more pleasant than before for workers in Britain, Germany, Scandinavia, the Low Countries and to a lesser extent France and Italy. In other parts of Europe, conditions changed little. In Russia and parts of eastern Europe, employers were almost entirely free to treat workers as they wished. Only in 1885 was night work for women and children prohibited in Russia; in 1897, the working day was reduced to $11\frac{1}{2}$ hours, but employers could still require their workers to work overtime to clean their machines. Factory workers could literally be locked inside the factory walls, and workers fined or dismissed for absences for marriages, sickness, or childbirth. They were fined or disciplined for losing tools, for damaging machinery, for producing products not up to standard and for failing to fulfil quotas. Such fines were duly recorded in the work book, a kind of record ledger which workers were forced to purchase so that their misdemeanours could be recorded. Even if the Russian case is one of the worst, throughout Europe the workers were badly lodged and fed, abused and mistreated, and paid a pittance for their labours. Faced with these problems, they had little choice except to try to find a job at a different enterprise or to migrate.

To be at once a worker and a woman was to be doubly disadvantaged. Working-class husbands, when able, removed their wives from the labour force, in this emulating the upper and middle classes. Women's place, they agreed, was in the home; yet in peasant and artisan homes women, perhaps indeed a majority of all European women, worked long, unpaid hours to maintain the family enterprise. The sorts of paid labour available to women were severely restricted: employment in a textile factory, as a seamstress producing ready-to-wear clothes, as a domestic servant, or as a prostitute. Domestic servants made up the largest category of non-agricultural employment in virtually every European country; a survey conducted in Berlin around the turn of the century concluded that nearly one out of every ten women between the ages of fifteen and sixty worked as a prostitute. Some change could be detected, spreading from west to east. The service revolution brought new opportunities to women, though their role continued to be severely restricted. For those with access to education, the rapid growth of primary education opened one new avenue. There were 100,000 more primary school teachers in Britain in 1910 than 20 years earlier. For less fortunate women, an increasing demand for sales staff, filing clerks and typists reflected the growth of services from another angle. At first considered a male occupation because of its alleged complexity, typing rapidly became a firmly female occupation. Telephone switchboards similarly came to be staffed almost exclusively by women. Outside the accepted 'female' occupations, women encountered only hostility, from workers' organisations as well as from the conservative social and political establishment.

In seeking to improve their lot, European workers

discovered that legitimate channels of protest were few – in many countries, democratic institutions did not exist, and in most countries suffrage was restricted to those who could pass literacy tests or paid a certain amount of tax. In Italy, the suffrage reform of 1881 had enfranchised only some seven per cent of the population; in 1907 Norway became the first European country to extend the vote to women. The bourgeois political parties evinced little response to workers' needs or demands and were tardy in sponsoring social welfare legislation. Faced with these difficulties, workers had two political alternatives: extraparliamentary action or the adoption of a new ideology appropriate to their condition. Extraparliamentary action could take the form of insurrection or industrial action against their employers. Insurrections were dramatic events but unsuccessful, and were invariably put down ruthlessly by the governments in power. As for strikes, workers again were faced with the power of their employers and the difficulty of finding alternative employment if they were locked out or dismissed.

Politically, a number of creeds during the nineteenth century had been attractive to workers, but the most important ideology adopted by the working class was that of Karl Marx. Explaining history as the history of class struggles, Marx called on proletarians to come together with the powerful slogan 'Workers of the world, unite'. Only working-class solidarity, Marx felt, could triumph over the exploitation of the masses by the holders of economic power, the owners of the means of production. Such a class war must aim at a complete change in the existing political, social and economic order. And such a change was historically inevitable, said Marx, for the development of capitalism would create the conditions for its own overthrow.

Marx wrote his *Communist Manifesto* in 1848 and for the next three decades the message of his followers became increasingly attractive to workers – and increasingly terrifying to the bourgeoisie and aristocracy. However, Marxism, confronted by the superior power of the rulers of society, had little practical success. Then in the late nineteenth century, a change occurred. The effects of the depression of the 1870s and 1880s served as an inspiration to class consciousness among Europe's workers, and the bourgeois governments gradually removed restrictions on working-class organisation. Thus were born the socialist parties of Europe; in the last three decades of the nineteenth century, a socialist party was established in virtually every country of Europe and an international association of the parties was created. By the end of the century, socialist parties were forces to be reckoned with in national parliaments.

Socialism was not just a political campaign. The socialist parties sponsored various institutions and activities for workers: newspapers and books, classes and meetings, even holiday resorts. The paid-up members of European socialist parties could live a great deal of their lives outside work in a socialist milieu, so the movement provided a cultural focus as well as a political one. A multitude of functions was also served by the French *bourses du travail* and the Italian *camere del lavoro*. These institutions, which also date from the late nineteenth century, were combination hiring halls, social centres and meeting places for the workers. Located in almost all major cities, they became a focal point for the creation of class consciousness among the working class.

Strikes, protests and other forms of action often emanated from socialist meeting halls or workers' institutions. A wave of strike action affected Europe in the 20 years before the First World War. In Italy, the 'Fatti di Maggio' in 1898 ended in the deaths of 1 policeman and 500 workers. There were over 1,000 strikes in 1901 and over 800 (with almost 200,000 participants) the following year. In 1904, there was a general strike, heralding a more concerted action by the working class in later years. The pattern was similar elsewhere in Europe, and striking workers were a familiar sight during the Belle Epoque. The reasons for strikes included lack of recognition of labour unions by management as well as protests against bad working conditions and inadequate wages. The achievements of strikers, as of revolutionaries, were few, again because of the power of employers. But these strikes did indicate the discontent among the working class and their new militancy.

Peasants

In spite of the industrialisation and urbanisation which seem so characteristic of the nineteenth century, by 1900 much of Europe remained rural and many Europeans could best be classified as peasants. If less than half the population of parts of western Europe lived in the countryside, then up to 90 per cent of those in eastern and parts of southern and northern Europe were rural dwellers. The peasantry was still a social category which implied particular economic relationships, a corpus of popular culture and folklore, and certain political rights (or, generally, a lack thereof). This points to the basic difference between a peasant and a farmer; a farmer is one who works in agriculture, who may or may not own his land, but who is inserted into a capitalist network of production and exchange. A peasant, by contrast, is someone who exists inside a traditional society of which farming is only one part and who is the inheritor of a body of traditions common to his region and work. Peasants produce primarily for their own subsistence, while farmers produce for the market. The peasantry in the early twentieth century was a declining class; it was shrinking with the migration to the cities and the move to industrial labour, while the old folklore and rituals were dying out under the influence of a centralisation of the state and of national culture through universal education, compulsory military service, and new forms of transportation and economic interchange. Nonetheless, neither the peasantry nor peasant life had disappeared.

In western Europe, peasants had been liberated from their legal servility long before the twentieth century. Serfdom had disappeared in Britain and parts of Scandinavia in the late Middle Ages. The remnants of feudalism had disappeared in France in 1789 and in Germany and the Habsburg empire in 1848. In these areas, peasants were legally free to move about the country, to buy and sell land and to change employment. Economically, they were less independent, as they often lacked the financial wherewithal to change their status substantially. Many peasants did indeed own plots of land in Britain, Scandinavia, France and Germany, as well as in the western Habsburg lands, but such plots were not always large enough to maintain their families; consequently many peasants were forced to rent or lease property or to sell their labour to a larger property owner. The number of peasant proprietors had increased in the nineteenth century; in France, it was said that more of the people who actually tilled the soil now owned land than ever before.

In southern Europe, the peasants' condition was less favourable. Plots owned by peasants were smaller, and sharecropping, which had practically disappeared from western Europe, was still common. In this arrangement, the peasant lived and worked on the land of a landowner, often an absentee bourgeois or noble proprietor, and paid rent to the master in kind, that is, with a share of the crops. Such a system was precarious, as landlords often retained the right to expel the sharecropper for lack of work or misdeeds; furthermore, extra profit often accrued to the landowner rather than to the peasant. In the large plantation estates of southern Europe, the latifundia, the sharecropping peasant was little better than a serf.

In eastern Europe, conditions were still worse. Former serfs in the domains of the Habsburgs continued to suffer under aristocratic domination after 1848, and even formal emancipation came only in 1861 in Russia and 1864 in Rumania. Throughout eastern Europe, emancipation settlements gave the peasants only a small share of the land, a share for which they paid dearly. In Russia, for instance, as many as 40 per cent of the peasants received allotments of land insufficient to support themselves and their families. The redemption payments – compensation owed to the government for their freedom – were set at very high levels, and would have extended for most until 1910 and for some until 1931 if they had not been abolished in 1905. Furthermore, most peasants in Russia were still tied to their village commune, the *mir*. The *mir* retained control of distribution of land and bore collective responsibility for all taxes levied on peasants as well as for redemption dues, and these arrangements severely limited the real freedom of the newly-emancipated serfs. The *mir* was also assessed for the taxes of deceased peasants until the next census removed them from the rolls, so the community often had to pay for the dead as well as the living.

In much of eastern and southern Europe, the peasant economy was still largely a question of polycultural production; peasant households tried to produce enough of the basic necessities of all sorts to feed their families. Grain or maize, a patch of vegetables, a few grapevines and perhaps a pig or a cow comprised peasant holdings. Surpluses were indeed sold at village or town markets, but except for large landholdings and the producers of specialty products such as fine wines and tobacco, most agriculturalists sold their output in the local economy. The vagaries of climate wreaked havoc on small and large farms alike; a major insect infestation, flood or spate of bad weather could ruin a peasant's livelihood overnight. Population was increasing and rose most rapidly in the poorest areas of the south and east. In Russia many *mir* redistributed land periodically on the basis of family size, and the number doing so increased, reaching nearly 90 per cent around 1900. Individual peasants therefore had little motive to improve their present holdings, but a strong motive to have as many children as possible. In southern and southeastern Europe the traditional division of holdings among heirs seems to have had the same effect. There were severe famines in Russia in 1891 and 1897 and in Spain in 1904–6. In many regions, productivity stagnated; owners lacked capital to change techniques, and smallholdings did not lend themselves to agricultural experimentation. Competition reduced profits; increasing quantities of wheat were imported into Europe from the plains of North America and the Ukraine, which meant that marginal cultivation was less feasible. Meat from Argentina, beer from Germany and cheap wines from Italy could hurt producers of these commodities in other areas, and the creation of an international economy therefore could have two-sided effects on the peasant economy.

Politically, peasants were also in a bad way. The main locus of contestatory political action lay in the factories and their industrial proletariat. Revolutionaries aimed their campaigns (and their theories) at the urban working class and very few attempts were made to organise the peasantry into a cohesive political force. One attempt, populism in Russia, did aim at taking the gospel of revolution to the peasant masses, but the effort was largely unsuccessful. Rural interests throughout Europe were represented in national parliaments by the bourgeoisie of the countryside, not the peasantry, and local elites dominated their spheres of influence. Political power at the village level lay with the priest, the landowner, the schoolmaster and the mayor, who did or did not cooperate with each other depending on the society in question.

Without representation, the peasants often turned to violence. Desperate poverty in the south and east combined with national, ethnic and religious divisions, and with hostility toward increasingly intrusive governments, to produce a chronically unstable situation. The rural uprising in Russia which contributed to the revolution of 1905 was the largest and most widespread since the eighteenth century. In Rumania in 1907 the government mobilised 120,000 troops to repress the peasant revolt, and at least 10,000 peasants died before order was restored. In Italy in 1908 a wave of violent agricultural strikes culminated in widespread land seizures, followed by eviction and repression at the hands of the army, police and private armed 'squads'. Any concessions granted in the wake of large uprisings were limited. In most cases the only result of protest was a disproportionately brutal repression, as in Italy, and increased surveillance and pressure – much of rural Russia was under martial law continuously from 1905 to the collapse of the tsarist government in 1917.

Peasants fared somewhat better culturally. Access to 'high culture' (art, literature and music) gradually opened with increased literacy and compulsory education. But peasants seldom became painters or writers themselves, and they participated in national culture largely as spectators. However, peasants did retain a vibrant and sophisticated culture of their own. This 'popular culture' consisted of a body of traditions and customs, often intimately bound up with religious observances. The festivals of the Christian year – Easter, Christmas, saints' days – all marked days of celebration for peasants. The peasant community naturally gathered in the church for the ceremonies marking these festivals. The ritual of Catholicism or Eastern Orthodoxy enriched peasants' lives with colour, music, symbols and gestures; even in the more austere Protestantism, church activities provided the central focus of peasant culture. Despite secularisation, most peasants were baptised and married in churches and hoped for a Christian funeral. Such events marked the turning-points of life, and the church was present to give its blessing. Particularly in Catholic and Orthodox countries, children were named after saints, and villages and guilds invoked the intercession of their heavenly patrons at festivals and masses. Customs included ritual confession and absolution by priests, partaking of the Holy Communion, participation in the activities of religious confraternities, and decoration of the homes with statues, crucifixes or icons.

Secular customs also bound together the village community: feasts to mark the end of the harvest season, practical jokes played on members of the community who had transgressed its social mores (the 'charivari', for example, in which effigies of adulterous or contumacious citizens were paraded on donkeys to the accompaniment of clanking of utensils and jeers), bonfires to mark the midsummer day and regular gatherings to perform certain tasks (repairing instruments, threshing grain or pressing grapes). Such observances integrated the society; baptism, for example, not only reflected the Christian belief of removing the stain of original sin from the new-born, but was also a ritual way of welcoming new members to the village community and recognising their legitimate membership in that body. Furthermore, the precise ways in which these customs were carried out was a mode of self-identification, separating peasants in one region from those in another.

This folk culture in many ways set the peasantry apart from other social classes. The canon of traditions was integrated into the economic livelihood of the peasantry, as can be illustrated by the number of rituals associated with breadmaking. Bread was the staple of life in many parts of Europe and was consequently treated with respect. In central

France, each loaf was marked with the sign of the cross before being put into the oven, the head of the household enjoyed the prerogative of cutting the loaf at the table, and there existed a variety of terms to distinguish the various kinds of bread – the butt of the loaf, the piece given to children, the crumbs which remained, and so on. At the end of the mass, after the distribution of Holy Communion, the priest in Orthodox countries and in many Catholic regions distributed pieces of blessed ordinary bread to the congregation, emphasising the parallel between the consecrated host of the Eucharist and the everyday basis of nourishment, and thus linking together peasant economy and peasant culture.

MIGRATIONS

The effects of social change can also be seen in large-scale migrations, one of the most important phenomena of the period. There were two kinds of migration: one from villages to towns and especially major cities and the other of migration from one nation (or continent) to another. Such migrations had marked earlier decades of the nineteenth century, but they reached a culmination in the generation before the First World War. Migration could be voluntary or forced; either people moved from one region to another because they hoped for some advantage from the change or because they were forced away from their homes by circumstances. Deportations, expulsions, boundary changes leaving ethnic groups isolated as minorities, and even treaties mandating movements were examples of forced movements. But there was also a somewhat less dramatic migration in which people packed their belongings in the hope of a better life elsewhere. In the generation before the First World War, people could migrate freely, and they did, in previously inconceivable numbers. Within Europe, peasants and artisans from the provinces migrated to factory cities or capitals. The booming industrial metropolises of the Continent became magnets drawing migrants into their economies and often into their slums.

More occupational choices existed in cities, but many were the migrants who failed miserably and did not acclimatise to their new environments. Some returned to their native regions.

Recorded increases in urban populations give only an approximate notion of net migration, and do not even hint at the much larger gross flows of persons to and from the cities. They remain astonishing nonetheless. Among capital cities, the population of London rose from 5.6 to 7.3 million from 1890 to 1910, that of Berlin from 1.6 to 2.1 million, and that of St Petersburg from 1.0 to 2.0 million. Smaller industrial centres grew even more rapidly: Manchester from 505,000 to 714,000, Düsseldorf from 145,000 to 359,000, Lodz from 113,000 to 408,000, Ekaterinoslav from 47,000 to 196,000.

An example of migration within one country is provided by Paris. As the political, economic and cultural capital of France, its magnetism was particularly strong. In the early nineteenth century, immigrants to Paris came primarily from the northern regions of France. By the end of the century, however, they came from all over the nation. They accounted for a large party of the city's population; in the last quarter of the nineteenth century, native Parisians totalled only 35 per cent of the city's population, while 58 per cent had been born elsewhere in France. As for occupational structure, over half worked in industry by the end of the century, and the second largest group comprised those working in commerce. The immigrants lived in peripheral neighbourhoods of the city, the only areas in which they could find housing; in particular, many lived in the eastern suburbs near Paris' factories. The immigrants had come to Paris because wages were higher there (about one and a half times greater than in the provinces at the end of the century); yet ironically, the higher cost of living cancelled out most of their increased earnings. Upward social mobility existed for immigrants to Paris, but there was also the possibility of actually failing. Migrants in Paris were often suspected of revolutionary activities and were thought by many to be a criminal element of the population. But the poor were not the only French to move to Paris. Successful members of the provincial middle class often wanted to try their luck in the capital, students came to acquire certification for entry into the professions, aristocrats came to participate in the social season, politicians took up their seats in the parliament and the cultural elite came to work in the garrets of Montmartre and Montparnasse (so, too, did the criminal – and these same areas of entertainment were also reputed to be centres for gangster activities in the early twentieth century). Immigration made Paris a microcosm of the entire nation.

Europe was also linked to the rest of the world by a large and accelerating intercontinental migration. More than six million Europeans moved overseas during the decade of the 1890s, eleven million in the first ten years of the twentieth century, and nearly six million again in the five years before the First World War. Not all Europeans showed equal readiness to move, however, and easy generalisations about the causes and consequences of the migration are therefore hazardous. The highly industrialised countries of western Europe, for instance, experienced widely differing patterns of migration. The number of emigrants from Britain had been relatively large throughout the nineteenth century, but the movement now increased. On average, Britain lost 76,000 persons through migration each year in the 1890s, approximately 2.3 persons for each 1,000 persons in the total population. Between 1900 and 1909, emigration rose to 132,000 per year, and between 1910 and 1914 to 214,000 per year, about 5.1 per 1,000. In contrast, France, the Low Countries, Switzerland and Germany experienced very little emigration during this period. Throughout the nineteenth century, French men and women moved from country to city but showed virtually no inclination to leave France. Belgium and the Netherlands gained slightly in the balance of arrivals over departures from 1890 to 1914, and though Switzerland suffered a small net loss through overseas migration, this was more than offset by an influx of workers from Italy. Germany had lost a large number of overseas emigrants during the 1880s, but the net loss dropped to negligible levels in the late 1890s when movements within Germany became more significant. Large areas of western and southern Germany resembled the Low Countries and Switzerland in the near balance of moderate inflows and outflows; the Rhenish-

Westphalian industrial district and Berlin, on the other hand, absorbed some three million migrants from Germany's eastern provinces, all of which lost heavily.

All of the countries of the perimeter lost population through emigration, most of the migrants going overseas, but again the patterns differed. In the north, emigration had been very heavy in the 1870s and 1880s, declined during the 1890s, rose again after the turn of the century, and then declined in the final years before the war. Migration from the east, far larger in absolute terms than from the north, remained smaller relative to total population until a sudden increase around 1900. Most eastern European migrants went to the United States. There, immigration authorities recorded 56,000 arrivals from Austria-Hungary in 1890, 115,000 in 1900 and 259,000 in 1910. Only 1,000 persons from Rumania, Bulgaria and European Turkey arrived in the United States in 1890, but the number increased to 25,000 in 1910. The Balkan Wars interfered with migration from southeastern Europe, but nonetheless 155,000 persons from Austria-Hungary and 18,000 from Rumania, Bulgaria and European Turkey landed in the United States in 1913. Russian emigration continued to accelerate until the outbreak of the First World War. Some 36,000 persons arrived in the United States from Russia in 1890, 91,000 in 1900, 187,000 in 1910 and fully 291,000 in 1913.

In the south, the timing of migration from Portugal, Spain and Greece matched that of eastern Europe, the flow of persons increasing rapidly in the final years before the outbreak of war. Portuguese and Spanish migrants settled primarily in former colonies in Latin America, especially Argentina and Brazil, while most Greek migrants went to the United States. Italian emigration, already heavy, increased further. Emigration from Italy had become significant in the 1880s, and the numbers of Italian migrants continued to increase, from 170,000 per year in the 1890s, to 373,000 per year from 1900 to 1909 and an extraordinary 507,000 per year from 1910 to 1914. During the final 5 years before the war, emigration averaged approximately 14.3 persons per 1,000 total population; had it not been for a substantial increase in the number of Italians returning from overseas,

Italy's population would actually have declined as a result of emigration.

Intercontinental migration was not simply the mechanical result of 'pressure' exerted by 'surplus' population. The risk and expense of moving from one continent to another not only required that opportunities for potential migrants be particularly favourable but also worked to restrict migration to those individuals particularly well prepared to take advantage of the opportunities. Only seven areas provided opportunities attractive enough to entice significant numbers of Europeans to leave their home continent: the United States, Argentina, Brazil, Canada, South Africa, Australia and New Zealand. Some British migrants settled in the United States but the large majority moved to the 'white' dominions. Following a depression in 1896, the explosive growth of industry in the eastern United States absorbed many migrants from agricultural regions in southern and eastern Europe who might have preferred to remain farmers in their new country; farming in the American midwest remained in the hands of earlier migrants from Germany and Scandinavia. Would-be farmers had greater chances in the wheat and meat industries of Argentina, Canada, Australia and New Zealand, and in the rubber and coffee industries of Brazil. In South Africa, the mining of gold and other minerals provided the most obvious opportunities. In all these countries, the immigrants' employment prospects multiplied as railways and road systems expanded to serve the growing export sectors, urban centres developed to handle the flow of goods and manufacturing industry (especially textiles) arose in response to growing local markets. This new overseas perimeter depended on the countries of western Europe for markets and supplies of capital, however – perhaps even more critically than the European perimeter. After the First World War, growth slowed and migration declined. Opportunity also depended on political conditions; the British dominions were generally unfriendly to non-British migrants, and in 1924 the United States Immigration Act effectively barred southern and eastern European migrants.

Domestic migration and international migration bear similarities. Europeans tended to migrate from rural areas to urban centres, both within Europe and overseas. Cities like New York and Buenos Aires became meccas for particular groups, like Italians, who settled in specific areas and concentrated in certain jobs. Most migrants also had very modest resources, little education and little job training; migration was a mass movement and therefore inevitably a lower-class movement. In some countries, 'migration' statistics simply recorded the numbers of steerage passengers on in and out-bound ships, and Italian authorities equated migration with the movements of Italian citizens 'in straightened circumstances'.

Whether the Sicilian or the Pole ended up in New York or Chicago, Milan or Lodz, he or she took a job at the bottom of the employment ladder. Intranational migrants were often disoriented in the big city, even finding it difficult to communicate since their native dialects might bear little resemblance to the language spoken in their new home. International migrants found the problems compounded in societies with entirely different languages, cultures and governments. The prejudice of the majority population in these societies made adaptation even more difficult; migrants in the United States were derogatively labelled 'micks', 'spics', 'wops', 'dagos', 'kikes', 'polacks', 'hunkies' or 'bohunks', and were the subject of outright discrimination and occasional violent attacks.

On the other hand, social mobility, though arduous, was not uncommon. Intercontinental migrants were not the truly impoverished or desperate. British emigrants came from the country with the highest wages in Europe and Russian migrants from the most advanced provinces of the empire. Italian migrants from both the north and the south were more likely to be literate and more likely to be skilled workers than the national average. Potential migrants were well-informed about conditions overseas; migration to each overseas area fluctuated quite dramatically from year to year according to the state of the local economy. Italian migrants clearly appreciated the fact that land was more expensive and entrepreneurial opportunities more restricted for them in the United States than in Argentina, as shown by the higher proportion of single males, lower proportion of farmers and higher rate of repatriation in the flow of migrants to the United States. The migrants' motives were not exclusively economic, however; migrants from eastern Europe frequently belonged to ethnic groups subject to more or less severe persecution. The Austro-Hungarian and Russian totals included many Poles. The Polish Academy of Sciences has estimated that between 1870 and 1914 some 2.6 million Poles migrated to the United States and 200,000 to other parts of the western hemisphere. Those Russian migrants who were not Polish were often Jewish, predominantly from the Baltic regions and other provinces of the northeast. Jews left Rumania in large numbers, and the Hungarian government's Magyarisation policies provided a motive for members of several ethnic groups to migrate if they could.

To aid in overcoming the challenges of their new environment, both those who moved abroad and those who settled in cities of their own countries tried to retain ties amongst themselves. Residents of the same village often moved to the same city where they could draw on the camaraderie and professional links of their compatriots. Migrants also took advantage of existing kinship networks; the male head of the family might migrate first and then later bring his wife and children and still later collateral relatives. Migrants tried to retain ties with their native regions and held on to parcels of property or returned home for visits when possible; in the case of international resettlement, such ties were obviously harder to maintain. Most migrants sent money back to their families who remained; in the case of certain groups, such as the Greeks and Italians, such remittances provided a major source of income in rural areas and accounted for a substantial portion of national revenue in aggregate terms.

The economic and social effects of the migration were at least as complex as its causes. On balance, intercontinental migration did not significantly reduce population pressure in the poorest rural districts of southern and eastern Europe; that massive task would only be accomplished by industrial development and urbanisation following the Second World War. Those migrants who returned often brought with them new or improved skills and sometimes significantly changed attitudes. The influence exerted by such persons is difficult to quantify, but the self-consciously 'modern' returned migrant with his American newspaper rapidly became as much a stock figure in the villages of rural Italy and Greece as the conservative local priest with his crucifix or icon. The majority of the migrants did not return, however, and their home countries lost a substantial faction of the best educated, most energetic and most adaptable of their workers. Those who remained overseas eventually ceased to send their wages home. Those who were more inclined to move with the intention of staying permanently, such as the ethnic minorities of eastern Europe, took what little capital they had with them and further reduced the already inadequate supply of investment funds in their home countries.

MASS SOCIETY

Economic disparities, class differences, political antagonisms, and cultural loyalties divided Europeans and often set them one against the other. However, other features of European life in this period forced a mixing of the population and created the conditions for the emergence of 'mass society'. Often these trends were connected with technological and economic developments. Such was the case with the new transportation networks. The first railway had been constructed in 1830 in England to link Manchester and Liverpool; during the next 70 years, railway lines crisscrossed the European continent, and Russia began a line to stretch all the way across Siberia. From 1875 to 1913, world railways increased from 311,000 to 1.1 million kilometres. The train provided a new, faster and cheaper means of transporting people and materials. Granted, Europeans would still be segregated by the class in which they could afford to travel, whether in the upholstered first-class carriages or on the hard benches of third-class compartments. But the railway brought together people from disparate regions and made it possible to migrate more easily than ever before. The train also allowed Europeans to go on holiday more easily; the advent of the new systems of transportation coincided with the period of increased tourism. The train linked villages and small towns with metropolitan centres and made possible movement across international borders. In the plush cabins of the Orient Express, connecting Paris with Istanbul, Europe's bejewelled elite could eat and drink and (at least according to the reputation the train acquired) make love and plot conspiracies. The ordinary 'milk runs' provided an opportunity for peasants to take their produce to market and for 'urban' and exotic goods to reach provincial shops. Since the price of a railway ticket dropped by half in 50 years, the train opened up travel to new classes of people, and provided a previously inaccessible geographical mobility which was sometimes a medium for social mobility. Within cities, another sort of train provided a more immediate mobility. The London Underground had opened in 1863, and in Paris the Métropolitain was built in time for the World Fair of 1900. Suburban systems surrounded such cities as Berlin and Milan; horse-drawn trams appeared in Thessaloniki in 1893 and electric railways in 1902. These urban trains made it possible for people to live in one part of the city and work in another, inaugurating the commuter age and, incidentally, encouraging the expansion of cities into suburban areas.

New leisure activities became available to Europeans at the end of the nineteenth century, too. The English mania for sport spread across the Channel, and Frenchmen joined such organisations as the Alpine Club, which was founded in 1874, and a Touring Club, dating from 1890. There was, in particular, the new sport of cycling; it was in the 1880s that the bicycle was perfected. Some observers worried about the effects of bicycle-riding on health – doctors discovered a new malady, called 'bicycle face', said to affect women who came under undue strain from the exertion of riding cycles – but the sport gained in popularity. The first Tour de France, the marathon bicycle race around the nation and one of the highlights of the European sporting season, was held in 1903. Soccer also attracted both participants and spectators. In Italy, the Juventus soccer club had been founded in 1893, and soccer was a focus of urban life in much of western Europe by 1910. Gymnastics became another aspect of the cult of physical fitness, a sport particularly encouraged for the working class because it trained them in discipline and the sort of prowess that might be useful for military purposes, at least according to some middle-class commentators. In 1894 the French Baron de Coubertin reconstructed an international sporting event modelled on the classical Olympic games. The event did not create international cooperation and harmony, as de Coubertin had hoped; but it did symbolise the consecration of sport as a pursuit fit for all.

Another phenomenon of the end of the century was the proliferation of cafés and similar establishments, like pubs in Britain and beer halls in the Germanic nations. Some, on the major streets, were still the preserve of the leisured classes, but the new ones served the working classes. All provided employment for their owners, managers, waiters, waitresses, cooks, cleaners and entertainers, as well as for distillers, beer-makers and other provisioners. The neighbourhood café or the corner pub served as a meeting place for local residents, a centre for social and political activities, and, of course, a dispenser of the alcohol that could dull the fatigue and boredom of industrial life. Alcoholism, in fact, came to be identified as a disease of the working class. Social commentators in France became obsessed with absinthe, a green liqueur with a liquorice taste. One series of French photographs shows a man having a drink one day, then more the next: 'The green poison troubles his reason and his eyes; from his heart no longer does he feel affectionate sighs'. He continues to drink, and the pictures show him hanging onto a lamp-post in a drunken stupor, brawling in a bar, being dragged into court, staggering home and dying from delirium tremens, leaving his wife and children to face life. The moral of the story was clear, but the social cause of alcoholism was also noted. One observer wrote in 1900: 'For the workers, the thirst for alcohol is not a cause of misery but an effect. It is the exception when a man who has enough to feed himself well becomes a drinker of alcohol; but when the worker does not have sufficient salary for food, natural necessity obliges him to turn to alcohol'.

Gradually, however, alcohol became less of a 'necessity' or 'food' and more of a recreational item, a semi-luxury in the same category as a cigar. An inebriated worker could destroy the complex and expensive machinery typical of the second industrial revolution, and large employers therefore instituted rules against drinking on the job and increasingly provided more suitable substitutes such as coffee, dispensed through factory canteens at subsidised prices. Socialist parties, partly because they worried about their members' health and partly because they worried about the public image of the working class, campaigned vigorously against excessive alcohol consumption. Socialist meetings and social gatherings also worked in a more subtle way to restrict drinking; they provided opportunities for relaxation, including moderate amounts of alcohol, but excessive drinking and certainly intoxication were actively discouraged. Governments found alcohol a convenient source of revenue – in Russia, the vodka monopoly provided nearly a quarter of government income – and their tendency to increase taxes on alcohol increased its price relative to other forms of entertainment, further restricting consumption.

Cafés also functioned as reading rooms, since many subscribed to newspapers. Advances in printing, such as rotary presses and linotype machines, facilitated the publication of inexpensive newspapers, the 'penny press'. Certain newspapers were specially written for the working class, including various publications of the new socialist parties. Others were scandal sheets whose 'yellow journalism' took its name from the cheap paper on which they were printed. The popularity of imperialism and the spread of anti-Semitism owed much to the search for sensation and profit of the owners of mass-circulation newspapers. Literacy rates were improving; by 1900, France and Great Britain had wiped out illiteracy and in Prussia only ten per cent of the population could not read or write at all. In southern and eastern Europe, the levels of literacy were far less praiseworthy, but across the Continent more people could now read than ever before, and there was more and cheaper reading material for them.

The spread in literacy was the effect of the new systems of primary education. By 1900, compulsory primary education was the rule rather than the exception in Europe; in practice, this often meant only several years of very rudimentary teaching in language and mathematics for the masses of the population. Nonetheless, even these basic skills gave peasants and proletarians access to a different culture from the one available in the mid-nineteenth century and lessened, albeit slightly, the distance between urban and rural and rich and poor. Other changes in public life had a similar effect. Perhaps the most notable example was compulsory military service. In the last decades of the nineteenth century, almost every European power instituted a period of obligatory military service for young men. It was still possible to avoid the service, or through education or money to procure an officer's commission. But now large numbers of ordinary boys were called up. In France, they were chosen by a lottery; in some other places, everyone was to serve. Military service meant that a peasant boy would be taught particular military skills, forced to submit to the discipline of the army and be transported far away from his native village to a training camp, military base, or imperial outpost. This exposed him to the wider world and confronted him with the differences between his own background and other contexts. For example, military service often pointed up the difference between peasant dialects and the national language, which the recruit had to learn in order to obey orders if he had not already had to learn it to please his schoolmasters.

Rising literacy and cheaper printing increased the market for the products of mass culture by providing a medium for advertising. The new newspapers and magazines blossomed with colourful appeals to potential purchasers of mass-produced clothes, household goods and foods. Margarine, for instance, was very much a product of the new age, a blend of scientific research, technology, imperialism and advertising. In 1869, the French government sponsored a competition among chemists to discover a cheap substitute for butter, partly in the hope of lowering the cost of feeding the army. The winning process synthesised a product from beef fat and sliced cows' udders. Further research isolated the chemicals involved and established that vegetable oils could be used in place of beef fat, though only in a refined and deodorised form requiring a large scale of production. Two Dutch firms, Van den Bergh and Jurgens, emerged to dominate the industry, though they were challenged after 1900 by other large margarine producers and by other users of vegetable oils, especially soap manufacturers such as the British Lever Brothers. Competition for oils led to a rush to acquire sesame, coconut, palm and groundnut plantations in overseas colonies. Competition for sales led to a proliferation of brand names, advertising intended to prove margarine was as good as butter and gifts of crockery, sugar, coffee or tea included with margarine sales. Before 1914, margarine was predominantly a food of the working class. In Britain, declining real incomes after 1900 may have induced urban working-class families to substitute margarine for butter. In Germany (the largest market), as incomes rose from a lower level, industrial workers may have added margarine to their diets. In Denmark (with by far the highest per capital consumption of margarine), agricultural workers laboured to produce butter for upper-class homes in Britain and Germany, but they themselves ate the cheaper substitute.

These changes mixed different groups together and brought ordinary people new possibilities for social and cultural activities and placed them in different sorts of contacts with their 'superiors'. In particular, the isolation of the old rural world, still very much a feature of Europe even after a century of industrialisation, began to break down. However, as the spreading unrest of the prewar generation demonstrated, Europe's institutions were inadequate to absorb the impact of economic and social change. Dissatisfaction with the existing order played an important role in the background to the First World War; the competition among social groups poisoned the atmosphere of the Belle Epoque within nations just as disparities in economic development and disputes over colonial possessions raised the level of international tension.

4
POLITICS AND IDEOLOGY BEFORE 1914

Politics may be viewed in either a wide or a narrow gauge. 'Formal' politics is based on parliaments, bureaucracies and other governing institutions and is an affair of heads of state, cabinet ministers and government officials. Politics can also be seen, however, as a host of activities occurring both inside and outside the chambers of legislatures – 'lobbying' and 'log-rolling', private and public 'pressure', demonstrations, strikes, acts of violence and other manifestations of 'extra-parliamentary politics'. Politics extends into other areas as well. Thus, the exaction of rent from a peasant by a landlord is both a political and an economic statement, as is the demand for higher wages from a bourgeois employer by a worker. The outlook which a landlord, peasant, bourgeois or worker holds is political. Beliefs adopted because of class, religion or education, both explicit ideologies and inchoate unexpressed attitudes, underlie all political actions. They do not determine them, however. The formal political realm always possesses a degree of autonomy; kings and presidents, ministers and bureaucrats, all have options, and their choices in turn affect extra-parliamentary action. The shape of politics consists neither of the rules governing formal political action nor of the social framework of extra-parliamentary politics alone, but of their interaction.

Among the questions dominating politics before 1914 was the very problem of who should have a voice in government. During the nineteenth century the suffrage had been widened and now there were calls for universal manhood suffrage and even for the granting of votes to women. Added to this was the competition of various political groupings – monarchist, conservative, liberal, radical and socialist – and debates about the roles of various institutions (including the army and the church) and interest groups in politics. Another important question was nationalism, a heritage from the surge of national unification in the 1800s, and failure to deal with it adequately ultimately led to the world war in 1914. Quarrels over disputed territories simmered and frustrations from previous wars remained, and the system of alliances increased rather than reduced tension. In domestic politics, disputes between ethnic groups, the question of military service and armaments expenditures, even questions of education, language and culture were part and parcel of nationalism. Another theme was the 'social question', an effort to better the lives of citizens through legislation concerning health care and pensions; the period saw a series of laws which treated these issues but did not diffuse socialist criticisms of exploitation of the workers. Yet another area for debate was economic development, particularly in those nations undergoing an industrial revolution for the first time at the end of the 1800s; the strategy of 'modernisation' involved not only economic theory but political choices. Finally, relations between the state and the various churches assumed an importance in the prewar period that is difficult for those of a later, more secularised age to appreciate. Especially in Italy and France, the state and church were at loggerheads and the rallying of Catholic-oriented parties in the 1890s did not solve the disputes.

The Dreyfus affair encapsulated the complexity of politics. In 1894, a cleaning woman in a French army office found a crumpled bit of onion skin paper which implied that French military secrets were being passed to the Germans; such a leak was extremely worrying to the French, still suffering from defeat by the Germans in 1870, and uneasy over conflict both in Europe and in the colonies. An investigation to find the treasonous spy resulted in the arrest of Alfred Dreyfus, an army captain, who, incidentally, was a Jew. Dreyfus refused to confess to the act; put on trial, he was convicted on the basis of documents provided by the army and sent to life imprisonment on Devil's Island. Dreyfus's brother then demanded a retrial, claiming that his brother was innocent. Meanwhile, a new chief of the French intelligence service found out that the espionage was continuing, which brought Dreyfus's culpability into question. He also found that the handwriting on the original document, supposedly Dreyfus's, was identical with that of another officer, a man called Esterhazy; Esterhazy, furthermore, had an unhappy personal life, in contrast to Dreyfus's, which might have motivated him to commit treason. For his trouble in bringing up these new matters, the government sent the intelligence chief to a new posting in Tunisia. However, before leaving, he had revealed his findings to an influential French senator, who asked the French president to reopen the case. The government refused, just as it had denied Dreyfus's brother's request for a retrial. They did agree to court-martial Esterhazy, although they informally promised him that he would be found innocent. All did not pass according to plan, however, because of the intervention of a number of well-known public figures. Foremost among them was the novelist Émile Zola, who in 1898 published a newspaper article, 'J'accuse', in which he accused the government of trying to cover up the truth of the case and suggested that Dreyfus was indeed innocent. Zola was tried and found guilty of treason, whereupon he fled to England. The intelligence chief returned to France and was dismissed from the army.

France now divided into pro and anti-Dreyfus factions. Ranged against Dreyfus were conservative politicians, members of the military, nationalists, monarchists, Catholics and anti-Semites. Many of them opposed the republic itself. They saw in the 'free Dreyfus' campaign a threat to France's military security and attack on the French courts. In Dreyfus himself, they saw a wicked Jew out to destroy the French state. Anti-Semitism was then in vogue in France; a book called *La France Juive*, published in 1886, the establishment of an Anti-Semitic League in 1889, and the foundation of a racist newspaper called *Libre Parole* in 1892 had whipped up sentiment against the Jews. Thus, the opponents of Dreyfus could combine their anti-republican, chauvinistic, religious and anti-Semitic sentiments in a campaign against the luckless officer. His defenders included the substantial Jewish population of France, many intellectuals and many protestants, an assortment of people who for various reasons felt out of step with the French elite and its attitudes. The socialists and syndicalists in particular supported Dreyfus because they feared his accusers would seek to overthrow the republic. France became an ideological battleground with pamphlets and newspapers, demonstrations and parliamentary debates, charges of anti-Semitism and injustice and countercharges of disloyalty, lack of trust in French courts and treason.

Dreyfus was brought back from Devil's Island and again put on trial – and once again he was found guilty and sentenced to ten years in the Caribbean prison colony. A new president took office in France in 1899, and he, unlike his predecessor, was neutral in the case. By a presidential decree, Dreyfus was pardoned ten days after the sentence. The Dreyfusards spent the next five years accumulating evidence to show the innocence of the captain; they proved that the original document on which he had been found guilty had been forged and that Dreyfus had not carried out espionage. The dénouement of the affair occurred in 1906, when a civilian court set aside the earlier judgements and declared them erroneous. Dreyfus was vindicated; the government awarded him a decoration and promoted him to the rank of major.

This long episode showed the extent to which Frenchmen could and did hold opinions on various political subjects and the ways in which those ideas could be marshalled. In a period of growing military competition, some blindly supported the army. The virulence of anti-Semitism could unjustly condemn a victim. And the long-standing quarrel between the church and the state, which would culminate in the separation of church and state in 1905, found fuel in the conflict between anti-Dreyfusards and pro-Dreyfusards. Thus, the *affaire* was a focal point for many of the social and political contests of the day, mobilising parliamentary and extra-parliamentary groups and showing the overlap of political and social issues.

POLITICS IN WESTERN AND NORTHERN EUROPE

In western and northern Europe, monarchs generally shared political power with the elected representatives of their subjects. The distribution of power remained a point of contention, however, and so did the question of participation. Suffrage was still restricted to a minority of the population, and parliamentarians generally came from the upper and middle classes. The dissatisfaction of members of those elite groups who desired more power was matched and exceeded by the unhappiness of those who had no power at all. The classic example is Britain. Conflict extending over 250 years had secured the dominance of the Houses of Parliament over the British crown and more particularly of the rule of the House of Commons. Commons won its final victory when in 1909 the House of Lords rejected a budget which would have raised taxes on wealthy individuals to pay for social legislation and a large naval construction programme. In return the Liberals engineered a bill in 1911 which gave the Lords power only to delay and not to veto legislation. However, though Commons represented the entire spectrum of political opinion in the kingdom, real power remained in the hands of the elite, and aristocrats and property-owners dominated the cabinets. Those campaigning for female suffrage and Irish independence, for instance, rejected the bland, gentlemanly consensus which ruled British politics.

In France the series of French revolutions had ended with the defeat of the Paris Commune in 1871 and the establishment of the Third Republic, which rested on the support of the middle classes and the property-owning peasantry. For twenty years conflicts between republicans and monarchists dominated politics; the Dreyfus *affaire* became a crisis precisely because so many did not accept the republic. With the conclusion of the *affaire* came a series of more stable governments from the left of the republican movement, the Radicals.

The unification of Germany in 1871 created a political and economic giant on the continent. Prussia, the state which had forcibly unified the nation through conquest, continued to dominate German politics. The German parliament, the Reichstag, differed from its English and French counterparts; elected by universal manhood suffrage, it had the right to debate government proposals and to impede or refuse to adopt laws, but enjoyed neither the right to initiate legislation nor control of the purse. New statutes were proposed by the chancellor; he, however, was responsible only to the emperor, not to the Reichstag, and thus was largely immune from parliamentary criticism. Taxation remained largely in the hands of the states, to which the constitution reserved powers of direct taxation. Therefore, even if the Reichstag rejected the imperial budget, the government still controlled considerable financial resources; the revenues of Prussia totalled more than those of the empire and they were entirely at the disposal of the emperor and chancellor.

Politics in the smaller states of western and northern Europe showed the conflicts over representation and parliamentary activity which emerged in the absence of a clear consensus. Ministerial responsibility to parliament had been won in Belgium in 1830 and in the Netherlands in 1868, but in neither country was the monarch entirely restrained by constitutional limitations. Leopold II, for instance, ruled the Congo until 1908 as his personal domain. In the Netherlands the voting population was doubled in 1887 and again in 1896 but still totalled only some 700,000 men. In Belgium, universal male suffrage was introduced in 1893, but remained qualified by a plural system whereby men with property, family and education received extra votes. In 1913 governments in both countries committed themselves to introducing universal suffrage, but the war delayed action until 1917 in the Netherlands and 1919 in Belgium. The essence of Switzerland's constitution was its balance between centralism and particularism, though the balance had been steadily tipping towards centralism. The very restricted franchises of some of the cantons could in effect be balanced by the possibility of passing federal legislation by national referendum.

In Sweden in 1865 the old four estates had been replaced with a two-chamber parliament, but in both houses voting and membership were based on wealth. Only 6,000 men out of a total population of almost 4 million were eligible to vote for members in the upper house. Norway's contrasting reputation for political liberalism derived in part from a long history of subordination first to Denmark and later to Sweden. The granting of suffrage to all men in 1898 and to women in 1907, in fact, had stemmed in part from the need to mobilise support in the nationalist cause of separation from Sweden, and the parliament remained firmly under the control of propertied interests. In Denmark the 1866 constitution severely limited the franchise to the upper house, making it the bastion of land and money; the struggle to secure ministerial responsibility to the parliamentary majority in the more representative lower house dominated Danish politics for the rest of the century. By the 1890s the power of the right had begun to decline in the face of the growing influence of small farmers, workers and urban groups. The change from open to secret ballot in 1901 led to the victory of the Left Reform Party and eventually to ministerial responsibility to parliament. In 1914 and 1915 the suffrage was extended to all men and most women and the age limit lowered from 30 to 25 years. Finally, Finland, though part of the Russian empire, still retained much of its autonomy. The Finnish Diet with its four estates, dating from the Swedish period before the Russian conquest in 1808, allowed political representation of all classes, despite the very restricted franchise. Then in 1906, after the revolution in Russia, Finland secured one of the most democratic parliaments in Europe, chosen by universal suffrage.

Compared to other parts of Europe and much of the non-European world, the politics of these nations was open, peaceful and representative. Governments of all western and northern European countries introduced various measures of social reform. Germany pioneered the field of social legislation with a Sickness Insurance Law in 1883 and parallel accident and old-age insurance laws in 1884 and 1889. The programmes were funded by contributions from both workers and employers, with additional contributions from the government for pensions. Legislation along the same lines continued after Bismarck's fall, with industrial courts to hear labour disputes in 1890 and improved factory inspection in 1891. In 1911 the accident and old-age insurance programmes were extended again, covering white collar workers for the first time. France lagged, but did restrict women and children to a ten-hour day in 1900 and all workers to a six-day week in 1906 and introduced an optional insurance plan in 1910. In Britain the Conservative governments in power from 1895 to 1905 passed a Workmen's Compensation Act in 1897, which made industrial employers responsible for injuries suffered by their workers, and an Education Act in 1902, which made all primary and secondary schools the responsibility of elected local governments and under which the number of secondary schools doubled in five years. The succeeding Liberal governments passed a Trade Disputes Bill which absolved labour unions of legal responsibility for illegal acts committed by their members and a new Workmen's Compensation Act which extended employers' liabilities in 1906, an old age pension for persons over the age of seventy in 1909 and national unemployment and health insurance programmes in 1911. The northern nations followed the German model of systematic legislation. Denmark introduced old age pensions and health insurance in 1891, and the government helped peasants to purchase land they had previously leased. In 1889 the Swedish parliament passed the first of several factory acts. Taxation was reformed and various archaic obligations were removed, such as the requirement that farmers along main roads supply hospitality and transportation for travelling government officials. Norway continued along the same lines after independence, and Swedish legislation passed from 1905 to 1914 included acts relating to industrial safety, old age pensions, government industrial arbitration and home loans.

Under the surface, however, the shape of politics was shifting. Governments recognised that industrial development created a class of workers with new and distinctive problems, but the ruling elites refused to share power with the workers' representatives. The German government hoped that social reform would win the working class away from socialism – Bismarck referred to social reform as the 'carrot' which he hoped to use along with the 'stick' of the anti-socialist law. Bismarck's downfall was precipitated by a quarrel with the new emperor, Wilhelm II, on the question of socialism. Bismarck had outlawed the socialist party in 1878, but in 1890 the anti-socialist law came up for renewal. Bismarck said that blood must flow to achieve his aim, and the new law was intended to provoke the socialists, operating clandestinely, to acts of violence, which would have allowed him to wipe them out altogether. The emperor disapproved, and Bismarck resigned. However, the workers failed to respond to the government's carrot. From 400,000 votes and 9 deputies in 1878, the socialist party increased to 1.4 million votes and 35 deputies in 1890 and finally to 4.2 million votes and 110 deputies in 1912. With 29 per cent of the popular vote, the socialist party had become the largest party in the Reichstag and the most powerful socialist party in Europe, but was still excluded from office under the empire's constitution. Meanwhile, in France a socialist had entered the French cabinet for the first time in 1899, though without the approval of his party. Now the socialists became powerful opponents of the republicans, gaining substantial support among France's growing industrial proletariat. The unification of the socialist parties in 1905 increased their organisational and electoral strength. In Britain too labour became progressively less content to have its interests represented by others, and during the prewar decade the Liberal Party was eclipsed by the Labour Party as the main alternative to the Tories. In 1900 15 members of the newly-organised Labour Representation Committee had stood for election, but only 2 were successful. Then in 1902 the decision of the House of Lords in the Taff Vale case that unions could be sued for the damage caused by strikes brought most unions to support the Labour Party, which gained 29 seats in 1906.

Independent workers' parties emerged in the smaller countries as well, most dating from the late 1870s and 1880s. Though they reflected common problems, their fortunes varied with local conditions. Denmark's fledgling socialist party received a tremendous boost in 1883 when the German socialists – forbidden to meet in Germany – held their party congress in Copenhagen. As it expanded during the 1890s the Danish socialist party moved towards cooperation with the representatives of small farmers. The Norwegian socialist party, dating from 1887, rode the tide of nationalism and the wider suffrage to gain a quarter of the vote in 1912. In Switzerland the two major socialist movements united in 1901, but the new party remained weak. The highly decentralised and regionally specialised character of Swiss industry impeded the emergence of a strong proletarian class consciousness, particularly as most Swiss workers retained a link with the land and were accordingly 'half-peasants'. The degree of popular control available in the referendum and initiative also deflected working-class discontent; sickness and accident insurance were instituted by referendum in 1889, and another referendum nationalised the railways in 1898.

Another potential fissure in political structures, one which could cut across or even swallow up the divisions among classes, was religion. In the Low Countries parties emerged in the 1880s grouped around radicalism, liberalism and socialism but the distinctions between the three remained blurred, compared to other countries. Religious lines were clearly drawn, however, and religious parties emerged whose central concern was clearly the role of the state, exemplified in the enduring and acrimonious debate over religion and state in education. Even the suffrage issue was ultimately only a means of extending the participants in this central debate, and the religious parties clearly sapped the potential strength of the secular socialist movement by competing for supporters from the ranks of the working classes. In France the 'Republic of the Radicals' favoured a strong position for France in Europe, the development of industry and agriculture, and a secular state. That last point was the *idée fixe* of the Radicals, who believed that the Catholic church enjoyed a nefarious influence in France. They were not anti-religious but anti-clerical, and they sought to reduce the privileged position of the Catholic clergy and religious orders. Monks and nuns in France numbered nearly 200,000 (grouped in over 3,000 different congregations), controlled extensive property and managed a system of powerful parochial schools. The church received subsidies from the state but was largely immune to state control. Its hierarchy was barely reconciled to the disestablishment of the monarchy. The church's undue domestic influence and meddling in foreign affairs led the Radicals to make it a point of honour to reduce the church's power. The 1880s saw a bitter debate over the role of the church in public education, and the dissatisfaction of the church hierarchy with the republic played a key role in the Dreyfus affair. Finally in 1905, a law declared freedom of worship in France and ended any privileged position for any church or religious group. Thus the Catholic church would no longer receive subsidies; furthermore, its property had to be turned over to so-called 'religious associations', and the state would take an inventory of church property to determine its assets.

The proliferation of organised interest groups revealed yet another way in which political concerns could be articulated. Bismarck had seriously considered a German parliament representing economic classes rather than individual voters. None of the chancellors who held office from the departure of Bismarck until the fall of the empire in 1918 had the power of the 'iron chancellor'. Indeed, they depended increasingly on the parties in the Reichstag. On the other hand, domestic politics in Germany became increasingly polarised. The conservative party supported the government, but its political base in eastern Prussia was eroding as industrial development centred in the west and the large cities. The Catholic Centre party, united only in its religion, reflected all the tensions in German society and had difficulty taking a stand on any but confessional issues. The liberal parties split, and the anti-Semitic parties appealed only to limited groups of peasants, artisans and shopkeepers, and then only in economic downturns. The failure of any party to win a clear mandate opened the way for various pressure groups, which lobbied for their members' interests. The Agrarian League sought government support for agriculture, the Central Association of German Industrialists pressed the case of heavy industry and other organisations sought places in the sun for light industry, commerce, shopkeepers and artisans. Except for the Catholic Centre each of the political parties came to represent one or another competing economic group: conservatives for agriculture and heavy industry, the various liberal parties for branches of light industry and commerce, and the socialists for the industrial proletariat.

In Germany and in most other countries, each interest group accused the others of exercising influence on the parliamentary process illegitimately. In Switzerland, in contrast, interest groups achieved substantial legitimacy. By 1900, in fact, they had replaced parties as the main contestants in the political process. They were the Vorort (the Swiss Confederation of Manufacturers and Industrialists – the employers' union) founded in 1870, the union of small traders founded in 1879 and the secretariats for labour and peasants dating respectively from 1879 and 1898. All four were subsidised by the government, which relied on their information for policy making. In explicitly recognising the legitimacy of economic interest groups and indeed employing them to overcome the divisiveness of competition among parties, the Swiss anticipated developments which elsewhere would not take place until after the Second World War.

POLITICS IN SOUTHERN EUROPE

Southern Europe presented another sort of politics. Parliamentary institutions were not so well established as in western and northern Europe, and in some cases important groups refused to recognise the legitimacy of the central government, their opposition obstructing legislation and administration and leading occasionally to violence. Lack of economic development, poverty and widespread illiteracy plagued Mediterranean Europe, local elites were more entrenched and the middle classes less developed. Furthermore, traditions of anarchism remained strong in the south even when they had been largely replaced by the new socialist beliefs in northern and central Europe. Finally, renegade groups of bandits in the Mediterranean region respected no political rules, and local interest groups (which sometimes collaborated with the local bandits) could be almost as powerful in their own spheres of influence as were the legitimate governments. Politics, considered in its broader definition, was thus as much a question of personal connections, influence, nepotism, informal arrangements – of 'clientelism' and 'patronage' – as of elections and political organisations.

The Kingdom of Italy had been founded in 1861, the northern and relatively industrialised state of Piedmont playing a role similar to that of Prussia in Germany. However, Piedmont had not succeeded as well as Prussia in reconciling conquered elements to its rule. In southern Italy, opponents of the central government carried on armed resistance for several years. One part of this tradition of opposition re-emerged in the widespread Sicilian peasant uprisings of the 1890s. In the meantime, the government had reached a tacit understanding with the local elites of the south, whereby the latter, urban lawyers and rural landowners, monopolised local administrative positions, manipulated tax assessments and government contracts to favour themselves and systematically exploited the sharecropping peasantry. In some districts the rule of the elite was enforced by violence carried out by secret societies, the most notorious of which was the Sicilian *mafia*. More openly hostile to the state was the Catholic church. In 1871 Italy finally acquired Rome and its hinterland, whereupon the Pope (despite a grant from the Italian government of an income equal to that previously received from the annexed areas) confined himself to the Vatican and forbade Catholics to participate in the political life of the new state. The ban was only lifted in 1904 when the Pope, in response to a general strike proclaimed by union leaders and radical socialists, granted permission for Catholics to take part in political activities involving the 'safety of the social order'. The church's active opposition greatly weakened the radical movement, and in return the state made important concessions, particularly in the area of education. However, the Vatican did not recognise the Italian government formally until 1929.

The structure of Italian parliamentary politics was *trasformismo*, ably managed by the most important Italian politician of the period, Giovanni Giolitti, who was prime minister during a great deal of the prewar period. An exceptionally shrewd political strategist, Giolitti combined with various interest groups and parliamentarians to keep power and carry out his programmes. *Trasformismo* was a matter of power politics and not ideological commitment, and for it Giolitti was labelled unprincipled. However, Giolitti saw as his vocation the creation of a modern Italy as a power to be reckoned with, economically as well as politically, a view shared by other leaders, including Giolitti's most bitter rivals. Whence came the attempt to stimulate economic development through the national bank, protective tariffs and military contracts let to favoured firms. Whence, too, came Italy's rapprochement with France, alliances with Austria-Hungary and Germany and especially new imperial ventures. Italy suffered a humiliating defeat at Adowa in 1896 in an effort to conquer Ethiopia and saw hopes for gains in Tunisia thwarted by France. So in 1911, Italy declared war on the Ottoman Empire, seizing Tripoli and beginning the conquest of the Libyan hinterland, hoping that it would be an area for economic development and colonisation through the migration of peasants from the overpopulated south, a 'fourth shore' for Italy. The colony was no great prize and the war in the interior dragged on to 1930, but Libya did give Italy a place in the imperial sun; along with alliances on the Continent, this made Italy a power, albeit 'the least of the great powers'.

Meanwhile, the government tried to contain peasant unrest and the growing power of the socialists. Laws passed in 1894 suppressed socialist and anarchist organisations, and the army put down the peasant uprisings in Sicily. Disorders in 1898 (with food shortages, military conscription and the defeat at Adowa as their background) were followed by a general strike in 1904 (the culmination of three years of violent strikes), another wave of industrial unrest which crested in 1906–7 and violent agricultural strikes in 1908. Official repression by the police and military units was extensively supplemented by armed 'squads' hired by the landlords. In 1914, another general strike began in Rome, in opposition to tax increases intended to pay for the looming war. The strike spread and some towns remained in the strikers' hands for a week or more. The army once again repressed the strike movement and as before enjoyed the assistance of unofficial but tacitly encouraged groups of armed men sponsored by conservative property owners, a foretaste of the violence which preceded the Fascist seizure of power in 1922.

Greece had fought a war of independence against the Turks in the 1820s, and the new state's small area had been augmented during the second half of the nineteenth century. Not all persons included in the new boundaries wished to belong to the Greek state, and many ethnic Greeks remained outside Greece's boundaries. In Greece, as in Italy, power was in the hands of the middle classes; the beginnings of economic development led to the primacy of entrepreneurs who owned the banks and shipping lines and landholders who owned the large estates. Though politicians identified with either a more progressive, liberal party or a more conservative, nationalist party, politics remained largely personal. The major question occupying Greece was still the 'Megali Idea', the 'great idea' of enlarging the nation's territory to include the ethnically Greek populations spread around the Balkans and Anatolia and, ultimately, to reconquer Constantinople. A war with Turkey in 1896–7 over Crete resulted in an overwhelming defeat for Greece, but the Balkan War of 1913 was more successful.

The heritage of the civil wars of the nineteenth century continued to haunt Spain; then came the defeat by the United States in 1898 and the loss of the Philippines, Puerto Rico and Cuba. All agreed that Spain must be 'regenerated', but what was to be done and for whose benefit remained unresolved questions. Conservative politicians envisaged a revolution from above, particularly the reform of local government. Others hoped for a regeneration of Spain by the army. One intellectual, Joaquin Costa, wanted to mobilise the 'productive classes' against the 'oligarchs'. On the left, a brand of Catholic reformism became popular in certain circles after the papal encyclical *Rerum Novarum* in 1891 had called for social action, and membership in socialist organisations increased dramatically. The most important left-wing current, however, remained anarchism, organised into a rival labour organisation in 1911.

In Catalonia, and particularly in Barcelona, a regional movement arose which demanded autonomy from central government administration. The movement took a cultural as well as a political form, emphasising the region's distinctive language and traditions. The Catalan middle class, the strongest and most industrially-oriented in Spain, had been especially hurt by the loss of Cuba, for three-fifths of Barcelona's textile production had been exported to the Caribbean. As an industrial centre, Barcelona had become a strong base for the growing socialist movement, and the industrial depression following 1898 contributed to an increasing radicalism.

The years from 1898 to 1908 were dominated by the conservatives, but the 'tragic week' of 1909 brought their downfall. The government had called up reservists to replace heavy losses in the colonial campaign in Morocco, anarchists declared a general strike in Barcelona, the movement spread to other Catalan cities, order disintegrated and all the forces opposed to the central government, the conservative party, the church and the oligarchs descended into the streets. Priests and monks were murdered, and in Barcelona 42 churches and convents were burned in a particularly severe outburst of anti-clericalism. The ensuing period of repression was no less severe, and the violence left deep divisions among conservatives, liberals, socialists and anarchists.

Portugal had been a constitutional monarchy since 1820. By the turn of the century, the republican movement was gaining ground. In 1910, republicans won majorities in elections in the two largest cities, Lisbon and Porto, a coup overthrow the monarchy and a republic was established. The new government pursued a progressive policy, legalising the right to strike, limiting the working week to six days, passing social insurance laws and establishing new kindergartens and universities. Yet the government never managed to secure the wholehearted support of its citizens – only 60 per cent of electors voted in the 1911 elections, for example, and most of the non-participants were unreconciled monarchists. Extra-parliamentary groups, either in favour of or opposed to the republic, emerged, including a Republican League of the Portuguese Women which demanded legal equality and suffrage for women and legalisation of divorce, and an anarchist labour union. The key problem remained underdevelopment; with few natural resources, Portugal had a traditional sort of agriculture and little industry, and three-quarters of the population was illiterate in 1911. Protectionism had been in force since the late 1880s, but the necessity of importing large quantities of wheat kept the 'bread question' at the forefront of debate. The country's imperialist urges founded outlets in Africa (in the areas which would become

Angola and Moçambique), but as in Italy and Spain the expenses of empire imposed a severe burden on the economy.

POLITICS IN EASTERN EUROPE

Politics in eastern Europe displayed the same institutional weaknesses as in the south, aggravated by economic underdevelopment, political autocracy and ethnic disputes. Bridging the gap between central and eastern Europe, Austria-Hungary was Europe's most contradictory state. Ethnically splintered into increasingly intransigent national minorities, politically it was an unwieldy Dual Monarchy, a two-headed compromise between Austria and Hungary arranged in 1867, in which the Habsburg ruler wore a double crown as Emperor of Austria and King of Hungary. Economically, the empire included great industrial cities and areas of wealthy mineral deposits, but it also included primarily agricultural Hungary and the Slav lands, where subsistence agriculture predominated. Socially, the empire included a glittering aristocracy at the courts in Vienna and Budapest, a wealthy middle class of industrialists and financiers, as well as hordes of state functionaries, a growing industrial proletariat and an impoverished peasantry in the Slav regions.

Presiding over this conglomeration was Emperor Franz Josef, who reigned from 1848 until 1916. Franz Josef's main aim was to keep his empire together, and he accordingly ruled it with a heavy hand. His ministers only rarely behaved as independent political figures, and the sort of parliamentary politics associated with England, France or even Germany was largely unknown in the Dual Monarchy. Austria-Hungary had a series of ministers, all of them hamstrung by the conservatism of Franz Josef and the obstructionism of the nationalists opposed to the Austrian Germans, of whom the Hungarians were the most troublesome. From 1900 until the outbreak of war, the Austrian half of the empire was ruled by non-parliamentary governments exercising their authority through imperial decrees. The introduction of universal manhood suffrage in 1907 was intended by the government to undermine the nationalist parties, but resulted only in a further fractionalisation of Austrian politics. In Hungary, the government threatened to introduce universal suffrage in 1906, which would have eliminated the Magyar majority in the Hungarian Diet. The Magyars moderated some of their demands and Hungary was ruled by a parliamentary majority until the war, though in 1912 a bill greatly increasing the size of the army (in which German, not Magyar, was the language of command) was only passed after the opposition deputies had been ejected from the chamber by force.

Outside parliament, Austro-Hungarian politics also ran across the entire spectrum. The socialist workers' movement espoused doctrines adopted from the German Marxists. The government's response was German as well: on the one hand, continued repression of socialist labour unions and political organisations, and on the other hand some very advanced social legislation, occasionally adopted verbatim from German models. Only prejudice could unite the citizens of the Dual Monarchy, it seemed; the anti-Semitic leader Karl Lueger adopted his programme quite consciously as more likely to lead to success than his previous liberalism and reformism. Uniting shopkeepers, artisans, workers and various nationality groups behind him, he was elected mayor of Vienna (over the opposition of the imperial government) and held office for nearly two decades until his death in 1910. Institutionalised anti-Semitism provided one of the background factors affecting the young Adolf Hitler, at the time an unemployed, frustrated artist on the fringes of Vienna's cultural life.

To the south of Austria-Hungary politics were equally divisive, but more personal. In Serbia two families whose ancestors had led rebellions against the Turks in the early nineteenth century contended for power, and another division separated the 'Austrian' party from the 'nationalists' who coveted Bosnia and Herzegovina and who looked to Russia for support. In 1893 a coup by the ruling family reduced the role of the legislature and therefore of the nationalists. In 1903 the king, his commoner wife and some 20 members of the court were brutally murdered by nationalist conspirators, who placed a member of the rival family on the throne and embarked on an expansionist anti-Austrian course. In

Bulgaria the German prince elected to the throne in 1887 survived the hostility of Russia and the other powers, plots, attempted assassinations and the intrigues of Macedonian separatists, and finally proclaimed himself tsar in 1908. The king of Rumania in turn protected himself with a deeply secret alliance with Austria, and the Rumanian oligarchy attempted to defuse discontent by exploiting popular anti-Semitism. All three, and Greece as well, claimed neighbouring territory, and all contained dissatisfied ethnic minorities. The Balkan Wars arose out of these claims, and one national minority, in Albania, managed to achieve independence because Austria and Italy did not want Serbia to obtain access to the Adriatic Sea. Others, such as the Macedonians, were less fortunate.

Politics in Russia, it has been said, was a question of absolutism tempered by violence. The tsar was a truly absolute monarch uniting his hereditary kingship with real control over the aristocratic elite and the masses of the peasantry, reinforced by his religious function as symbolic head of the church. The reigning tsar from 1894 until the Revolution of 1917 was Nicholas II, a weak-willed reactionary. Nicholas and his wife Alexandra maintained a sparkling court in St Petersburg, but they themselves were under the spell of a sleazy religious figure who claimed to be able to cure their son's haemophilia.

Russia's defeat by the Japanese, a crushing blow to the prestige of the state, and the abortive 1905 revolution which followed it, provoked some rethinking of government policy. Against a background of economic slump, peasant unrest and the war, a priest led a peaceful procession of workers through the streets of St Petersburg in January 1905. They carried a petition asking for economic and political change and professed their loyalty to the 'little father tsar'. However, the tsar's troops fired on the demonstrators and killed many of them; sympathy strikes broke out, the most dangerous being the movement among the railway workers. The government still possessed a reliable instrument of repression in the army, however, and in addition the tsar called an economic reformer to the prime ministership and issued a manifesto which led to the creation of what has been called a 'semi-demi-constitutional monarchy'. A new legislative assembly, the Duma, included an upper house with members elected by the provincial councils, the church and various other bodies, but an equal number of members who were nominated by the tsar. The lower house was elected by males over the age of 25, but voting was neither direct nor by secret ballot, and suffrage was further restricted in the elections to the third and fourth Dumas. The prime minister and other ministers were responsible to the tsar not to the Duma. The government could dissolve the Duma (as it did in 1906 and 1907) when criticism became too strident, and retained the power to issue decrees in times of national emergency or when the Duma was not in session.

Piotr Stolypin, who became prime minister in 1906, carried through a series of reforms including social insurance, improved education, rural self-government and, most importantly, the land reforms. The government had seen the *mir* as a source of stability in the countryside. However, rural violence had increased during the 1890s, and the peak of peasant outbreaks in 1905 had contributed to the revolution. Since the *mir* had failed in its purpose, Stolypin was willing to abandon it, to 'wager on the strong' rather than relying on the communes. Stolypin's plan was to transfer title to the land from the commune to the individual peasant, in order to create a class of substantial independent farmers who would raise agricultural productivity and support the government. By the First World War, over half of peasant households possessed hereditary tenure, but most of their property remained unconsolidated, segmented in inefficient parcels. The result had been not so much a general liberation of the peasantry, as a moderate expansion of the class of wealthier peasants, the so-called kulaks. These peasants were resented by the poorer, often landless peasants and were feared by the nobility, which opposed further reforms. Unrest did not disappear from the countryside, and large areas lived under martial law from 1905 to 1917.

Meanwhile, the Russian socialist movement was developing. The socialists had been meeting regularly, often abroad, since 1898, but, like their counterparts elsewhere, they were divided amongst themselves. The most severe rift occurred at the socialists' second congress in 1903, which saw the split between the Mensheviks and the Bolsheviks. The Bolsheviks, headed by Lenin, were the more hard-line group; although they took as their name the Russian word for majority, they were actually in the minority. The Mensheviks, who were less optimistic about the prospects of one great revolution than the Bolsheviks, thought that it was necessary to acquiesce to parliamentary rule in order that the 'bourgeois revolution' could be effected – as Marx's theory had argued – before the 'proletarian revolution' could take place. Both groups managed to recruit widespread support. The socialists' natural base, the proletariat, was relatively small in Russia, but the total number of strikes rose from 466 in 1911 to 2,032 in 1912 and 3,534 in 1913, and the number identified by the police as 'political' in motive from 24 to 1,300 and 2,401. Workers' demands tended to become more extreme, and the estimated one million 'political' strikers of 1913 tended to support the most extreme radical parties, especially the Bolsheviks. The stage seemed set for a showdown; the outburst of patriotic enthusiasm at the outbreak of the war in 1914 showed that the system still possessed some reserves of stability, but these were not sufficient to survive the shock of repeated defeats.

EXTRA-PARLIAMENTARY POLITICS

Formal politics in the Belle Epoque thus ranged from a democracy dominated by the privileged classes in western Europe to an only slightly tempered absolutism in the east. Everywhere as well, political action also took place outside the legislative chambers, another indication of the 'emergence of mass society'. Europeans were becoming more politicised through rising literacy, education, military service, migrations and the activities of political organisers. For some, these extra-parliamentary activities were the only available means of making their voices heard, since they were denied access to the more 'legitimate' formal means of political persuasion. For others, they were adjuncts to regular electoral activity. In a few cases such as Switzerland formal and extra-parliamentary politics merged in the officially-supported interest groups. Some of the extra-parliamentary demonstrators, such as the suffragettes, aimed at getting the ballot, while others, such as the anarchists, rejected the parliamentary system altogether. Demonstrators enjoyed some support among the elite groups. But the state often used the means at its disposal – statutes, censorship, imprisonment, the police and the army – to quell anything resembling insurrection among the populace.

One sort of extra-parliamentary protest was revolution pure and simple, a European tradition in the nineteenth century. The Russian revolution of 1905 and the Rumanian peasant revolt of 1907 were repressed, but radicals dreamed of continuing the tradition. Not all revolutionary attempts came from the extreme left wing, however. In 1909 a military coup in Greece brought to power a prime minister more favourable to the interests of the middle classes and the army, in 1910 a coup of moderate republicans overturned the Portuguese monarchy and the 1903 coup in Serbia replaced one dynasty with another.

Isolated individual acts of violence also punctuated the years before 1914. A French president, a Spanish prime minister and the Empress of Austria-Hungary fell to assassins, and bombs killed and injured hundreds. Contemporaries referred to such incidents as 'anarchist outrages' and tended to attribute them to a single shadowy group of conspirators. They were wrong; terrorist violence arose from several sources, each reflecting in a different way the failures of the existing social and political system. The philosophical conviction that no government can ever be legitimate – anarchism – led a few individuals to the belief that government could be destroyed by the assassination of individual leaders. More commonly, however, terrorism arose from despair. Assassinations and bombings were the desperate acts of those who had become convinced that only fear could force concessions from the elite, or those who hoped that violence would publicise their cause and create sympathy for their goals.

A continuing sort of activism was provided by the increasingly powerful trade unions in Europe established in the late nineteenth century after the removal of legislation forbidding their existence. In some regions, workers joined unions grouping together those from specific professions – miners, textile workers, and so on – but in most places they were also affiliated with national organisations bringing together various occupations, such as the Trades Union Congress in Britain or the General Confederation of Labour in France. Such organisations had powerful political leverage and enjoyed widespread support inside parties of the left. But the unions also were able to pressurise employers directly by calling on their workers to participate in strikes or other industrial action; the incidence of this sort of protest grew significantly from the late 1890s to the First World War. In France the widespread strikes between 1906 and 1911 showed both the dissatisfaction of the working classes and their strength, in Britain an outbreak of strikes in 1911 and 1912 brought railwaymen, dock workers and coal miners into conflict with the government and in Germany a series of massive strikes and lockouts were planned by the major unions and employers' organisations in 1914. Striking workers demanded recognition for their unions, better pay and improved working conditions; these 'economic' demands were also sometimes linked with political demands for better representation or for social legislation. Successful actions were the exception rather than the rule, as neither governments nor employers wanted to treat with what they regarded as rebels. In the Netherlands, for instance, the government broke the railway and dock strikes of 1903 with military force.

An extension of the strike was the general strike, a stoppage of work by all workers in the nation to achieve political ends. In Belgium a general strike in 1893 forced the introduction of universal suffrage, though still with plural votes, and another in 1913 ended when the government promised to eliminate plural voting. The Norwegian labour movement had threatened a general strike in 1905 if Sweden refused to grant independence. Swedish workers called a general strike in 1902 to press for extension of the franchise and again in 1909 to combat pay cuts and a lockout by employers. Both failed, however, and the 1909 defeat caused a large decline in union membership. Failures, in fact, were far more common than successes – as a German union official said in 1905: 'It's hard enough to organise an ordinary strike, let alone a general strike'.

A form of extra-parliamentary activity intended to extend the sphere of formal politics was the women's suffrage movement. In Britain especially, such campaigners as Emmeline Pankhurst organised marches, petitions to parliament and publications to demand women's suffrage. The responses they received were generally negative, male legislators claiming that women were incapable of rationally deciding for whom to cast a vote, or that they played no real role in the politics of the country, or that their husbands knew better than they how the country should be run. Faced with this intransigence, the suffragettes took to more direct action, including attacks on political leaders, sabotage and bombings. Imprisoned protesters went on hunger strikes. The government retaliated with forced feeding of the prisoners, a gruesome degradation of the women and a telling symbolic answer to their demands. In 1913 Emily Davison threw herself in front of the king's horse at the Derby, becoming a martyr to the cause and showing the determination of the protestors. Later the king inquired after the jockey, and the queen after Miss Davison. Six thousand women attended her funeral. Where parliamentary politics was more restricted, women such as Rosa Luxemburg in Germany and Alexandra Kollontai in Russia gravitated to extra-parliamentary creeds designed to change the system rather than merely broaden participation in it.

National minorities also resorted to extra-parliamentary action to achieve their ends, which involved the dismemberment of existing states and creation of new ones. The Habsburg empire was very nearly hamstrung by disputes among its constituent nationalities. The Irish question showed even the longest-established and most stable of the western European states was not immune. The ruling consensus simply dissolved whenever Ireland was mentioned. A Home Rule Bill which would have created an Irish parliament but provided for continued Irish representation in the Westminster Parliament was proposed in 1912 but provoked bitter opposition from the House of Lords, the Conservatives and especially the Ulster Unionists, who threatened violence and began to recruit and arm large numbers of volunteers. Finally adopted in 1914 after being passed by Commons three times, it pleased neither the Protestant Ulstermen nor the advocates of complete independence for Ireland and the government agreed to postpone its introduction until after the war.

In the Balkans the Macedonian movement in what is now southern Yugoslavia, northern Greece and western Bulgaria provided a revealing example of new forms of extra-parliamentary action and the limitations still imposed by traditional political and diplomatic structures. Certain elements in the Bulgarian government supported Macedonian claims for independence in the hope that in freeing themselves from the Ottoman empire they would then fall to Bulgaria. In 1893 the Internal Macedonian Revolutionary Organisation (IMRO) was founded, and in 1895 an 'external' organisation with its headquarters in Sofia. From bases in Bulgaria IMRO bands raided 'Macedonian' territory in the Ottoman empire. A former Bulgarian prime minister was murdered, as were a number of Rumanians, the latter leading to trials and acquittals by Bulgarian courts in 1901. An insurrection in Macedonia in 1902–3 was supported from the bases in Bulgaria – by this time the Bulgarian government had lost control of its protégés. In 1903 and 1904 Russia and Austria, 'acting for the European powers', proposed plans for limited autonomy and a local gendarmerie composed of Christians and Muslims in proportion to their share of the population, with foreign officers and a foreign general, as well as a reorganisation of the province's finances under an international control commission. When the Turks baulked, an international naval 'demonstration' and occupation of the island of Lemnos forced the sultan to yield. The powers did not consider Macedonia as strategically important as Albania, however, and therefore permitted Serbia and Greece to retain their conquests after the Balkan wars – creating new national minorities for the future.

IDEOLOGIES

All political groupings espouse an ideology, even when their actions betray more the characteristics of narrow political strategy aiming at getting or keeping power than consistent allegiance to a coherent creed. Most of the parliamentary parties throughout Europe agreed on the ground rules of politics. That is, they subscribed to the ideas of laws being made by chambers of representatives chosen in direct or indirect elections. Even in the east where law was still felt to be the pronouncement of the monarch himself, all governments found it necessary to adopt the forms of parliamentary government. Another belief of the mainstream parties was in the relatively free operation of the economy. Property might be gained through inheritance, purchase or gift, but it became the right of the owner to use and dispose of it without constraint. Acceptable constraints such as entails derived from the wishes of previous owners; in most countries any other restriction, from taxation to the state's right to sequester property, was hotly disputed. The socialists denied the right to private property; otherwise, few were the renegades who refused to accept the sacredness of a man's possessions.

In western Europe members of the ruling classes believed that the market should be free to operate subject only to its own laws of supply and demand. All agreed that the state should really aim to act only when it was a question of something too big for the private sphere to handle. The most sophisticated professional justification of this western European capitalism was provided by Alfred Marshall in his *Principles of Economics*; first published in 1890, it achieved instant acclaim among economists. Synthesising and extending the conclusions of the 'marginalist' economists, Marshall provided a coherent explanation of the interaction of supply and demand. Consumers, according to Marshall, allocated their incomes among commodities to maximise their satisfaction. Producers, in turn, allocated their capital among factors of production to maximise output. Consumers and producers both determined their allocation on the basis of declining marginal utility, the principle that additional units of a single commodity yield progressively less satisfaction and that additional units of a single factor of production yield progressively smaller increases in output. In the short-term 'market period', supplies of all commodities and factors were fixed and therefore their prices could rise suddenly in response to an increase in demand. However, in the 'long-run normal' period, if the change in demand proved large and permanent, firms would enter or leave the industry, bringing factors of production into the industry or leading to their movement into other industries. The explicit introduction of time into economic analysis was perhaps Marshall's greatest achievement, but it was an abstract, soothing sort of time. Marshall's system always tended toward equilibrium, yet at the same time it led to continual progress. Competition among the many small 'representative firms' led to the best possible allocation of resources. Increasing efficiency led to increased income, not only for the owners of the firms, but also for their employees. The system might not permit everyone to become wealthy, but it placed the 'noble life' within reach of all; further, with increasing affluence the moral tone of society would improve, because all groups would learn to behave more honourably towards one another.

In eastern Europe, political and economic ideas were quite different. In the Ottoman Empire, in theory, all land was owned by the sultan, who granted its use through his graciousness to the concessionaries of agriculture, commerce and industry. The industrialisation of Russia was a sort of state capitalism, with the government playing the major role as entrepreneur and banker, though relying on the cooperation and financial input of foreign stockholders. Professional economics reflected these differences. The dominant approach on the Continent was the 'historical school'. German economists in particular considered the British emphasis on competition and free trade a rather crude reflection of Britain's national interests. In concentrating on individual consumers and firms, they said, British economists had neglected the fundamental fact that in every case, unique historical developments provided the context for economic action, and that consequently economic behaviour would vary from place to place and time to time. The context was provided by the national community, which the historical economists conceived as an organic entity superior to any specific individual or social group. Gustav Schmoller, whose *Outline of General Economic Science* published in 1900 synthesised the approach of the historical school, concluded that the German state had exerted a powerful positive influence on society and the economy. However, he also favoured restricting the right of workers to organise. State intervention was always conceived in the interests of existing elites; historical economists supported government attempts to foster and guide economic development but never contemplated significant interference with private industrial or agricultural enterprise.

A third plank of dominant ideology was a belief in the efficacy of various institutions promoting social harmony and social mobility. Primary among these were the institutions of education and the church. Throughout Europe, there was a great belief in the value of education and the importance of education in providing a sure path of upward social mobility. Governments founded new universities and mandated compulsory childhood education. Government charters granted seals of approval to professional organisations of lawyers, doctors, engineers and others working in particular fields, entry to which was based on training and education. This meant, too, a belief in the ability of the individual to rise in status through hard work. Education, for many, was the panacea in this programme. Religion was a subject of greater debate, but in general, most political parties and the political elites believed in the value of religion both for its moral and its social effects. They lamented the secularisation of society and were aghast when researchers in the new discipline of sociology pointed out the decrease in religious practice. Even anti-clericals still thought of religion as the fountain of ethical conduct and the proper exemplification of membership in society.

Finally, the bourgeois parties believed in the nation and in the need to defend it. Not all of the mainstream parties were chauvinistic and imperialistic, but all believed in the distinct characteristics of their nations. They exalted the heritage of the nation: its artistic patrimony, its economic wealth, its political organisation. Looked at in a wide frame, this seems confusing; the French harked back to the Revolution of 1789, while the English were proud of not having had a revolution in the eighteenth century and the Russians were appalled at any revolutionary cries. But each national elite was true to the traditions of its own country, feeling that it had achieved some identifying mark, whether revolution or national unification or the creation of an empire on which the sun did not set. Translated into political programmes, nationalism meant the stockpiling of arms and the strengthening of the military forces to combat competitors in the colonial world, to guard against aggression by the nation's neighbours and to suppress rebels at home. The dangers of domestic violence and foreign war were recognised, but nationalism was generally seen as a good thing, proof of loyalty to a particular cultural and political group and willingness to defend the flag when necessary.

Other groups which increased in importance or emerged on the scene in the late 1800s and early 1900s did not accept these general principles, either because they demanded a wholesale change in the economy and society (the socialists) or because they emphasised particular exaggerated features (such as some of the right-wing groups). Such movements attacked the centrist consensus, and during the Belle Epoque new ideas fermented in Europe; they would then polarise in the interwar years. Although some of these groups were small, they were vocal and achieved a significance far greater than their numerical strength.

For the right-wing groups, centrist beliefs became highly distorted: instead of nationalism, they espoused a blind chauvinism; instead of protecting the territorial integrity of the homeland, they aimed to enlarge it through conquest; instead of social and cultural integration of the country, they wanted the elimination of different beliefs and different minority groups; instead of a strong central government, they preferred dictatorship. Yet it is otherwise almost impossible to make generalisations about the right-wing groups. For example, the *Action Française*, a newspaper established by Charles Maurras in 1899, brought together a fanatically nationalist group of disgruntled aristocrats, opportunist intellectuals and monarchists; despite the atheism of its founder, it gained the support of many Catholics and the sympathy of the Pope. The anti-Dreyfus groups combined distrust of modern liberal society with strident nationalism and anti-Semitism.

Anti-Semitism was a major theme for many of the nationalist groups of the period. They saw the Jews as a pernicious and dangerous influence in society, grabbing economic power and subverting the morals of the nation. The most frightening new development in their arguments was racism; for these demagogues, it was not the Jewish religion but the Jewish race which was the culprit. The Austrian Georg Ritter von Schönerer talked about the 'racial peculiarities' of the Jews and said the 'race makes for the filth'; he predicted that the evils of the Jews would ultimately be revenged 'on their bodies'. Such figures drew on a widespread popularisation of Darwin's biological theories which differentiated between various races and attributed to them particular characteristics. Another element was the idea of the *Volk*, the race of people sharing a certain language and culture whom the propagandists saw as having a right to hegemony over society and over a particular territory. The stalwarts of their movement were the troopers who would cleanse society and protect the *Volk* against foreign encroachments, and they would bear the standard of their cause against foreign enemies, traitors (such as the Marxists) and all and sundry who did not support them. Their objective was a moral revival of a cleansed body politic, strong and triumphant. It is easy to see how such beliefs turned to violent acts and how, later, they would be institutionalised in fascism and Nazism.

Totally different from these groups, both in the cogency of their theory and in the ideas which they expressed, were the socialists. Since the days of Marx socialism had become at once an economic analysis of history, a political philosophy, a parliamentary grouping and a cultural phenomenon. The basic ideas of Marx on the class struggle, the dialectic, the ownership of the means of production and the inevitable collapse of capitalism remained the canons of the theory. But the various theorists and parties differed on the way to gain power. The reformist wing of the socialist movement, including Edouard Bernstein in Germany, many members of the parliamentary socialist parties on the Continent and the Labourites in Britain, thought that socialism could win power by peaceful means, that is, by elections. Inside parliament, socialist deputies could work for the amelioration of the conditions of workers while awaiting the demise of capitalism and the advent of a socialist society. The more radical socialists, including such figures as Lenin and Rosa Luxemburg, considered parliamentary cooperation a surrender to the ruling classes; real socialism could be achieved only by a revolution in which the proletariat would take power and expropriate the bourgeoisie's economic and political power. Such quarrels meant that a great deal of time was spent in doctrinal warfare, censorious debate, and even excommunication from the movement. The dispute was personal – rivalries for control among the leaders – but also ideological; how was socialism to be achieved?

Some of the socialist leaders managed to surmount these fraternal disputes; foremost among them was the Frenchman Jean Jaurès. A brilliant student, a creditable historian – he wrote histories of the working class and of the French revolution – an eloquent orator, and a member of parliament, Jaurès symbolised the socialist ideal of intellectual cogency and political action. Jaurès was a reformist, saying that the class struggle was not necessary in a parliamentary society. He was a nationalist, even supporting the acquisition of colonial territory, and working with the centrist governments of the time. But he personally managed to reconcile the demands of different socialist factions in the programme he authored for the party, the Toulouse declaration of 1908. Jaurès said that the ultimate aim of the movement was the acquisition of complete power, a plank which pleased the left wing of the new unified socialist party; he added that circumstances might dictate the use of the general strike and rebellion, which pleased syndicalists; and, for immediate purposes, the document advocated electoral campaigns and parliamentary activity. Jaurès showed the ability of the socialist movement to participate in the parliamentary system without abandoning its revolutionary ideals or its mass base of support; ironically, his murder on the eve of the First

World War brought to a close a short-lived unity of the French socialist movement and ended the career of one of the most attractive statesmen of the epoch.

Socialism during this period achieved importance not only as a parliamentary force, but also as a form of analysis. Although intellectual life in Europe was still dominated by the concepts of liberalism and capitalism, socialism was making inroads as a methodology. It was also gaining support among the intellectual and cultural elite; Bernard Shaw in England was a Fabian, and many of the avant-garde in France were socialists. Ideas of the economic basis of history, the primacy of the class over the individual, the dialectical view of progress emerging from conflict – all were gaining intellectual respectability.

Not only were European intellectuals rejecting many of the received notions, but they were inventing new methodologies to investigate them. New academic disciplines emerged to look at the changes in society, analyse them, and project changes in the social order. One of these was the discipline of sociology. Auguste Comte coined the word in the early nineteenth century, but it was only at the end of the 1800s that sociology attained academic independence. The new sociologists tried to fathom the social changes around them and look for general explanations for social trends. Ferdinand Tönnies, a German scholar, published a treatise in 1887 in which he identified modern social change as a shift from *Gemeinschaft*, a community with symbiotic ties among its inhabitants, dominated by the links and commonality of the structure, to *Gesellschaft*, a new social organisation with individualistic action and contractural relationships, but lacking the unity provided by the old bonds. Emile Durkheim, a French sociologist, made a study of suicide, linking certain sorts of suicide to *anomie*, an alienation from society in the industrial age, in which individuals, feeling untethered to the world around them, kill themselves. Max Weber, a German, looked at economic history, the connections between Protestantism and capitalism, the social role of bureaucracy and the possibility of creating models or 'ideal types' for the analysis of society. Meanwhile, anthropologists began to study the so-called 'primitive' societies of Asia, Africa and the Americas, and psychologists, the best known of whom was Freud, turned their gaze inwards to study the unconscious workings of the mind.

Social theory had immediate political relevance. Analysis of society could provide the basis for political action. If man was irrational, then could politics be rational? If economic exploitation was caused by the monopoly of the means of production in the hands of the bourgeoisie, then should not the entire capitalist system be overthrown? If the society of industrialism could drive men to suicide, then what changes should be made in that society? If non-European societies did operate with a logic of their own – and their residents were content with them – then what could be the logic for the imposition of foreign norms through imperialism? From several different directions social scientists were undermining the assumptions on which most Europeans still based their view of the world.

Politics did not take place in a vacuum. Ideologies could be based on scientific or pseudo-scientific enquiry. Political groupings could be a question of factionalism, clientelism or personality cults as much as formal parties or rational choice. Economic and social groupings determined the context of politics, and in many parts of Europe they directly controlled politics. The politicisation of the masses, and their mobilisation by political parties, changed the actors in the political scene, and extra-parliamentary politics brought into the arena those who were denied adequate access to more regular channels of debate. The conflicts of classes were matched by ideological battles, as well as by the ins and outs of political strategy and vote-getting, a politicisation of society which would continue to be a feature of twentieth-century Europe.

5

THE FIRST WORLD WAR

THE FAILURE OF DIPLOMACY AND THE FAILURE OF STRATEGY

On 28 June 1914 a nineteen-year-old Bosnian named Gavrilo Princip shot and killed the heir to the Habsburg throne, Franz Ferdinand, and his wife Sophie in Sarejevo, capital of the Austrian province of Bosnia-Herzegovina. After a flurry of diplomatic activity and a series of ultimatums and mobilisations, the First World War broke out 39 days later. England, France, Russia and Italy faced Germany and Austria-Hungary, each side with their allies, in a war that would last for four years. The conviction that great events must have equally great causes has led to repeated attempts to identify some form of logic to the outbreak of the war. Those adopting the methods of diplomatic history have analysed the structure of international relations and the specific decisions leading to the war, seeking to identify the crucial policy or irreparable error making war unavoidable. Others, taking their lead from social and economic history, have seen the war as the more or less inevitable outcome of processes at work beneath the surface of politics and diplomacy. Each approach illuminates some but not all of the picture. The decision for war was in all cases a political, not an economic or social, event. The rigid alliance system with its precarious balance could have permitted any serious dispute to grow into a major war. However, this war was a mistake, the outcome of a series of errors. Previous crises in the Balkans – notably the wars of 1911 and 1913 – had been resolved without war among the great powers. Social and economic analysis, though equally unable to explain why this particular war should have broken out when it did, can contribute to an understanding of the background factors increasing the disposition to war, and is essential to an appreciation of the way in which the war's impact diffused through European society.

For a generation, the international atmosphere had become increasingly competitive, as the number of potential rivals increased and new technologies threatened existing power relationships. Strategic plans crystallised in elaborate mobilisation timetables. At the same time increases in military spending, and the introduction of new technologies which they implied, threatened to upset the careful calculations on which strategic assumptions were based. The naval arms race between Germany and Britain is the classic example. German determination to build a battle fleet large enough to pose a 'risk' to British domination of the seas called forth an equal British determination to maintain superiority and permanently embittered relations between the two countries. Along more conventional lines, Russia had been extending strategically important railways since the war with Japan in 1904–5 and had embarked on an extensive programme to modernise the army after the crisis arising out of Austria's annexation of Bosnia and Herzegovina. France extended the period of military service from two years to three in 1913, hoping to compensate for a low rate of population growth, but was still caught up in debate over the necessary increase in taxation to pay for the reform when the war came. The German General Staff, deeply worried by improvements in the armies of Germany's two likeliest opponents, was pressing for a massive investment in new railway lines to make possible the more rapid deployment of troops, a programme which inevitably would conflict with the ambitions of the navy enthusiasts. The temptation to strike a pre-emptive blow while in a position of superiority could add danger to any international dispute. Some German experts had pressed for a preventive war in 1905, and Austria's determination to crush Serbia in 1914 sprang in part from fear for the future.

Military spending linked government and industrial interests in all countries. In western Europe, though industrialists generally opposed actual hostilities as being bad for business, they waxed enthusiastic about contracts to supply military hardware. In Germany and Britain, naval chauvinism developed a regional focus in the shipbuilding districts which benefited most directly. Elsewhere in Europe, government military spending constituted a key element in industrialisation programmes. This might take the form of favouring domestic suppliers, as in Italy, or of encouraging spillover from foreign firms, as in Spain and Russia. Military exports from industrialised to less developed countries played important roles in both diplomacy and economics. Serbia's shift from Austrian to French suppliers after 1903, for example, announced and made possible a new and more aggressive Serbian policy towards Austria.

None of the responsible leaders of the great powers proved able to resist the currents of diplomatic and military insecurity, and key ambassadors and chief advisory personnel proved no better. The foreign ministers all failed to recognise the nature of the crisis or to respond effectively. The French president was en route from St Petersburg to Paris at the height of the crisis, leaving his ambassador free to encourage Russian bellicosity. Austrian leaders assumed that Russia would not intervene, Russian leaders that Germany would not respond to Russian mobilisation, German leaders that Britain would remain neutral, and British leaders that the crisis would somehow resolve itself short of war. As their original, unreasonably optimistic assumptions proved wrong, all resorted to a panicky grasping at straws, and then retreated into a gloomy fatalism. The German chancellor attempted ineffectively and too late to restrain Austrian belligerance, then moaned that 'we have lost control and the landslide has begun'. After his return to Paris, the French president attempted with equal lack of success to restrain Russia, after which French policy focused on placing the blame on Germany in order to ensure British entry into the war. British leaders, including the foreign minister, only gradually realised that their policy over the preceding decade in fact committed them to support France. British attempts to act as mediator failed, indeed appeared disingenuous or worse to the other powers, and gradually the prime minister and others came to believe they simply 'must face it'.

There is, therefore, more than enough blame to be shared among the leaders of all the European nations; indeed, it is their general failure of talent and imagination which requires explanation, not individual weaknesses or specific errors. Most belonged to the aristocratic landowning classes, and despite their common language (French) and their superficially sophisticated cosmopolitan milieu, they had little knowledge of industrial society and less understanding of the social changes taking place around them. They believed implicitly in their right to rule, yet sensed vaguely that increasing numbers of people disputed that right. All the governments in which they served had more or less consciously developed the technique of exploiting mass enthusiasms in support of government policy while attempting to deny genuine mass participation in the formulation of that policy. The technique was effective, but only so long as policy could be made to appear 'successful', and therefore popular pressure could powerfully affect policy once enthusiasms had been aroused.

For all governments and ruling elites, the war provided a convenient escape from particularly intractable domestic difficulties. Popular enthusiasm appeared to submerge divisions among the nationalities of the Habsburg monarchy, and some Austrian leaders saw in the prospect of annexing large amounts of Serbian territory with their Slavic populations a possible counterweight to Hungarian Magyar pretensions. In Russia the large number of strikes viewed by the police as 'political' rather than merely 'economic' had seemed genuinely threatening, but they evaporated as war fever spread. In Germany the Social Democrats were the largest party in the Reichstag, held at bay only by the empire's peculiar constitutional structure, and in 1914 a massive confrontation between employers' organisations and labour unions loomed on the near horizon. In France the assassination of socialist leader Jean Jaurès in 1914 tragically symbolised the gap between right and left and the fact that even in a republic many felt the working class had no right to representation, but all Frenchmen agreed that France must stand by Russia. Britain seemed on the verge of actual civil war over the question of Irish home rule, and the assurance given by Irish Protestant and conservative party leaders that they would stand behind the Liberal government in a European war played an important part in the decision to intervene. From this perspective, the war's outbreak resembles previous outbursts of imperialist enthusiasm. Writing in 1916 with the benefit of hindsight, Lenin still developed a theory of imperialism which seemed to predict the wrong war in the wrong place at the wrong time. Contrary to Marxist belief, the war resulted from conflict among the least developed of the great powers; it did not result from disputes over colonial territory and involved economic interests only tangentially. The conflict in the Balkans did resemble previous imperialist crises, however, in that 'success' would become a symbol of national prestige, and that each country's rulers could use foreign enemies as an external focus upon which domestic hostilities could be concentrated. Imperialism and expansionism were neither autonomous forces nor direct consequences of economic development, but specific programmes advanced by governments in part because the passions they aroused could be useful in deflecting the attention of the majority away from the very real shortcomings of the existing political and social system.

Ignorance of the possible effects of a major war made it easier for European leaders to contemplate war as a policy option and facilitated the slide into war in 1914. No country possessed any sort of plan extending beyond the deployment of existing forces and use of existing military supplies. Military and civilian leaders alike assumed that even a general war would be short and involve only limited consumption of resources. During the debate over British intervention, the English foreign minister asserted that 'for us, with a powerful Fleet, which we believe able to protect our shores, and to protect our interests, if we are engaged in war, we shall suffer but little more than we shall suffer even if we stand aside'. The war, said the publicists, would be 'over by Christmas'. Similarly, most German military experts thought the war would be over in six months, and the most pessimistic estimate held that the war could not last longer than two years. Like Britain, Germany possessed no plans to increase military consumption or to allocate labour. Russia and the other countries of eastern Europe, possessing only limited industrial sectors, relied on promises from their more advanced allies to supply their wartime needs.

Those who thought about the matter at all had concluded that industrial societies were incapable of engaging in long wars without collapsing. The chief German military strategist, Schlieffen, had said that the mechanism of industrial society 'with its thousand wheels, upon which millions depend for their livelihood, cannot stand still for long', and this belief had led him to propound the plan for a quick victory which bore his name. A corresponding belief held that it was neither necessary nor desirable for governments to interfere in the economy during wartime. In Britain, it was confidently asserted on all sides that 'business as usual' would continue during the war.

Not only all leaders, but all classes shared the enthusiasm for war. Most socialist leaders, who had actively opposed militarism and war before 1914, managed to convince themselves that this particular war was defensive and supported their respective governments. The leader of the Austrian socialist party had earlier said that 'it is better to be wrong with the working class than right against them', and decided to support the war in view of the overwhelming support for it among the workers and the futility of opposition in the face of censorship and martial law. In Germany, the leaders and press of the socialist party at first opposed the war, but Russian mobilisation made it appear that Germany was under attack by reactionary tsardom and uncivilised masses of Slavs. Socialist leaders were not arrested, as they had expected to be – indeed the chancellor himself took them into his confidence – and the mood of the party's rank and file members was unmistakable. One socialist deputy decided to vote for war credits after hearing reservists marching to join their units singing socialist party songs, and being told by his constituents: 'We are going to the front with an easy mind because we know the Party will look after us if we are wounded, and that the Party will care for our families if we don't come home'. Only in Serbia did the two socialist deputies actually cast their votes against the war.

The factors predisposing Europe to war in 1914 also help to explain the general failure on the part of all belligerents to realise how soon and how completely their strategies had failed. In retrospect, the end of the war and its political consequences seem clearly foreshadowed by the end of 1914, after only three months of fighting. In the east, Russian units scored tactical successes, but Russian technological backwardness revealed itself in inadequate transport, leading to slow deployment, and German commanders also benefited from the failure of the Russians to encode their radio messages. Austrian inefficiency was similar to but worse than Russian, and on 8 September Austria's foreign minister warned Germany that without immediate aid Austria would be forced to make a separate peace. The German General Staff's system worked to perfection and Germany's invasion of Belgium was a great success, but the Germans failed to take Paris. The French expected to neutralise the German advance through Belgium by hitting the Germans on their southern flank, and by an offensive of their own into southwestern Germany, but assaults by the French and British failed to dislodge the Germans from their positions. By November 1914 the western front extended from the tip of Belgium across northern France to Switzerland, and did not move more than ten miles in either direction until 1918.

THE BATTLES OF 1915 AND 1916

Strategically, the war was over. In the east, the miserable performance of the Austrian armies already heralded the collapse of the Habsburg empire into its constituent nationalities. The Russians in turn suffered defeat whenever they faced the Germans, and the magnitude of their losses far exceeded the capacities of their relatively small industrial sector and backward agriculture. Though new Russian armies might be raised, equipped and fed, the costs would inevitably reopen the social fissures temporarily covered by patriotism. Germany, forced to prop up the Austrians in the east and carry the whole burden of the war in the west, already lacked the manpower to deliver a decisive blow in either direction.

The war had become a war of attrition, a war which Germany could not win, even before the crushing addition of the United States to the balance of manpower and economic resources.

The total failure of strategy in the early months of the war had no impact on strategic thinking. An entire generation of military leaders had been raised in a tradition emphasising offence and movement; static lines and defensive strategy they considered marks of incompetence and even cowardice. Joseph Joffre and the 'young Turks' of the French General Staff believed that a spirited offence by enthusiastic individual soldiers would prevail against any defence. British commanders emphasised a 'war of movement'. Many British officers had been influenced by colonial wars, especially the Boer War, where cavalry had played a large role in the huge open spaces of South Africa. British recruits were taught that the bayonet was the decisive weapon, for supposedly bayonet charges had decided hundreds of battles against native armies in Asia and Africa.

The German version of the offensive strategy was the belief in the 'decisive battle'. The bitter dispute which wracked the German General Staff concerned not strategic philosophy but rather where the decisive battle would be fought. The 'easterners' wanted to follow up their initial successes, but the chief of staff replied that victory would come in the west. For the French, with so much national territory in German hands, offensive action in the west was an article of faith. The British shared their faith, however. Doubters had their plans restricted to the status of 'sideshows'. A corollary to the doctrine of offensive action was the belief in the need to attack and defeat the strongest enemy forces. They were clearly on the western front, and there was no easy and obvious 'back door' to Germany and Austria. Therefore, all commanders concluded that their initial losses had to be made good, new larger armies raised, and new allies found to break down the enemy and achieve a decisive victory in the west.

Through early 1915, the French and British battered at the German lines. None of the offensives gained significant territory, however, and the attackers always lost more men than the defenders. Commanders resolutely ignored these facts, and the summer was spent preparing for a great autumn offensive by the French and British, intended to break through at two separate points and catch the Germans in a great 'pincers' movement. The attacks continued through September and October, but after yielding a bit, the German lines held again.

The German commanders, too, failed to learn the lessons of 1915. In early 1916 the Germans attempted to 'bleed France to death' and score a decisive psychological victory by capturing Verdun. In 1792, the fall of Verdun to the Prussians had caused panic in France's revolutionary government and set off the infamous 'September massacres' of aristocrats, priests and suspected traitors. In 1915, the fortress city lay in an exposed salient in the French lines and was actually rather lightly held. In late February, following a massive concentrated artillery bombardment by some 1,400 guns along an eight-mile front, the Germans succeeded in taking Verdun's outer defences. The French commander, Joffre, actually favoured yielding and retreating to a shortened defensive line. French political leaders, believing the fall of Verdun would severely damage morale and cause the fall of the government, ordered Verdun held at all costs. Despite the difficulty of supply through the narrow salient, Philippe Pétain indeed did defend the main fortress against repeated German assaults in March and April. A series of French counterattacks in May was succeeded by German attacks until mid-July, by which time they and the French had each suffered some 350,000 casualties. In December, the French attacked again, driving the Germans back some two miles and recapturing the outposts lost in February.

The French and British, still pursuing the elusive 'breakthrough', began their next offensive on the Somme. The Somme has become a paradigm for the western front. The British lost 60,000 men on the first day alone, some 21,000 killed, most of them during the first hour of the attack on the morning of 1 July. Between July and November, the British and French gained some 125 square miles of territory, but failed to break the German lines. Though they inflicted between 400,000 and 500,000 casualties on the Germans, the

British lost 400,000 men and the French a further 200,000.

Both the attack planned as a 'battle of attrition' and the attempt to gain a 'decisive breakthrough' had failed as strategic concepts. Both sides had mastered the tactics of defence with mines, barbed wire, trenches and, above all, machine guns. Properly constructed front-line trenches had parapets, firing platforms, concealed firing slits, support trenches some 200 yards behind and reserve trenches a further 400 yards behind. Dugouts at regular intervals provided shelter from artillery fire. All trenches were laid out with regular 'traverses' or kinks to prevent the enemy from firing along the trench once he reached it. A second line of trenches with their own support network lay behind the front line, sited just out of effective artillery range, and a third line behind that. Telephone lines buried as much as six feet below ground linked the front with headquarters. Commanders on the defensive dispersed their forces whenever possible and held reserves and counterattack units well to the rear until needed. Western Europe's dense railway network made it easy to move reserves from one sector of the front to another. The attackers could get a temporary advantage in numbers, but the defenders could call for reinforcements by telephone and the necessary units could be moved by train. The attackers meanwhile would have to move on foot, and would have no communications with their rear after the beginning of the attack.

No defending commander could possibly be surprised when an attack came, moreover, because an artillery barrage announced each attack well before it began. Even better for the defenders, though worse for the attackers, the artillery bombardment, though visually and aurally impressive and even intimidating, did not kill very many of the defenders or destroy the all-important machine guns. The British stockpiled 2,960,000 artillery shells along the Somme front, and for seven days the German defenders huddled in their dugouts without sleep and without warm food while the entire 21,000 tons of shells, and a quantity of chlorine gas, descended above their heads. Their dugouts, however, excavated as much as 30 feet underground, could withstand any of the British artillery except perhaps a direct hit from one of the

1,400-pound shells lobbed by the 15-inch howitzers – but the British possessed only 6 of these. Direct hits were unlikely in any case, for all howitzers had an aiming error of at least 25 yards. The British gunners hoped to hit the entrances to the dugouts and entomb the Germans, but could not see their targets and would have needed luck to hit them if they had. The British also hoped that the large quantity of shrapnel shells they fired would destroy the German barbed wire, but though the experienced troops at the front already knew high-explosive shells were more effective against both barbed wire and trenches, not enough high explosive was being produced in England to supply these shells in sufficient quantity.

Most of the defenders would survive the artillery barrage, then, and race up from their dugouts to reoccupy their trenches and reassemble their machine guns before the attackers could cross no-man's-land. At the Somme, the British planned to climb out of their own trenches, arrange themselves in long lines or 'waves' and walk a mile or a mile and a half, through the German barbed wire which should have been destroyed, and seize the German trenches from the remaining defenders, most of whom should have been killed. In fact, the Germans saw the British forming up through their periscopes, and some British units came under machine-gun fire before they could advance. Other British units advanced but found the German barbed wire only slightly damaged, and the resulting delay only increased the effectiveness of the German fire. A third of the British units failed to cross no-man's-land. Some of the remaining units actually succeeded in their objective of taking the German trenches, but merely forced the outnumbered Germans to retreat to their second line, from which they would have to be dislodged some other day.

In eastern Europe the thin railway network reduced the ability of the contending armies to bring up reserves to resist attack. The relatively thinly-held front was therefore more mobile, and large amounts of territory could be gained or lost in a few days. Strategically, however, the east did not differ so greatly from the west. Attackers inevitably ran ahead of their communications, supplies and reserves, and defenders eventually could assemble their reserves for a counterattack. The war in the east was therefore also a war of attrition, but again commanders failed to draw the proper conclusion. To German commanders in particular, the greater movement of the front seemed to promise the opportunity for the 'decisive battle' which had eluded them in the west. The battles spread to Italy and the Balkans but neither there nor in eastern Europe were conclusive victories gained; eleven battles at Isonzo, Italy, failed to move the front more than 20 kilometres in either direction. The only real result was carnage – in the Brusilov offensive, the Russians lost over a million men.

THE ORGANISATION OF SOCIETIES AND ECONOMIES FOR 'TOTAL WAR'

The appalling losses of the war's first months decimated existing armies, and typically the best units suffered the heaviest losses. Britain's small professional army disappeared in the opening battles of 1914, and those units lucky enough to have been stationed overseas suffered in their turn at the Somme. France lost 850,000 men killed, wounded or taken prisoner from September–December 1914 alone. Austrian and German losses were equally distressing, and Russian casualties mounted beyond the tsarist government's ability to count. The expectation on all sides of a short war meant in addition that commanders made no attempt to conserve matériel. German supplies of ammunition had disappeared by October 1914. In December 1914 Grand Duke Nicholas told his allies that Russia would be incapable of further offensive action because of the supply shortage, and in early 1915 as many as a quarter of new Russian conscripts were being sent to the front without weapons and told simply to pick up rifles and other supplies from the dead.

All governments of course saw the need for more men, and more gradually all came to realise the connection of the supply of men with the supply of weapons. The German response seems in retrospect the most rational and best organised, in part because Germany could build on the existing cartel organisations and tradition of cooperation between industry and government. The sudden shortage of ammunition caused its price to rise steeply, but output slumped at first because of a labour shortage. All reservists had been called up regardless of occupation, including a large number of workers in the munitions industries. The government therefore almost at once introduced exemptions for workers in strategic industries. The crucial shortages would emerge in raw materials, however, and already in August 1914 the government adopted the plan of Walther Rathenau, head of the AEG electrical combine, for an agency to exercise central control over supplies. The resulting War Raw Materials Office expanded and subdivided rapidly, and by 1918 25 'war corporations' had emerged, each with responsibility for specific products. Formally organised as private corporations, these agencies also functioned as official 'trust organisations'. Scarce materials were simply declared 'confiscated' and distributed by the war corporations to selected firms.

In Germany central control over supply and distribution of raw materials was accompanied by industrial reorganisation and new investment in certain areas. Compulsory cartelisation could be drastic, particularly in areas not considered strategically crucial. The number of shoe manufacturing firms, for instance, was forcibly reduced from 1,500 to 400. Government and industrial spokesmen justified cartelisation in the name of rationalisation, simplicity of structure, and increased efficiency. Despite occasional gestures towards small industrialists, however, the benefits of wartime reorganisation went almost exclusively to large firms, and generally to those with the best inside connections with the administrative bureaucracy. New investment moved in the same direction, though it did sometimes have the effect of bringing a new process into large-scale operation sooner than might otherwise have occurred.

Although Britain at first relied on volunteers, and British legislation continued to have a somewhat ad hoc quality, the exigencies of war imposed structures strikingly similar to those which emerged in Germany. Kitchener called for volunteers – 'Your country needs YOU' his image proclaimed from thousands of posters. The army bureaucracy expected to induct some 100,000 men within 6 months and about 500,000 total, target figures selected because they were the largest number of new soldiers which existing plants could provide with uniforms, weapons and ammunition. Popular enthusiasm had run well ahead of official planning, however, and the army was inundated with 500,000 volunteers in 1 month and an average of 100,000 each month for the following year and a half. Because anyone could volunteer, by the summer of 1915 the munitions industry had lost 20 per cent of its labour force, and the complaints of field commanders over the insufficient quantity and poor quality of ammunition led to an open scandal which contributed to the fall of the government.

Britain's wartime organisation originally came under the Defence of the Realm Act, under which the government possessed wide rights of requisition. However, the government remained reluctant to use such powers directly, and preferred compromise, particularly when the need to increase production impinged on existing interests. Initially, the owners of munitions plants attempted to overcome the sudden shortage of skilled workers by increasing mechanisation of production and by employing greater numbers of semi-skilled and unskilled workers, especially women. The craft unions, jealous of their members' status, wages and working conditions, opposed this 'dilution' of the labour force, seeing the employers' moves as an unsubtle attempt to use the wartime emergency to undermine the unions' position. The dispute threatened for a time to become serious, but was overcome by the Shells and Fuses Agreement of March 1915, under which the unions agreed to 'dilution' as a temporary measure for the duration of the war, and employers undertook not to dismiss skilled workers or to cut their rates of pay.

In June 1915 Lloyd George became the head of a new Ministry of Munitions which expanded over time into an approximation of the War Raw Materials Office in Germany. Lloyd George, proud of his 'businessman's ministry', bypassed the War Ministry whenever possible to get estimates of requirements directly from field commanders. Their demands, considered excessively high by the War Ministry, were

assembled into an extremely large estimate by the Ministry
of Munitions, an estimate which not only proved correct but
which in fact had to be increased further. The Ministry
of Munitions always worked in close cooperation with
industrialists, assuring them from the outset that there would
be no government 'control' of private firms. Nonetheless, the
government did invest in new plants and oversee the
conversion of non-munitions plants to wartime production.
The number of government-owned plants increased from 70
in late 1915 to some 200 by the end of the war. The new
plants were larger and more efficient than the old, using
more highly mechanised techniques and less skilled labour,
and the price of a standard 18-pound shell declined by 50 per
cent during 1915.

Within all countries politics continued as usual. The issues
and cleavages which had divided Europeans before the war
emerged again as the initial burst of patriotic enthusiasm
passed. The bloody Easter Rebellion in Ireland in 1916 put
Britain on notice that Irish nationalism had not disappeared.
In Germany industrialists regarded cooperation with labour
unions as a regrettable temporary necessity, and conservatives
began to view victory and massive annexations as a way
to avoid political reform. In Austria, national and local
parliaments were suspended and the entire monarchy placed
under martial law. Though for a time the army, acting under
the War Service Act of 1913, could claim that 'everything
goes at a more rapid pace now', the willingness of Czechs,
Poles, Rumanians, South Slavs and Italians to submerge
their interests in the struggle to maintain an empire
dominated by Germans and Magyars disappeared rather
rapidly. In Russia the prewar political groupings also
reappeared. No central agency to control wartime production
and distribution could be established because of competition
among existing government departments and between the
government and the political parties.

The failures of 1916 led to the replacement of military and
government leaders but did not lead to changes in strategy or
to serious attempts to end the war. In most countries the
groups responsible for policy formulation became smaller,
further reducing the possibility of discussion of strategic and

political options. Wartime leaders believed implicitly that the war had to be continued, and that it had to lead to 'victory', in order that the immense sacrifices already made would not have been in vain and in order that the politicians and generals could keep their jobs. The new French premier, Georges Clemenceau, told the Chamber of Deputies: 'You ask me for my policy. It is to wage war. Home policy? I wage war. Foreign policy? I wage war. All the time, in every sphere, I wage war'.

Only in Russia did political changes seem to promise some change of direction. Disorganised transportation and the steady refusal of the peasantry to sell their crops at any price had reduced urban food supplies to desperate levels. In St Petersburg exasperated workers called a strike in January 1917 to mark the anniversary of the 1905 revolution and protest the war, and fully 40 per cent of the city's workers flooded the streets in the ensuing demonstrations. During February the strike movement spread, and when army units stationed in the cities refused to fire on the strikers, tsarist autocracy collapsed and yielded to the Provisional Government, a coalition of opponents of the old regime led first by Prince Lvov and later by Alexander Kerensky. However, the leaders of the Provisional Government did not see themselves merely as the first stage of what we now identify as the Russian Revolution. Rather, they expected to be able to organise the country to prosecute the war more effectively.

The plans of the new leaders in all countries required further mobilisation of human and industrial resources. Britain actually introduced conscription in January 1916, before it was necessary, but by 1918 the demand for yet another 900,000 soldiers required the abolition of exemptions for even skilled workers in munitions industries. Control over industrial production extended, as the sense of crisis overrode concern for violations of free trade principles. Germany embarked on a programme of increased military production and passed the 'Patriotic Auxiliary Service Law'. In theory the Auxiliary Service Law placed all males between the ages of 16 and 60 not already in military service under the authority of the war minister. In fact the army commanders were forced to compromise with other government agencies, business interests, the parties in the Reichstag and even labour organisations. Despite the creation of a new War Office, competition among procurement agencies and the absence of clear priorities drove prices up. This primarily benefited large industrialists, who continued to reject government control over their firms. In France, new factories coming into production in 1917 made the Paris region a centre of heavy industrial production for the first time. Russia's factories, few in number but very large and relatively efficient, had been shifted to military production by a series of War Industry Committees under the leadership of private industrialists. Austria began to suffer from shortages of raw materials but received no help from Germany, and Italian requests for aid from Britain were rejected because the British insisted they required all available industrial output to support a new offensive in Flanders.

The policy of 'business as usual' – the quasi-official British phrase – emerged most clearly in the industrialists' demand that they earn profits on war production. Rathenau and other German planners in fact pressed for maximum levels of profit, arguing that high prices were merely the normal consequences of the crisis and shortages. In 1916 the German war ministry attempted to restrict rates of profit, setting off a bitter debate within the government and between the government and industry, with all sides attempting to justify their positions by appealing to the increasingly difficult military situation. In Britain and other countries the situation was similar. At first no one contemplated controlling prices, and as supplies disappeared prices increased accordingly. Gradually governments intervened to ration scarce commodities and impose maximum prices but never at the expense of profits. Even the new, lower prices on munitions imposed by the British government during 1915 allowed ample profit to industrialists.

By 1916 increased food prices and shortages were bringing hardship to the civilian populations of all countries. As prices rose, not only the amount of food but also the quality of available food declined. Governments attempted to control prices and ensure supplies through distribution and rationing schemes but achieved only partial success at best. The British were in the most fortunate position, despite their heavy reliance on imports. Approximately 90 per cent of prewar food supplies were still available in late 1916, though prices had risen substantially because of increased freight rates and general inflationary tendencies. The intensification of Germany's submarine campaign led the government to introduce comprehensive controls over the purchasing, shipment and distribution of imports. The government also intervened directly in domestic agricultural production, planning an increase of 7.5 million acres in the area sown, 40 per cent over the prewar average. Soldiers and prisoners were allocated to farms for planting and harvesting, as were seeds and fertilisers. Substantial numbers of tractors were distributed to central depots in each district.

The outbreak of the war deprived Germany of perhaps 500,000 seasonal farm workers from Russian and Austrian Poland as well as the millions of men conscripted into the army. Many rural women and children had already been working full time; even though more women were employed and eventually nearly 900,000 prisoners were assigned to German farms, the losses could not be made good. Germany had used large amounts of chemical fertilisers before the war, but the demand of the munitions industries for nitrates now took precedence over the needs of agriculture. The army requisitioned large numbers of draft animals, and farm machinery was in desperately short supply as well. Farm output therefore declined progressively. Worse, the occupied areas of Belgium and northern France required food imports, while Poland, Rumania and the Ukraine yielded only moderate food exports.

The German government attempted to leave the control of food prices in the hands of local officials, with disastrous results. Farmers withheld supplies from towns which set low prices, and officials therefore competed with each other to set higher prices to ensure supplies. By the time a national Food Control Office was established in May 1916 much food was already being traded on the black market. After the imposition of the maximum price for pigs in November 1915, for instance, officially recorded sales had dropped from 61,000 to

15,000 per week. Rationing extended further and pressed more severely on consumption than in Britain, eventually dropping to 1,000 calories per day. Unlike Britain, however, the official rations were easily avoided by those with money or connections. Those without either suffered proportionately more. Newborn infants and children declined in weight compared to prewar averages, while the incidence of rickets and tuberculosis increased. By 1917 the mortality rate of children aged 1–5 had risen 50 per cent, and that for children aged 5–15 nearly 75 per cent.

The position of other countries in western, southern and northern Europe depended on their initial position and capacity to import food. France suffered a drastic decline in production because of losses of territory and absence of labour reserves. Women, children and prisoners were mobilised unsystematically though quite ruthlessly, but the wheat harvest dropped some 40 per cent. Rationing was severe, but France retained access to overseas supplies. Italian farm output, conversely, did not decline until 1917. However, as Italian consumption began at a lower level, the Italian government was less able to organise markets than the French government. Italy was less able to afford imports and the Mediterranean sea routes remained more dangerous than the Atlantic. Italians therefore suffered more than the French, especially in urban centres.

In eastern Europe, the Habsburg empire had been in approximate balance before the war, with Hungary exporting grain to Austria. Fighting in the eastern half of the empire reduced supplies. In addition, the Magyar owners of large estates in Hungary held grain off the market to feed their animals, hoping to maintain the size of their herds to ensure their market position after the war, and Czechs and Croats objected to central control over food supplies on nationalist grounds. Nonetheless a central food agency was established in Austria in late 1916 and extended to Hungary in 1917. Rationing embraced even potatoes in late 1917. In 1915 two meatless days per week were declared, increased to three the following year. Horsemeat consumption doubled. In December 1914 bakers had already been ordered to cut the wheat content of bread to 70 per cent, the rest being barley and rye. By 1915 bread was a mixture of potato flour, corn meal, rye and 'very little wheat' and by 1916 available bread was a mixture of barley and oatmeal. In Vienna civilian food consumption had declined by half by early 1916, and observers commented on widespread rickets, tuberculosis, and hunger oedema among children.

Russia mobilised some ten million men for military service, about a third of the male agricultural labour force. Russia had been a large exporter of grains, but now the cultivated area declined substantially, and because the rations issued to soldiers were actually higher than average peasant consumption, demand increased. The Russian distribution system was inadequate, partly because of the thin transportation network and partly because of government mismanagement. By 1915 grain shipments had declined by a third from prewar levels. Prices rose sharply, doubling in most country areas and increasing as much as eightfold in some cities. The stage had been set not only for the revolution but also for the mass starvation of the civil war period.

In wartime Europe, prices rose not only for food but for all consumption goods, and they rose not only because of actual shortages but also because all governments financed the war through inflation rather than through tax increases. All countries had abandoned the gold standard, most indeed before the war had actually begun. Britain alone among European nations preserved the forms of the gold standard, but administrative regulations made it impossible for individuals to exchange notes for gold or to export gold from Britain. National monetary systems therefore were isolated, and governments financed their domestic purchases of military supplies with loans from the banking system. Credit creation increased the supply of money and government purchases reduced supplies of goods, and prices therefore began to rise almost at once. Belligerent governments financed their purchases from allies and neutral countries first by selling assets held in those countries and then by credits advanced by the exporting countries. This was the origin of the decline in British assets held overseas and of the 'war loans' advanced by allies to one another, the largest being the credits granted by the United States to Britain and France.

General increases in taxation were rejected out of hand. The French finance minister asserted that higher taxes would add too much to the existing burden of the war. No tax was imposed on wartime profits. The French government was also typical in that although some taxes were raised to cover 'ordinary' expenses, the much larger cost of the war itself appeared only in a separate 'extraordinary' budget, whose payment was postponed to the future. The finances of less sophisticated governments declined rapidly into disarray. The Russian government, for instance, had drawn about a quarter of its prewar revenue from its monopoly of alcohol production and another quarter from the income of the state railways. A proclamation of August 1914 forbade Russians to consume alcohol for the duration of the war; brewing and drinking continued, of course, but government revenue from these activities disappeared. Meanwhile government agencies monopolised traffic on the railways, and railway revenues therefore merely transferred credits from one government department to another. Taxes on incomes and profits introduced in 1916 were ineffective and came too late to halt the inflationary spiral.

Inflationary finance, regretted by all, was introduced everywhere as a temporary measure in the belief that the war would be short and that the enemy would pay. The German finance minister spoke for all belligerents in asserting that 'the instigators of this war have brought upon themselves the leaden weight of billions; it is for them, not us, to drag it with them for decades to come'. As the war dragged on, government officials continued to resort to inflation, believing that 'normal' conditions could be re-established at the war's end at the enemy's expense, and their commitment to this belief increased their intransigence in the war's prosecution. Ordinary people continued to accept and use their country's inflated currency because of their faith that its diminished value would be restored. War bonds, whose sale served to absorb some of the excess civilian purchasing power accumulating in all countries, found a generally enthusiastic reception because people believed in the good faith and creditworthiness of their governments.

As governments came to appreciate the need for the mobilisation of entire economies for war, they placed increasing emphasis on measures of 'economic warfare'. The British 'hunger blockade' infuriated Germans, and German submarine attacks seemed to the British to provide the final evidence of German inhumanity. The passionate denunciations have an ironic aspect, for neither policy succeeded. All leaders overestimated the importance of international trade in economic development and hence in a nation's capacity to wage war; all underestimated the resilience and flexibility of their domestic economies. In contrast to expectations, all nations proved able to reorganise their domestic economies to mobilise unprecedented resources in isolation from the international economy.

Britain, with overwhelmingly the strongest navy, naturally led the way in establishing and extending a surface blockade of enemy ports. Complex regulations were imposed on neutral countries, not only to deny Germany and Austria-Hungary supplies but to guarantee their sale to Britain and France on favourable terms. The original agreements covered only re-exports, not the neutrals' own products, and the Scandinavian countries in particular continued to sell goods purchased in Britain to Germany. In March 1915 Britain declared an unrestricted blockade on shipments to Germany, an illegal act under international law. Britain also imposed export quotas on sales to neutral countries to prevent re-exports to the enemy, blacklisted firms dealing with Germany or Germany's allies and threatened to cut off fuel supplies to neutrals which refused to conform. The United States bitterly opposed these infringements on the traditional rights of neutrals until entering the war, after which American spokesmen became the strongest advocates of the unrestricted blockade.

Overall the blockade failed in the early years of the war and was only moderately successful even in the war's later stages. The blockade did not cause the food shortage in Germany and Austria-Hungary. Neither nation had depended on food imports before the war; in both, agricultural output declined because such large numbers of farm workers were mobilised. Germany in particular expanded production of artificial *ersatz* products to replace imports, most notably in the case of nitrates. Deprived of foreign markets, Germany's large export industries could be turned to war production. Germany and Austria-Hungary increased their imports from adjacent neutrals, further diluting the impact of the blockade. Food, timber and metallic ores continued to flow from the Netherlands, Denmark, Sweden and Norway. Production in occupied territories also contributed to the German war economy. The mines and factories of northern France and particularly of Belgium were exploited by the Germans, while some grain and substantial amounts of oil were extracted from Rumania. Germany and Austria-Hungary were suffering from shortages of all resources by 1917, but would have even without the blockade because they would have had in any event to compete in international markets with the much stronger financial powers of Britain and the United States.

The German submarine campaign also failed. Unable to use the surface vessels acquired at such great financial and political cost, the German navy commanders developed an unjustified faith in the submarine and pressed for its unrestricted use against enemy shipping. In fact in 1915 Germany possessed only 27 submarines, most of which could not operate in the open sea, and could maintain only 3 'blockade stations' of 1 vessel each off the west coast of Britain. After the sinking of the *Lusitania* and ominously strong American protests, the German government forbade further sinkings without warning and cancelled all operations west of Britain in September 1915. The naval commanders continued to press for an expanded submarine campaign, and in 1916 bypassed the chancellor and appealed directly to the emperor. By late 1916 an expanded 'restricted' campaign was actually sinking some 300,000 tons of shipping a month. The navy argued that an 'unrestricted' campaign could sink 600,000 tons a month, and that losses of this magnitude would force Britain to sue for peace in 5 months. German naval experts considered convoys of merchant ships escorted by naval vessels impossible for both technical and economic reasons, and also calculated that even if the United States should enter the war, no effective intervention would be possible before Britain collapsed.

The German navy proved wrong on all counts. British losses did mount to 866,000 tons in the single month of April 1917, approximately 1 in 4 ships cleared for British ports. The target figure of 600,000 tons per month for 5 months was met and exceeded. But Britain did not sue for peace. Worse, the new convoy system proved almost completely effective, and by late 1917 losses had declined to 300,000 tons per month. In the meantime the use of standard designs and interchangeable parts had revolutionised shipbuilding and by 1918 two new ships were being built for every one sunk. Worst of all, the resumption of unrestricted submarine attacks brought the United States into the war, and this new addition of potential manpower and matériel placed Germany and its allies at a hopeless disadvantage.

COLLAPSE

Increasing hardship and continued purposeless slaughter eventually undermined both civilian and military morale in all countries. Where the figures are at all reliable, they indicate that prices had risen from two to four times and that real wages had declined from one-third to two-thirds by 1917. Conditions worsened from west to east, and an especially severe winter in 1916–17 added to the misery. Strikes in Britain, France and Germany served notice that the carefully balanced agreements among governments, employers and labour unions were tottering. Reductions in food rations led to disorders in Leipzig and Berlin, workers in Milan and Turin were openly mutinous and food riots erupted in most of the major cities of Austria-Hungary.

In April 1917 the French commander ordered his army forward once again in pursuit of a 'breakthrough', despite knowing that the Germans had withdrawn to shorter, more easily defended lines in the area of the planned attack. The attack in addition was known in advance to the Germans, and their defence was therefore even better prepared than usual. The predictable massive French losses finally pressed morale down past the breaking point. Whole regiments went to the front bleating like sheep in passive protest. Others refused to go to the front at all, and refusal spread, eventually affecting over 50 divisions. Officially, over 100,000 courts martial found some 23,000 soldiers guilty, though only 49 were actually shot. Unofficially, a large number of soldiers suffered more summary execution as a warning to their fellows.

In Russia, hunger had already led to revolution, but supporters of the Provisional Government wanted to continue the war. They believed that national honour required them to stand by their allies and that victory would restore Russian territory occupied by the enemy. They hoped in addition that the war itself and the eventual victory would work to postpone discussion of fundamental political and social reforms until a later and more favourable moment. Their calculations were not as hopelessly unrealistic as they now appear. However, the Provisional Government, after initial concessions to enlisted men, attempted to reimpose and increase discipline. The families of soldiers who refused orders or deserted were to be denied food rations, and Kerensky wanted strikers interfering with the war effort such as railway workers treated as military criminals as well. The government organised demonstrations to show support for a new offensive in July 1917, but suffered a serious blow to its prestige when most of the demonstrators appeared with banners and placards demanding instead an end to the war. After initial successes, the offensive stalled, and a German counterattack threatened St Petersburg itself. The army melted away, creating a power vacuum into which Lenin and the Bolsheviks stepped in November.

Meanwhile in the west, a new offensive resulted in the extraordinary battle of Passchendaele in 1917. Eight British attacks cost over 300,000 casualties, while the German defenders may have lost 200,000. The soft, boggy ground was soaked by rain and churned up by artillery fire. In the resulting muddy morass men sank to their waists and heavy equipment simply disappeared. Visiting the front for the first time in November, the British Chief of Staff broke down and cried, 'My God, did we really send men to fight in that?' and his companion merely replied, 'It's worse further up'. The British gained some five miles of territory but merely made the salient from which they had attacked more inconvenient than before, and so even these pathetic gains were quickly surrendered to the next German attack. In the meantime the British army had become very nearly as demoralised as the French.

Early in 1918, the Germans scored military successes against Russia, and began to advance towards St Petersburg. The new Bolshevik government, without an army, had no alternative but to accept whatever peace terms the Germans would offer, and Lenin decided to sign the Treaty of Brest-Litovsk, by which Russia gave up Lithuania and Transcaucasia in addition to recognising the independence of Poland, the Ukraine, Byelorussia and the Baltic states. Brest-Litovsk was a propaganda disaster for the Germans, however; particularly in France the growing antiwar sentiment was replaced by a resigned conviction that only Germany's defeat would lead to an acceptable peace. The defeat of Russia did free over 40 German divisions for operations elsewhere, and though the Americans were certainly coming, they were not 'over there' yet. The Germans therefore gambled on a final attempt to achieve a 'decisive victory' in the west before American troops arrived in large numbers, but the effort failed. A series of counterattacks by the French, British and Americans pushed the Germans back.

Contrary to all expectation, the strategically decisive battle took place neither in the west nor in the east, but in the Balkans. On 15 September 1918, some 700,000 Italian, Serbian, French, British and Greek troops attacked along the northern border of Greece. The Bulgarian army opposing them collapsed, and Bulgaria asked for an armistice. The Allies demanded free passage throughout Bulgaria for their troops, opening the front all the way to the Danube. On 29 September, the German commander Ludendorff, hearing of the collapse of the Balkan front and pressed in the west by new British and American attacks, demanded that the German government conclude an immediate armistice.

Before Germany could secure an armistice, however, the Austrian army crumpled and the Habsburg empire dissolved.

Rations had deteriorated to the point where the dwindling supply of horsemeat was reserved for the officers. Still, the Austrians concentrated their resources and attacked the Italians, which resulted in a clear defeat for the Austrians. Domestically, the Austrian Empire was in a pitiful state. Already in 1916, 24-hour shifts had not been able to compensate for shortages of raw materials; during that winter each household in Vienna was permitted to heat only a single room, and in consequence thousands of water pipes froze and burst throughout the city. By 1918 an air of unreality pervaded accounts of the Austrian war effort. On the one hand the government demanded the surrender of kitchen pots and door latches to be melted down and used for munitions, while on the other hand a plan promulgated in August created an elaborate Building Trades Association with eight carefully defined occupational groups from architect down – at a time when all construction activity had been suspended for lack of either materials or labour. The army was collapsing, ethnic groups were in open revolt and the final military defeat and the end of the empire were inevitable.

In Germany, the liberal Prince Max of Baden became chancellor, but his initial appeal for an armistice was rejected by the Americans, who would negotiate only with a democratic government and after Germany had evacuated all occupied territory. Then naval commanders decided to order the fleet to strike at the British in what could only have been a suicide mission. On 28 October the sailors at Kiel mutinied, and during the next week the revolt spread to the other ports of northern Germany, where workers', sailors' and soldiers' councils patterned on the Russian soviets sprang into existence. On 7 November a similar revolt broke out in Munich. On 9 November Emperor Wilhelm refused Prince Max's suggestion that he abdicate; Prince Max proceeded to announce the abdication even without Wilhelm's approval, but the smooth transition to a constitutional monarchy desired by most political leaders was scuttled by the sudden proclamation of a republic to a waiting crowd in Berlin. The new republican government accepted the Allied terms two days later.

Firing ceased on the western front at 11 a.m. on 11 November 1918, four years, three months and a week after the German army first crossed the border into Belgium. The announcement of the armistice provoked wild rejoicing in the cities of the victorious powers. Some of the celebrations turned riotous and were only ended by police intervention. Riots of a different sort soon followed in western army camps as soldiers protested delays in demobilisation. The killing and dying continued; full-scale military campaigns in Russia, Poland, Hungary, the Balkans and Turkey, civil war in Ireland and serious disorder in Italy and Germany exacted a heavy enough price, though not so heavy as hunger and the diseases which preyed on the hungry. No one knows the cost, but estimates of deaths from starvation in eastern Europe and from the worldwide influenza epidemic have been placed nearly as high as the number of soldiers killed in battle.

The cost of the war is incalculable in several senses. No one knows how many died; historians have adopted the conventional round figure of ten million soldiers killed in battle, but estimates of civilian deaths are guesses. The conventional figure of 20 million wounded soldiers is equally uncertain. A higher percentage of the wounded survived than in earlier wars, but the surgical principle of removing damaged tissue which saved soldiers' lives also left a high proportion of veterans missing part or all of a leg or an arm. No one knows the monetary cost of the war; indeed, one of the war's effects was to destroy the old certainty in the value of money itself. Political and territorial changes are easily enumerated: the end of the Habsburg, Hohenzollern, Romanov and Ottoman empires, the creation of the new and reshaped states of central and eastern Europe and the emergence of the world's first avowedly socialist regimes. The social and economic changes were both broad and profound. The price of these changes continued to burden Europe for decades.

6

ECONOMIC DEVELOPMENT
1918–39

CYCLES AND TRENDS BETWEEN THE WARS

Two trends – psychological and social, rather than strictly economic – dominated the interwar years: a pervasive desire to do everything possible to restore the economic system which existed before 1914 and an equally pervasive desire to create a new system. The former, rooted in nostalgia for the past and embodied in the bureaucratic and property-owning elites, suffered from several fundamental misconceptions concerning the prewar economy. The latter, aiming towards utopian visions of the future and embodied in dissatisfied intellectuals and social classes, could take both left and right-wing forms, but it suffered in both cases from equally fundamental misconceptions regarding the ease with which economic and social structures can be transformed. The absence of a social consensus reflected the increasing severity of the tensions inherited from the generation before the First World War and explains many of the economic problems which spilled over into social, political and cultural life.

Each of the sub-periods into which the interwar years are conventionally divided reflected the division between those who would restore and those who would create. Divisions over reconstruction foreshadowed later conflicts. For the elites in the victorious nations, the sacrifices justified the restoration and maintenance of their system; defeated nations looked to the future. For the masses of peasants and workers heretofore excluded from participation in public life, the war justified visions of a better world and attempts to make the visions reality. Many feared a massive depression and unemployment with the demobilisation of the armies, but instead all industrial centres not disorganised by the war boomed. Those who favoured economic and social reconstruction based on the long-range planning techniques developed during the war were shunted aside. 'Demobilisation' was defined narrowly as the rapid dismissal of soldiers from the army, on the least expensive terms possible. In France each soldier received something over a month's wages and a promise that he could return to his old job, a promise not binding on employers. Meanwhile, in response to demands for 'home rule for industry' (the British phrase), governments removed most price controls. However, they also continued their wartime practice of currency inflation, in some cases because inflation permitted them to refund their short-term debt cheaply, in others because a declining exchange rate would stimulate exports. Four years of frustrated demand and increasing supplies of money drove prices up; the boom lasted in each country until the government restricted credit to 'stabilise' the currency. The succeeding slump and unemployment – in 1920 and 1921 in western and northern Europe, in 1923 and 1924 in central and eastern Europe – were extremely severe but short in most countries.

The later 1920s seemed to justify those committed to restoring the prewar economy. Led by an investment boom in the 'new' industries of the second industrial revolution, manufacturing output in most countries expanded strongly. Then between 1928 and 1932 investment ceased and depression struck country after country, lasting in some until 1935 and others until 1938. In the new crisis, governments again restricted credit, deepening the depression and exacerbating social discontent. Revolutionaries on both right and left attempted to seize power to remake the economy in their preferred image. Though instituted by governments of radically different persuasions, the policies which began to overcome the depression were broadly similar. Public works alleviated unemployment and restored personal income, while government investment stimulated industrial recovery. In the later 1930s, however, government investment and increasing shares of national income were channelled into military spending. Recovery became rearmament, and war again approached.

Politics and economics, then, seem more closely intertwined than before 1914, but economic fluctuations did not simply reflect political developments and policy decisions. Business cycle theorists have little trouble fitting interwar events into a pattern. In this view, the outbreak of war in 1914 delayed an impending depression by maintaining investment. The peak reached in 1919–20 was correspondingly high, and the succeeding slump correspondingly severe. The upswing in the late 1920s, the new peak in 1929 and the slump of the early 1930s mark the return to the normal decade-long investment cycle typical of the nineteenth and early twentieth centuries. The depression of the 1930s was no more severe than several in the nineteenth century, indeed was less severe in some countries than the slump of 1921, and recovery was well advanced by the end of the decade.

For believers in long swings in economic development, the interwar period must logically be a 'downswing' between the 'upswings' of 1896–1914 and 1945–70. Again a case can be made which organises many phenomena comprehensibly. The preponderance of bad years over good, the absence of major technological breakthroughs and chronic overcapacity mark the interwar years off from the previous generation. Most significant is the movement of prices, which showed a persistent tendency to decline following the currency stabilisations of the early 1920s. Prices slipped downward in part because of restrictive government monetary policies, the direct link between the supply of money and gold having been broken. However, prices also declined because of increasing productivity – another and more positive way of viewing 'excess' capacity.

The 1920s and 1930s were years of crisis for agricultural producers throughout the world. Worst affected in Europe were producers of staple commodities such as wheat and sugar. Increased demand and disruption in traditional producing areas in northern France, eastern Europe and the Balkans had led during the war to a large extension of cultivation, particularly in the Americas. By 1925 European production had been largely restored (though Russian wheat had yet to return to world markets), and in the meantime yields had improved as well, the result of seed selection, breeding of new strains and more efficient extraction in the case of sugar. As output rose, prices declined and farmers clamoured for protection. Restrictions imposed on trade in agricultural commodities contributed significantly to the downward spiral in the early 1930s.

Meanwhile, the 'traditional' industries on which Europe's wealth and power depended – cotton textiles, coal, iron, steel, heavy machinery and shipbuilding – all suffered, as did the regions in which they had concentrated. World demand for cottons and coal rose very slowly compared to the prewar generation, while for heavy metals, machinery and shipbuilding, world demand declined from wartime peaks. All these industries suffered from increased competition. Sometimes the pressure came from other branches of industry; synthetic fibres captured much of the textile market, and electricity had become a serious competitor with coal as a source of power. More frequently, and more openly and obviously, the pressure came from the new industrial centres. The war had accelerated developments already in progress, as textile, mining and metallurgical firms in the United States, South America, Japan, Australia, India and South Africa had leapt to fill the vacuum created by war. In the postwar period, reconstruction of western European industry and the resumption of industrial development in eastern Europe not only restored old capacity but also increased potential output, the new plants being larger and more efficient than their prewar predecessors. Again as in the case of agriculture, producers demanded protection, and the resulting restrictions accentuated downward pressures and hampered recovery.

The 'new' industries of the second industrial revolution – steel, advanced machinery, chemicals and electricity – continued their spread. Automobiles and aeroplanes had become items of mass production and individual bicycle mechanics could no longer expect to enter the field as serious competitors. In chemicals and electricity, the heavy dependence on formal research subsidised by governments, universities and large firms continued to increase. The war had accelerated the spread of production to new centres. In the case of dyes, for instance, Germany had produced 80 per cent of the world's output before the war. Belligerents and neutrals expanded their production when German supplies were cut off, and Germany's share of world output dropped to 46 per cent in 1924. In this and other cases, the new and expanded firms demanded protection from foreign competition after the war, reinforcing the general tendency to restrict trade and competition.

In part, the problems of industry during the 1920s and 1930s originated in a fundamental and expensive transformation. The typical pattern of nineteenth-century industrial location resulted from the distribution of raw materials, expecially coal, and of skilled labour, the heritage of previous generations of artisan manufacture. Specialised firms tended to concentrate in single regions, which became highly dependent on the fortunes of particular industries. The typical pattern which emerged in the twentieth century resulted from the need to locate as near as possible to urban, middle-class markets, and to large pools of unskilled or semi-skilled labour. With improved transportation and electric energy, both raw materials and power could be brought to the factory. Large, diversified firms tended to disperse branch plants for extraction, production, assembly, packaging and distribution rather than concentrating in single districts as formerly. Increased flexibility also made industry more mobile; firms could relocate branch plants within a country or across national boundaries relatively easily and on relatively short notice. Older, specialised regions, especially those located at a distance from the largest urban centres, began to decline in the 1920s as these developments gained momentum. Older firms and older industries demanded government aid and protection. They also attempted to cut costs by lowering wages and increasing the hours of their workers. In turn, the workers, usually highly skilled and exceptionally well organised, resisted. The resulting conflicts polarised economic, political and social life, and contributed directly to the rise of radical movements promising a way out of the impasse.

The 1920s and 1930s witnessed a striking number of consolidations, combinations and cartelisations in industry, as well as the establishment of associations, marketing organisations and stabilisation schemes in agriculture. In part, this continued a trend from before 1914 which had been accelerated by the economic controls imposed during the war. In eastern Europe, prewar governments had sponsored cartels as part of their industrialisation programmes, and their successors now continued that tradition. In western Europe, some cartels may have improved efficiency. In the German iron and steel industry, the number of plants was reduced from 55 to 45 between 1924 and 1929, and the average output per blast furnace increased from 1,655 to 2,567 tons per week. Many of the diversified firms which came to dominate the world economy resulted from combinations carried out in the interwar years, such as Unilever, a firm created in 1930 by a union of British and Dutch enterprises whose control over both raw materials and processing led to immediate dominance in the soap and margarine industries. Their behaviour during the depression of the 1930s conformed exactly to an economist's prediction of the behaviour of monopolistic firms: savage reductions in investment, dismissals, lowered output and attempts to hold prices high.

Financial and industrial leaders probably enjoyed greater public confidence during the interwar period than ever before or since. When politicians faltered, there were calls for cabinets of 'experts' to deal with financial and economic problems. Non-expert governments sought their advice and aid. The advice, typically deflation to lower export prices in combination with tariffs and subsidies to stimulate investment, was both faulty and inconsistent. Their aid, always expensive, sometimes passed over the line to the illegitimate. The spectacular case of Ivar Krueger illustrates some of these themes. Head of the Swedish timber and match company of Krueger and Toll, Krueger arranged a merger in 1923 with the American firm Lee Higginson & Co., the resulting conglomerate becoming the International Match Company. Krueger's empire was complex, but his basic approach simple; he borrowed money and lent it to hard-pressed governments in return for an official monopoly of production and distribution of matches. Most of his loans went to eastern European governments, regarded by Krueger's creditors as poor risks, but in 1927 he lent 75 million dollars to the French government, and in 1928 another 125 million to the German government. The 'Swedish match king' was regarded as a genius, but in the world financial crisis he found it difficult to continue borrowing and forged collateral in an attempt to secure new loans. In March 1932 he was found dead in his Paris apartment, a presumed suicide. The Swedish stock exchange closed for a week, Krueger's principal bank required substantial assistance from the Swedish government to prevent its collapse and the Swedish prime minister was forced to resign after falsely denying receipt of a large gift from Krueger.

STRUCTURAL PROBLEMS IN WESTERN AND NORTHERN EUROPE

The malaise of affluence affected western Europe only; the shifts among old and new industries, the problems of balance among old and new industrial regions, and the debate over the subtleties of financial and economic policies only affected countries where high levels of economic development were a fact of long standing. Still, the problems were real enough. The older, simpler forms of development were giving way to a far more complex set of relationships within each country, among the western European countries as a group, and between western Europe and the rest of the world. Older, simpler policies repeatedly proved themselves inadequate, but only gradually – and only at disproportionately high cost – did new approaches emerge to take their place.

Britain

The difficulties of the older industrial centres were most severe for Britain. Textiles, coal, iron, steel and shipbuilding all bulked large in the British economy, and all had slipped behind international competitors in technique and proved unable to adapt to changing conditions. Cotton textiles, an industry importing all of its raw material and exporting four-fifths of its output, obviously depended on its technical excellence and ability to adjust to world market conditions for its survival. British cotton firms possessed some advantages, particularly easy access to high-quality Egyptian cotton and a pool of skilled labour experienced with the more complex types of machinery. As competition increased in simpler, less expensive types of cloth, British firms should have moved rapidly to the higher-quality products. They did not, however, and traditional British markets were lost to foreign competition. In 1912, Britain had produced 8 billion yards of cottons and exported 6.9 billion. In 1921, with world demand nearly restored to prewar levels, British production was only 5.6 billion yards and exports only 4.5 billion. British exports to India (the most important market throughout the nineteenth century) declined from over 3 billion yards in 1913 to fewer than 2 billion in 1930, the Indians now producing over half of their cottons themselves and importing the remainder from Japan. The Japanese had also cut into British exports to China, as had Italian producers in the Balkans and the eastern Mediterranean and United States firms in Latin America.

British coal output peaked in 1913 and stagnated at around 80 per cent of that peak figure during the 1920s before the onset of the depression. British mines were old; 57 mines employing nearly 50,000 workers indeed were over a century in age. They were therefore deep, and their seams were thin and difficult to work. The mechanisation enthusiastically embraced by Britain's competitors found only a slow and grudging acceptance, however, and British unions resisted mechanisation. Lord Birkenhead, referring to the coal strike which led to the 1926 general strike, said: 'It would be possible to say without exaggeration that the miners' leaders were the stupidest men in England if we had not had frequent occasion to meet the owners'. The owners refused to consolidate, except when resisting the unions, and avoided new investment. They preferred to reduce costs by lowering wages and increasing hours. Output per shift rose only 14 per cent in Britain between the wars, compared to 54 per cent in Poland, 81 per cent in the Ruhr and 118 per cent in the Netherlands.

The iron, steel and shipbuilding industries repeated the

story of textiles and coal. In iron and steel, world output rose, but British consumption and exports declined. In 1925, nearly half of British pig iron capacity and nearly three-fifths of steelmaking capacity lay idle. Technical backwardness and high prices made exports to Europe difficult, and British firms therefore confined their attention increasingly to the Empire. In shipbuilding, a shortage following the war had led to rapid expansion, and when the bubble burst in 1921 Britain was left with a large amount of capital sunk in excess capacity which proved impossible to redeploy into more productive areas.

The 'new' industries – electricity, chemicals, advanced machinery, and the automobile – did better. Indeed, they did quite well, employment rising from 745,000 in 1924 to 914,000 in 1930, and exports holding steady at over 80 million pounds in 1930 despite depressed world demand. However, their impact was limited; too small in their aggregate size to balance the decline of the old industries, they concentrated in the Midlands and around the urban market centres of London and Manchester-Liverpool. In some cases their expansion increased British imports, particularly of petroleum, and in most cases they employed primarily semi-skilled and unskilled labour, generally young and often female.

Government policy unquestionably worsened the economic situation. The report of the Cunliffe Committee echoed an overwhelming consensus in its search for 'the steps required to bring about the restoration of normal conditions'. For most, this meant the restoration of the gold standard and an avoidance of any direct intervention of government in the economy which might be construed as 'socialistic'. Prices were to be held low to make British exports more competitive, which led to excessively severe deflationary policies in 1919 and again in 1929. At the same time, the value of the pound had to be maintained at its prewar level, in the hope of maintaining Britain's position as the world's chief financial centre – an impossible task, as Britain's reduced earnings from foreign investments and 'invisibles' could not cover the increasing deficit in the trade balance and permit the high level of British foreign lending which had stabilised the international economy before the war. The pound was overvalued in 1924, most severely hampering exports of precisely those basic industrial commodities in which Britain specialised and in which international competition was most intense. Domestically, continued attempts to reduce British prices by reducing wages rather than increasing investment led to labour unrest. Internationally, the search for sources of raw materials and markets culminated (after the gold standard had been abandoned) in the adoption of a protective tariff and bilateral trade agreements negotiated with the stronger dominion countries and imposed on the colonies and weaker trading partners in Latin America and eastern Europe. Even this complete turn away from traditional policy availed little. Britain's share of world trade was lower in 1937 than in 1929; increased exports to 'protected' markets forced rivals into 'unprotected' markets, where their competition may have cost more than the gains.

Britain's recovery, when it came, was largely internally generated, the result first of a housing boom and then increasing military expenditures. The government lowered interest rates by reducing rates on the public debt and by restricting foreign lending, in the hope of stimulating investment generally. Direct subsidies channelled through local councils and the prevailing low prices of imported construction materials concentrated much of the new investment in housing. The new homes tended to be built in the suburbs of the southern cities, a development closely connected to the rapid recovery of the automobile industry, but one which reinforced the trend running against the northern industrial centres. It was only rearmament which began to absorb large numbers of unemployed industrial workers. In 1937, the government announced a five-year arms programme, of which some 30 per cent would be financed by borrowing; by 1939–40, annual spending had risen to over twice the original target figure and two-thirds was to be borrowed. By early 1940, Britain was spending nearly as large a fraction of national income on the military as Germany.

France

In France, a family returning in 1918 to the place where their village had stood in 1914 might have been forgiven for wondering whether they had won the war, or lost. Not all of the family would have returned; ten per cent of the males of working age had died, and more had been incapacitated by their wounds. Seventy years later, farmers still regularly uncovered unexploded shells while ploughing the former battlefields. Much French industry was located in the north as well; overall, French industrial production declined by two-fifths during the war, with the most severe contraction coming in the consumer industries. The Bolshevik repudiation of the tsarist government's debts cost French investors fully half of their foreign assets. Understandably then, fear of socialist threats to property and a bitter insistence that Germany must pay for France's losses marked French public life between the wars.

The war accelerated trends already evident in the French economy before 1914; the metal-working industries increased relative to textiles, new large industrial plants concentrated near Paris and the number of farmers declined. France experienced the postwar boom and depression, though in more moderate form than Britain, and then boomed through the 1920s. Foreign trade in 1929 was two-thirds greater than in 1913, and French industrial production had risen by two-fifths. Reconstruction helped to raise the rate of investment. The government processed nearly three million claims for assistance. Roads and railways were rebuilt, the railways in substantially improved form. The 300 rebuilt coal mines included much new electrically-powered equipment. Half a million homes and a quarter of a million farm buildings were reconstructed. However, most of the nearly 8,000 factories rebuilt with government grants were merely restored to their original state. The opportunity for a thoroughgoing modernisation of northern industry therefore passed unexploited.

French growth in the 1920s replicated the British patterns, with traditional industrial sectors suffering a relative decline and newer areas growing rapidly. France benefited from a smaller commitment to the older areas and from more substantial growth in the new industries, stimulated by buoyant exports and the beginnings of large-scale purchases of consumer durables. Industry in the Paris region continued to expand, the urban market acting as a magnet similar to London. The French chemical industry had also grown in response to wartime demand, and growth continued. Production of artificial fibres, 11 million kilograms in 1913, reached 197 million kilograms in 1928. In southern France, a large petroleum refining industry sprang into being. The oil supplies from the Near East, previously controlled by Germany, had fallen to France as reparations; the demand arose from the explosive growth of the automobile industry. French automobile production rose from 40,000 in 1920 to 254,000 in 1929. André Citroën, inspired by Henry Ford during a stay in Detroit, pushed for mass production and lower prices. His firm had captured 40 per cent of the French market by 1925. The chemical industry and new branches of metallurgy such as aluminium also benefited from the rapid growth of hydroelectric capacity in central and eastern France. French output climbed from 3.5 to 17 million kilowatt-hours between 1920 and 1929. Even agriculture, traditionally the problem area in the French economy, advanced, output rising 10 per cent during the 1920s despite a substantial reduction in labour power.

It would be wrong to overestimate the differences between France and Britain, however. Agricultural advance concentrated in the northeast, in wheat and sugarbeet, both of which required high tariffs to survive; in much of the rest of France, agricultural methods remained traditional. Electricity and automobile output in 1929 were approximately the same as Britain's. French exports benefited from the sharp decline in the value of the franc, especially compared to sterling. Investment was made easier by domestic inflation, and inflation in turn resulted from continual borrowing by the government to cover the costs of the war and reconstruction. In 1929 it could no longer be assumed that Germany would pay these costs, which had amounted to nearly three times the 'ordinary' budget. With the worldwide depression (and an overvalued franc in a world where other countries had abandoned gold), exports dropped 60 per cent between 1929 and 1935. This depressed domestic industry and stifled investment. New company issues dropped from 22 billion francs in 1932 to 4 billion in 1934. Citroën, having borrowed heavily to retool his plants to produce a new front-wheel drive model intended to capture a larger share of the market, was refused an extension by his creditors in 1934; his firm collapsed, and he later died following an operation for ulcers. Until 1936, the government followed the conventional wisdom by reducing expenditures in the hope of reducing prices. The Popular Front government elected that year attempted to restore production and investment by raising demand, but distrust of the socialists led to a flight of capital, resulting in inflation without growth. The succeeding government introduced a large number of measures to stimulate private investment once again, but though industry began to recover in 1938, the French economy in 1940 was still producing not much more than it had in 1913.

Germany

The largest and most problematic of the western European nations was Germany. As in Britain, old industries and regions suffered from the new higher levels of international competition. As in France, currency manipulations fostered economic expansion, but only for a time. As in all countries, the initial attempts to combat depression with protection and deflation only served to turn depression into disaster. Finally, the turn to authoritarian government and the emphasis on military spending as a means of overcoming the crisis also reflected broad trends, though in Germany they took on peculiarly destructive forms.

Though defeated, having experienced a revolution, and burdened with reparations payments demanded by the victors, Germany boomed through 1922 while other industrial economies faltered, and unemployment averaged less than three per cent. Germany had suffered only the indirect damage of neglected maintenance and delayed replacement during the war. However, the government allowed the exchange rate to slip and made credit available through the

Reichsbank, especially to large industrial firms. German industry therefore was well placed to take advantage of the reopening of international trade and supplied the demands frustrated through four years of war as well as the large amounts of raw materials and finished products stipulated in the reparations settlements. Favoured firms could obtain credit from the Reichsbank, purchase their less fortunate competitors, repay the loans in depreciated currency, and repeat the cycle with new loans. This process was well under way before the Ruhr crisis of 1923. Business leaders enjoyed exceptional prestige, as did catchwords derived from the image of the burgeoning American economy – 'Fordism' for mass production and 'Taylorism' for increased labour productivity. Large firms grew larger, the absorption of smaller firms and closure of plants justified as 'rationalisation' and assumed automatically to produce greater efficiency.

The government of 'experts' which came to power in late 1922 was dominated by commercial and industrial interests. The chancellor himself had been head of the Hamburg-America Line, much of whose assets were in foreign currencies, and the government's supporters in industry had amassed large short-term debts for investment and acquisition. The government therefore had little interest in supporting the value of the mark, and when French and Belgian troops entered the Ruhr in 1923 to enforce payment of war reparations, the government took the patriotic step of calling for 'passive resistance' – in effect a government-sponsored general strike. Because increased taxation would have been unpopular, however, the government supported the Ruhr workers and their families by printing money, at the same time permitting bank credit to expand at ever higher rates. At the height of the resulting inflation, over 30 paper mills, 150 printing firms and 2,000 printing presses were working 24 hours a day to supply the demand for money. They failed; the amount of money in circulation rose less rapidly than prices and indeed declined late in the year. The velocity of circulation of money increased as the public became less and less willing to hold currency. Strange things began to happen. Notes denominated in the tens of thousands of marks had to be overprinted in the millions before they even left the printing plants. Workers received their wages in shopping bags and even wheelbarrows full of currency, twice a day, the morning payment made in time for the money to be spent during the lunch hour, before the afternoon foreign exchange quotations were announced and prices increased again. When the price of coal passed out of sight, some burned their evening wages in the kitchen stove. At the end an American dollar would purchase 4,200,000,000,000 marks, assuming anyone with a dollar were willing to make the exchange.

The government fell, passive resistance ended, and the French, whose own currency had declined by a quarter in late 1923, were more willing to moderate their reparations demands. The new Rentenmark, exchangeable for one trillion of the old marks, was in theory based on a mortgage on all the real estate in Germany, but in fact depended on the German public's desperate desire for a new stable currency and on a large loan from Britain, France and the United States. The stabilisation of the currency was accompanied by drastic attempts to reduce government spending and balance the budget, measures intended to lower prices and so stimulate exports. Some 700,000 government employees were dismissed, and overall unemployment rose to 10 per cent. Germany's internal debt had disappeared; both German governments and German industrial firms emerged stronger financially than their counterparts elsewhere, but local governments borrowed to finance construction projects of questionable value, and industrial firms borrowed to create new combinations rather than for productive investment. Unemployment remained high; after dropping to 7 per cent in 1925, it rose to 18 per cent in 1926, dipped to 8 or 9 per cent in 1927 and 1928, and then began to rise in 1929.

The glitter and prosperity of the later Weimar years therefore had a shadowed aspect, even in the centres of large industry. In textile centres and in the still large artisan sector, things were worse, and in the countryside they were worse still. Textile firms found themselves in much the same position as British firms; thousands of artisan families tried their hand at selling or repairing products they had formerly made, with indifferent success. Small farmers, though their debts disappeared and they had food to eat even in the most difficult times, suffered from heavy-handed government direction (the price paid for compulsory deliveries of rye to the government in 1922 was 6,999 marks per 1,000 kilograms, while the domestic free market price was 31,500 marks), and from a persistent tendency for industrial prices to rise more rapidly and decline more slowly than agricultural prices. The large landlords of the east, bitterly hostile to the republic in any case and not mollified either by the reduction in their debts or government aid advanced in the later 1920s, continued to see their position as specialised grain producers erode as it had for a generation before the war. When the depression struck, these groups were the worst hit, and they responded by attacking the republic.

In 1928, German net investment began to decline, and the decline continued through 1929. By the end of the latter year, agricultural investment had dropped to zero. Net investment in industrial plant and equipment had dropped as well. The most important factor, however, was the decline in inventory investment, by half in 1928 and by another two-thirds in 1929. German business, always relatively heavily dependent on short-term bank credit, borrowed heavily in the international short-term market in the late 1920s because of a shortage of domestic credit resulting from the 1924 stabilisation, reparations and continued balance of payments deficits. When American interest rates began to rise in late 1928, they worked to accelerate a decline already in progress. Declining investment, concentrated at first in the consumer goods industries, caused rising unemployment. More than one million workers were already jobless in early 1929 and nearly two million in early 1930.

In 1930, the German economy was still no more depressed than in 1924 and less so than in 1926. However, world conditions would not provide the basis for recovery as they had before. German exports dropped from 10.8 billion marks in 1927 to 4.9 billion in 1933. Unemployment had exhausted the insurance scheme, planned for a maximum of 800,000 recipients, leading to a government deficit which the socialists proposed to cover through new taxes which would have fallen primarily on employers and government employees. The resulting political crisis brought Heinrich Brüning to power at the head of a coalition excluding the socialists.

Brüning typified the orthodox approach in his commitment to deflation. He feared inflation (1923 was still a recent experience), disliked the idea of giving money to the unemployed and believed Germany could not afford an extensive public works programme. He knew that deflation would worsen the depression, but he hoped to lower prices enough to stimulate exports, and in addition he hoped that a depression would prove Germany's inability to pay further reparations and lead to their cancellation. Without an effective parliamentary majority, he issued a series of decrees under the emergency authority granted the president under Article 48 of the Weimar constitution. Government expenses were reduced, old taxes increased and new ones introduced (including a tax on unmarried persons). When the decrees were submitted to the Reichstag for retrospective approval, they were rejected, the Reichstag dissolved and an election held – in which the Nazis won 107 seats and the communists 77. Brüning persisted, ruling by decree, and his programme climaxed with a series of measures in December 1931 reducing prices, wages and rents by 10 per cent, limiting interest rates to 6 per cent, further increasing taxes and further reducing government spending, especially on social services and unemployment benefits. By mid-1932, when Brüning resigned after a dispute with President Hindenburg, German industrial production had declined to about half its 1929 level, and the number of registered unemployed had reached six million, or something like one-third of the entire labour force. In the elections of July 1932, the Nazis gained 230 seats, and the communists 89, making a majority coalition impossible.

In January 1933, Adolf Hitler became Chancellor of Germany, and in March an Enabling Act granted him dictatorial powers for four years. A moderate programme of public works had already been undertaken following Brüning's resignation, and the Nazi government now announced a massive construction programme as the centrepiece of a four-year plan. Labour unions were dissolved and replaced by the Labour Front; workers with agricultural experience were encouraged to return to the farm, women were encouraged to return to the home (either as wives and mothers or as domestic servants) and young people were encouraged to join the Labour Service which assigned them to construction camps. Later, the Labour Service was made compulsory, limits were placed on the number of women in educational institutions and industrial workers were forbidden to change jobs without permission. In addition to the six billion marks allocated to public works, grants were made to industry to stimulate private investment. The results, initially, were quite spectacular. Unemployment declined to four million during the first year of Nazi rule and had effectively disappeared by 1937. Industrial output in 1937–8 was 122 per cent above the depressed level of 1932–3 and 30 per cent higher than 1929. Internally, the public works programme was financed initially through bills discounted by the banks, but later government spending was largely covered by taxes on corporate profits and personal incomes and by forced loans from both businesses and individuals. Externally, strict controls over foreign exchange and a series of very favourable bilateral agreements with eastern European countries maintained exchange equilibrium and produced a positive balance of payments, though Germany's exports did not recover as well as did Britain's.

The Nazis' second four-year plan of 1936 announced a turn towards military spending, though most of the increase came only in 1938 and 1939, and none of the competing agencies succeeded in gaining exclusive responsibility for economic planning. The boycott of Jewish businesses of 1933, the Nürnberg Laws of 1935 depriving Jews of citizenship rights, and the attacks on Jewish property – followed by a massive fine levied on the Jewish community – announced another aspect of the Nazi regime. The greatest positive factor in economic life continued to be the highway construction programme, accompanied by a trebling of automobile registrations. Highways and automobiles had military importance (the Volkswagen was intended as an all-purpose military vehicle as well as a civilian automobile), and whether the stimulus provided by these and more directly military investment would have been forthcoming from private sources cannot be known. In the event, the Nazi economic programme required violation of most of the party's ideological principles. The emphasis on military expansion inevitably favoured heavy industry at the expense of shopkeepers, artisans and small farmers, the groups the party was pledged to protect. Labour continued to flow from country to city and from agriculture to industry, and eventually even the restrictions on female employment had to be lifted. Such inconsistencies did not bother the majority of Germans, enjoying renewed prosperity, or the minority of committed party members, obsessed by their vision.

The Low Countries, Switzerland and Northern Europe

The war had affected Belgium, the Netherlands and Switzerland in drastically different ways. The Germans invaded and occupied Belgium, drawing what they could from Belgian industry. Some of the bitterest fighting of the war took place in Flanders' fields, and by 1919 Belgian agriculture was a shambles and industrial production had sunk to half its prewar level. The Netherlands, though technically neutral, maintained an army fully mobilised throughout the war for fear of the Germans, while suffering from the illegal blockade and trade restrictions imposed by the British. As elsewhere, chemical plants had to be constructed to supply products previously obtained from Germany; Philips, for instance, set up a plant to extract argon gas for its light bulbs. In this, the Netherlands resembled Switzerland; Swiss industry expanded rapidly under the stimulus of wartime demand. However, both Dutch and Swiss industrial producers began to suffer from shortages of raw materials, and in all three countries food began to run dangerously short. Labour unrest increased as food supplies dwindled, though both the Dutch socialist uprising in 1918 and the Swiss general strike of 1919 were repressed.

Belgium fared perhaps the best in the postwar recovery period. The government took responsibility for reconstruction and, aided by German reparations payments, launched a systematic programme of modernisation. Coalmines were expanded and mechanised, and the iron and steel industry was completely rebuilt. By 1924, pig iron output had reached prewar levels, and by 1927 capacity was half as large again as in 1913. On the other hand, the 1926 stabilisation of the

Belgian currency at a level somewhat higher than the French franc hampered exports and slowed growth. All three countries suffered, as did their larger neighbours, from the loss of overseas markets and from excess capacity – in the Dutch and Swiss cases, plants constructed during the war now had to compete once again with prewar suppliers (especially German) as well as new competitors overseas.

Industrial output slumped and unemployment soared in all three countries between 1929 and 32. The responses of the three governments were also similar, reflecting general trends. All three assumed 'temporary' decree powers – in 1933 in Switzerland, in 1934 in the Netherlands and in 1935 in Belgium. Having attempted to maintain the value of their currencies while cutting government spending, all eventually devalued their currency, attempted to ensure export markets through bilateral agreements and began to increase government spending. In the Netherlands, the emergency government imposed restrictions on agricultural output and began a programme of public works to create jobs. In all three countries, however, widespread recovery began only after the government had begun to spend heavily on armaments. Belgium began to arm seriously in 1933 in response to the Nazi seizure of power in Germany, Switzerland extended the period of military training (after a plebiscite) and greatly increased armaments spending in 1935 and the Netherlands followed in 1936.

In the north, the wartime experiences of Denmark, Norway and Sweden paralleled those of the Netherlands. All remained neutral, and all suffered from the attacks of German submarines and the increasingly rigorous British blockade measures. All in addition found their exports in demand by both sides. Swedish industry benefited particularly, and the stock market boomed. Norwegian fish, copper and sulphur pyrites went almost exclusively to Britain, which threatened to embargo coal and other supplies unless given priority. Danish farmers discovered that Germany would pay high prices for every bit of food they could produce; the Danes also discovered a taste for luxury imports and by 1919 imports of champagne had risen by a third, lesser wines and tobacco by 200 per cent and fruits and chocolates by 400 per cent. The Danish positive trade balance disappeared, but government attempts to impose foreign exchange controls failed in the face of the farmers' opposition. By 1917, even in Denmark, the pressures of the war began to tell, especially on food supplies, and there were bread riots in Sweden in 1918. All three governments entered the postwar world determined to return to the gold standard at prewar parities and accordingly adopted strict deflationary policies to reduce prices and wages. The ensuing depressions were severe – in the case of Sweden, substantially worse than the downturn of the 1930s. On the other hand, all returned more or less to their prewar paths of development in the later 1920s – again especially Sweden, whose industry boomed in response to strong export demand.

Around the Baltic, Finland, Lithuania, Latvia and Estonia all seized the opportunity of the Russian Revolution to proclaim their independence, and for all the struggle against Russian attempts at reconquest lasted through 1919. The national movements were social movements as well; agrarian legislation broke up the large estates owned by ethnic minorities (Swedish in Finland, German in the other three states) and distributed the land to small farmers. Agricultural cooperatives fostered development on the Danish pattern, Estonia and Latvia succeeding particularly in exporting butter and bacon. Forestry products, especially from Finland, also found a ready international market. Latvia, despite the heavy expenses of postwar reconstruction, reduced government spending, raised taxes (and collected them in a new currency unit tied to gold) and became one of the first nations to stabilise its exchange rate. Finland, in contrast, devalued its currency, but though Finnish exports proved more buoyant than those of Denmark and Norway, they did no better than those of Latvia.

The depression touched the northern countries relatively lightly. Industrial production declined 12 per cent in Sweden, 8 per cent in Norway and only 6 per cent in Denmark between 1929 and 1932. Finland, however, suffered a 20 per cent drop in industrial production, and Baltic forestry and agricultural exports fell victim to declining demand and increasing tariffs. During the later 1930s, economic development in Lithuania, Latvia and Estonia was overshadowed by the increasingly threatening political situation. Of the four remaining countries, Denmark and Norway recovered quite slowly, while Sweden and Finland recovered strongly, industrial production in both countries in 1937–8 having risen more than 50 per cent above its 1929 level.

In Sweden in 1932 a liberal government had imposed tariffs and devalued the currency. In 1933 the new Socialist government's budget explicitly accepted responsibility for managing the economy and announced a large programme of public works intended to have a counter-cyclical impact. Proponents of both policies claimed credit for the ensuing recovery. Swedish exports rose rapidly. In particular, the krone had been devalued more, relative to the British pound, than the Canadian dollar, and Swedish wood pulp, paper and newsprint drove their Canadian competitors off the British market. Later, the British housing boom, and still later British rearmament, contributed to Swedish exports. When the new public works projects began in 1934, a quarter of the unemployed workers had already been given relief work by the government. Government spending maintained the domestic market, laying the foundations for a rapid expansion of housing construction and consumer durables investment. By 1935, the government considered recovery far enough advanced to begin repaying the debts incurred in 1933 and 1934. They may have been too optimistic; nearly 12 per cent of the labour force was still without work in 1937, and only a large increase in military spending made inroads on that figure before the war. Sweden was also fortunate compared to Denmark, for instance. The Danes had devalued by roughly the same amount as New Zealand, but their exports to Britain were severely limited because of quotas imposed on bacon, ham and butter. Denmark also had disarmed almost completely in 1926, and did not increase military spending during the 1930s, as nearly all other countries did.

MEDITERRANEAN EUROPE

In southern Europe, the war worsened the unsolved problems and deepened the social cleavages of the prewar period. Industrial development, encouraged in some sectors and some districts by the war, remained too limited in extent to transform society; at the same time, its rapid growth and high concentration brought together masses of workers alienated from the existing social and political system. Agriculture, deprived of workers and (except in Greece) still controlled by a class of deeply conservative large landowners, stagnated where it did not actually decline. Rising prices led to unrest; the strikes and rioting in Spanish and Italian industrial centres in 1917 were suppressed by the military, but the outbreaks foreshadowed the confused disorders of the postwar period. War – whether civil, colonial or foreign – precluded the establishment of anything approaching 'normal' economic conditions. The regimes which eventually came to power promised a new social order but proved unable to stimulate the economic development on which it might have been based.

Conditions in Spain, Portugal and Greece degenerated rapidly after the war to something approaching chaos. A confused series of uprisings and coups in Portugal left little time or energy for economic development. Spain had fared the best, industry in Catalonia and the Basque region expanding rapidly. Prices had risen as well, however, fuelling the chronic discontents of the working class, and the postwar depression worsened conditions further, stimulating separatist sentiment in addition to class conflict. In addition, the expense of the war in Morocco bore heavily on the economy. The two developments coalesced following the disaster at Anual, and in 1923 the crisis brought a military regime to power. Spain did well once again during the boom of the later 1920s; textiles, iron and steel and electrical output all rose rapidly. However, the depression added to the already bitter hostility between republican social reformers and conservative, monarchist, military and clerical forces and in 1936 Spain was engulfed in an extraordinarily destructive civil war.

Greece suffered a crushing defeat at the hands of Turkey in attempting to seize territory granted as part of the Versailles settlements. To the cost of the war itself were added the problems of absorbing 1.3 million ethnic Greeks transferred from Turkey between 1923 and 30. As in Spain, the depression worsened the chronic conflict between republicans and royalists. A coup in 1936 brought a dictatorship to power, which held food prices low, increased wages and improved social security measures on the one hand, and extended government control over industry, began a large public works programme and increased military spending on the other hand. Suppressed inflation led to shortages, discontent and a revolt in Crete in 1938, but the regime survived until the German invasion in 1941.

In Italy, the war reinforced structures and trends evident in the prewar period. Unemployment and economic disorganisation in the war's aftermath obviously provided the setting for Mussolini's seizure of power. Ironically, Italy's economic outlook contained substantial bright patches. Fighting had been confined to the extreme northeast; most of Italy's factories and farms had been spared, and indeed the need to expand industrial capacity had resulted in substantial improvement in certain sectors. The general shift to electricity would continue to benefit Italian industry, overcoming the lack of coal resources; from 1.3 million kilkowatt hours in 1910, output rose to 2.6 million in 1915, and 4.0 million in 1920. In addition, export markets awaited anyone with the capacity to supply them. By 1922, just as Mussolini was coming to power, Italian industrial output was beginning to exceed prewar levels, and the boom continued through four more years.

The Fascist industrialisation drive of the early 1920s actually employed policies traditional to Italy and typical of the programmes of countries in southern and eastern Europe before the war. Easy credit from the central bank and direct grants to industrialists from the government encouraged investment, while tariffs and subsidies helped to secure markets. The close relations between industrialists and the government were symbolised in the 1925 Palazzo Vidoni Pact uniting the Confederation of Italian Industry and the

Confederation of Fascist Trade Unions. Labour relations were regulated in the industrialists' interests through pacts which outlawed strikes and lockouts. Independent labour unions had disappeared; in their place were the Fascist corporations in which power was exercised by bureaucrats and employers, and the Labour Charter of 1927 – which did, however, guarantee a maximum 50-hour week.

There were excellent harvests in 1923 and 1925, and by 1926 industrial output was 42 per cent higher than prewar. Electricity and chemicals led the way, and Italy's rayon industry led Europe. More traditional industrial sectors fared nearly as well; cotton textiles boomed as Italy invaded markets previously the domain of British, Belgian and German producers, pig iron output quadrupled, and steel output and shipping more than doubled. Even the closing of America to Italian migrants had little effect at first, because of the demand for labour in the reconstruction programmes of France, Belgium and Luxembourg. Nearly as many Italians emigrated each year in the early 1920s as had before the war.

Italy's success did not continue through the late 1920s, however. Iron and steel output stagnated and cotton production actually declined between 1925 and 30. Extremely poor harvests in 1926 and 1927 depressed the economy. Emigration declined and repatriation rose dramatically as northwestern Europe completed reconstruction and the United States remained closed. The completion of reconstruction and the recovery of Germany meant the re-emergence of formidable competitors in international markets. The need to settle war debts with the United States and Britain also weighed on the economy in 1926 and 1927. Most important, however, was Mussolini's decision to stabilise the value of the lira. The target value was set high, for reasons of national prestige. In order to maintain the new exchange rate, domestic credit was sharply reduced in the hope of lowering the domestic price level. This was the same policy pursued in Britain, and it had the same consequences; the shortage of credit caused a depression in Italy, while the excessively high value of the lira worsened matters by increasing export prices just as international competition began to increase.

Italy held the lira at a high level through the 1930s, attempting to minimise the deflationary impact through tariffs, quotas, prohibitions and subsidies. A 'battle for wheat' extended production in the Pontine marshes and imposed compulsory marketing pools on grain producers. Continued credit restriction led to the failure of small firms, their absorption by larger firms and calls by all industrialists for state intervention in their favour. Government bodies established in 1933 granted funds to industry directly and assisted large banks to do so as well. Because the banks themselves owned large shares in major firms, the government found it convenient to organise industries into large agglomerations which were easier to finance and plan. Increased military spending worked in the same direction. Economically, the Fascist state was not much of a success. National product per capita probably did not increase at all between 1929 and 1939. The conquest of the Libyan hinterland and of Ethiopia – both small wars – strained Italy's resources severely, suggesting how limited they remained.

EASTERN EUROPE

The economic position of eastern Europe before the war had been bleak enough. Partly because of the pattern of prewar government support, significant industrial centres existed only in Bohemia, Vienna, Budapest and Upper Silesia. Czechoslovakian industry employed 37 per cent of all workers in the early 1920s, Austrian industry 33 per cent and Hungarian 20 per cent. The rest of Poland swamped the Polish portion of Upper Silesia, Warsaw and Lodz; industry employed only 9 per cent of all Polish workers, placing Poland at about the same level as Yugoslavia, Rumania and Bulgaria. Even these percentages were optimistic, since 'industry' included construction and artisan manufactures along with the modern mechanised sector, and the totals probably understated agricultural employment. Backward agriculture resulted in low savings and restricted domestic markets, which hampered development. Exports were concentrated in a narrow range of commodities, usually primary products, often controlled by foreign interests. Such development as had occurred before the war had often required heavy foreign borrowing, and many of these debts continued to burden the struggling economies after the war as well. Wartime losses were heavy throughout the east and reached horrendous levels in some regions. Occupied territories suffered worst. Armies had marched through Galicia, now part of southern Poland, four times; villages had disappeared, fields had not been cultivated for four years, and the survivors subsisted on bread made of perhaps a twentieth part of rye flour mixed with whatever roots, grass, nuts and heather came to hand. Serbia, now part of Yugoslavia, mourned war dead amounting to fully ten per cent of the entire prewar population. When the fighting finally ceased, parts of the Balkans had been at war for ten years. Disease spread through hungry and tired populations; influenza killed tens of thousands, and in Poland a serious typhus epidemic raged as well.

The postwar political settlements did not promise much for future economic development. Along the 20,000 kilometres of new borders drawn from Finland to Greece, toll stations arose. Of the eight million Austrians, two million lived in Vienna, an industrial and imperial metropolis now deprived of its hinterland. Previously, Viennese weaving firms had obtained their thread from Bohemian spinning plants. Cut off from each other and from their previous markets elsewhere in the empire, both industries stagnated in the later 1920s. Hungarian industry, centred in Budapest, had likewise been cut off from its raw materials and markets. Recreating in part the divisions which had marked the Habsburg empire, Germans, Czechs, Slovaks and Ruthenians contended for power in Czechoslovakia. National divisions in Yugoslavia found concrete expression in the railway, which combined sections of five systems using four different gauges. The new boundaries of Poland and Rumania included large stretches of territory coveted by their neighbours and populated by dissatisfied national minorities.

Eastern Europe received little outside help. In the crisis of

1918 and 1919, Britain and the United States had mounted an extensive famine relief programme, especially in Poland. However, only a tenth of the funds was a gift. The remainder was in the form of loans, and the programme was sharply cut after the peace treaties were signed. Even before the armistice, the United States had adamantly rejected any extension of controls over supplies or prices of raw materials. In the resulting inflationary boom, eastern European countries borrowed to purchase scarce materials at high prices, but then, in the succeeding deflationary depression, could not earn enough from their exports to cover the interest payments. In Yugoslavia, Rumania and Bulgaria, the depression added immediately to existing problems. Austria, Hungary, Czechoslovakia and Poland all maintained exports through 1921 by devaluing their currencies, but only Czechoslovakia managed to restrain the resulting domestic inflation. In Poland, a 'cabinet of experts' instituted a deflationary programme in 1923. Austria and Hungary did receive loans from the League of Nations in 1922 and 1923, but only after their currencies had already collapsed and only in return for deflationary policies carried out under League supervision. In 1926 Bulgaria also received a League loan to resettle some of the Macedonian refugees. In all three cases, the League acted too late and imposed overly restrictive conditions. But in this, League officials merely reflected the consensus of both public and private bankers in western Europe and the United States, who considered the countries of eastern Europe poor credit risks. After 1929, western Europe and the United States were unable to lend, and in addition imposed or increased tariffs on eastern European exports. The bilateral agreements offered by Nazi Germany, though unfavourable, were the only option open.

Even had there been less destruction and more foreign assistance, the problems would have been formidable. Foremost among them was agriculture, now even less efficient than before the war. Only in Czechoslovakia, where the land reform of 1919 was accompanied by state aid to the new owners, did output and productivity increase. The Magyar elite which still ruled Hungary prevented any land reform; nearly half the land remained in large estates while some three million peasants owned no land at all. Poland's land law of 1925 was limited and the distribution of ownership remained much as in Hungary. In Bulgaria, the Peasant Party government completed the distribution of land to small peasants by breaking up state lands and all 'estates' over 30 hectares. The king of Rumania promised land reform in 1917 because he feared Bolshevik agitation spreading through the army might otherwise lead to a revolution, and by 1921 some 2.1 million hectares had been assigned to 1.4 million peasants. Land reform in Yugoslavia proved inevitable when the peasants began to seize the land in 1918 and 1919. Half a million families received over two million hectares, about a quarter of the land.

Where the land was redistributed, output declined, most drastically in Rumania and Yugoslavia. Facing chronic deficits in their budgets and balance of payments, governments did nothing to provide the peasants with capital. Rather, in desperate need of revenue, they raised taxes, which bore most heavily on the peasants. The peasants did what they could to increase production of cash crops, but their poverty precluded any major improvement. In Bulgaria, for instance, production of tobacco increased, but in 1936 there were still 450,000 wooden ploughs compared to 254,000 made of iron. Bulgaria's population was increasing rapidly; well over half of the agricultural population was 'excess' in the sense of being unnecessary for actual production, a situation typical of the Balkans and Poland as well. The United States immigration law closed a possible escape route and foreclosed the possibility of accumulating capital through overseas remittances as well. World markets collapsed in the 1930s; even without Russian competition, eastern Europe's agricultural exports were a quarter below prewar levels. Governments suffered from the loss of foreign exchange; peasants, dependent on the market for supplies and food, found themselves trapped between the prices they received and the prices they paid and went hungry.

The answer, as all the new governments realised, was industrial development. All introduced programmes similar to those of the prewar period. Tariffs tended to be much higher (Czech tariffs were twice the old imperial duties, for instance), indeed were often set unreasonably high so that large reductions could be offered in negotiations without reducing protection. Bilateral arrangements, clearing agreements, quotas, prohibitions and embargoes emerged in the 1920s and expanded in the 1930s. Formal purchase and sales monopolies or informally organised cartels dominated trade. Domestically, governments employed capital grants, loans, tax rebates, preferential freight rates and subsidies to stimulate industry, as they had before the war. The programmes achieved only limited results, however, due to the lack of capital. The general failure to stimulate private domestic investment or to attract foreign capital led to an expansion of the state sector, a development well advanced even before the depression and the rush to increase military spending in the later 1930s.

THE SOVIET EXPERIMENT

The new socialist regime in Russia built on the foundations of the tsarist economy. Before the First World War Russia already had possessed a large manufacturing sector, highly concentrated, technically advanced and rapidly expanding. On the other hand, this industrial sector employed only a small fraction of the total population. The agricultural sector remained large and extremely backward, and the possibility of substantial improvement remained doubtful. In certain respects the Soviet Union merely repeated and extended these patterns. The fundamental method of advance remained the same as well; the peasantry was taxed, indeed starved, and capital was drained from agriculture to finance heavy industrial development. However, there were important differences as well. In contrast to tsarist Russia, the Soviet Union had virtually no access to foreign capital and imported technologies. Though the tsarist government was certainly ruthless and repressive, it never exercised the degree of control over the economy or the sheer extent of physical coercion suggested by the two value-laden phrases 'central planning' and 'red terror'. Finally, the Soviet Union eventually underwent a virtually complete social revolution.

The Bolsheviks did not possess a programme for re-establishing order in 1917. Lenin's famous programme of 'Peace, Land, Bread' remained without content. As a group, the Bolsheviks were hostile to private property, to 'trade' and to the peasantry. The period of transition to a new economic organisation, however, as Lenin himself admitted confidentially, might be quite long, particularly as a Bolshevik government would have to avoid alienating the peasants. In the meantime, the Bolsheviks identified themselves publicly with the peasantry as well as the proletariat. Already in November 1917 it was announced that the land would be nationalised and distributed to the peasants, as well as that workers would oversee factory production. The national bank was seized and in December the Supreme Council of National Economy or Vesenkha (after its Russian initials) was established to set and enforce 'general norms' in industry and carry out nationalisations.

By mid-1918, however, the Bolsheviks seemed on the verge of losing control. Soldiers, afraid that they might not receive land if they remained at the front, returned to their villages, taking their guns with them. The army dissolved. Industrial workers began to seize control of factories. The Germans imposed the treaty of Brest-Litovsk, the peasant-populist social revolutionaries led violent opposition to the central government and several anti-Bolshevik armies sprang into being with the active assistance of British, American and Japanese troops.

The Bolshevik response was a series of radical measures grouped under the label 'war communism'. Lenin announced the need for 'businesslike' efficiency in industry and for a 'single will' to manage each industrial enterprise. In 1918 industry was placed under quasi-military control, and a radical nationalisation decree extended and formalised the process of nationalisation which had already been under way. The 1917–18 harvest was an extremely poor one, and hunger and a typhus epidemic added to the miseries of the civil war. The official bread ration in St Petersburg declined to 50 grams per day. As suppliers dwindled and government prices remained fixed, food disappeared into the black market. The government responded with a 'crusade for bread' and a 'food dictatorship'. Workers, police and army units moved into the countryside to seize stocks of food from the peasants, and a campaign was launched against the 'kulaks' (in theory, large peasants, but in practice anyone in the villages opposed to the government). The peasants reduced their plantings, and the food supply dwindled further. Individuals had to purchase on the black market to survive; as little as 30 per cent of all food may have moved through official channels, and the Bolshevik government was forced to declare some unofficial trade legal. Individuals in both the cities and the countryside were understandably reluctant to hold paper currency, and its value collapsed.

The Bolsheviks defeated their opponents in the civil war, but not too much credit can be given to their economic policies. Heavy industrial production in 1921 equalled only 21 per cent of 1913 output. Vesenkha had decreed that small establishments were not to be nationalised, but the order had been ignored by local party organisations, and of the 37,000 nationalised enterprises, fully 5,000 employed only 1 worker. The arbitrary terror imposed by local party members on these artisan establishments reduced their efficiency and output while increasing opposition to the government. In the countryside, the government continued to use force to collect food from the peasants.

In 1921 Lenin shifted his ground and began a return to a market economy, later formalised as the New Economic Policy, or NEP. Instead of requisitions, the government would content itself with a tax on the peasantry, at first assessed in kind, then in money after the currency was stabilised in 1924. Private trade was legalised once again and spread rapidly. The nationalisation of small enterprises was revoked; the state would now seek to control only the 'commanding heights' of the economy. Many firms were returned to their former owners, and many of those remaining under Vesenkha's control were leased to private entrepreneurs.

The movement away from War Communism was probably accelerated by the disastrous famine which struck in 1921 and 1922. The 1920 harvest was about 54 per cent of the average for 1909–13, and in 1921 the yield sank to 43 per cent of the prewar average. A drought in the eastern and southeastern regions added to the burdens imposed by war, revolution, civil war and terror. The national averages conceal the fact that in some districts there was simply no food at all, and millions died. The repercussions extended wavelike throughout the economy, with mass migrations imposing direct hardship on areas close to the famine centres, while the overall decline in purchasing power created industrial depression further away. A glut of industrial goods emerged in the midst of drastic overall shortages and forced industrial workers out of work despite the decline in the industrial labour force to only half its prewar level.

From the low point of 1920 and 1921, the economy recovered rapidly to 1926. A limited amount of foreign trade alleviated the food shortages, repairs to the transportation system restored it nearly to its prewar level of efficiency, a new currency was introduced and the government budget was balanced. Small business was again nearly entirely in private hands, but state ownership of large industrial plants and transportation gave the government effective control over distribution and prices of industrial goods. The crucial factor in recovery, however, was the relatively abundant harvests of 1922 and 1923, gathered in by the small peasants who at this point controlled 98 per cent of the land.

An increasingly bitter debate now began within the government and within the Party over the future direction of economic policy. No one had seen the NEP as anything more than a temporary expedient, but opinion varied as to its optimal extent and duration. As owners of private property, the peasants were unlikely to become enthusiastic communists. Their small holdings were highly inefficient, exposing the economy to the danger of famine and limiting the amount of capital which could be extracted from agriculture and used for industrial development. Officially, however, any peasant who increased productivity risked being labelled a kulak and expropriated. During the NEP period, peasants had in fact been allowed to make profits. However, a study produced by Vesenkha showed that, without new large sources of capital, industrial growth would slow after 1927; this possibility was rejected by the majority of Party members, who favoured rapid industrial growth for defence against the western imperialist powers, as a means of maintaining enthusiasm and support for the revolution and not least for its own sake. Huge new projects such as a linking of Ural iron ore with central Siberian coal could not only bring economic benefits but also prove the superiority of the Soviet system. In the background, Stalin's success in gaining control over the Party bureaucracy and the police also meant the victory of this line of thought.

In 1926 the government began to dismantle the NEP. Surcharges of 100 per cent were levied on private goods shipped on the railways. 'Temporary' taxes were imposed on profits, and taxes on the peasantry were sharply increased, with additional taxes imposed on those unfortunate enough to be designated kulaks. The Criminal Code provided for confiscation of the property of anyone guilty of 'evil intentioned' price increases. The First Five-Year Plan was adopted in 1927, after considerable discussion within the government and some truly heroic statistical work by teams of economists.

The peasants remained the crucial problem. The government had been holding prices of both industrial and agricultural products artificially low. This reduced peasant incomes and deprived them of industrial goods which were snapped up by enterprises and individuals close to the factories. The peasants therefore were reluctant to deliver any of their output, preferring to eat it themselves. Stalin, to solve both the economic and political problems at once, decided on collectivisation. Scattered, small, inefficient peasant holdings were to be combined into large, highly mechanised, efficient farms. In 1929, the goals of the five-year plan were revised, to increase industrial production and to collectivise the peasantry immediately. The campaign was interrupted in 1930, then resumed. Half of all peasants were in collectives in 1931 and 90 per cent by 1936. The cost of collectivisation was quite extraordinary. The peasants slaughtered and ate their livestock and reduced the area planted with crops; the government employed the most extreme measures to obtain food supplies and punish 'offending' areas. In Kazakhstan, to take one example, the 20 million sheep and goats recorded in 1928 had declined to 3 million in 1935, and the recorded population dropped by 20 per cent between 1926 and 1939. The 1932 harvest would have been poor in any case and was made worse by the confusion and desperation in the countryside. Officially, there was reported to be 'an extremely grave food shortage'; in fact, there had been massive famines.

The state farm (*sovkhoz*) employing wage labour was the ideologically preferred form, because it was analogous to factory organisation, without remnants of private property or 'trade'. Nonetheless, the inconvenient necessity of paying the employees of state farms led the government to prefer collective farms (*kolkhoz*); systematised in 1935, their organisation remained virtually unchanged until the 1960s. Initially, some 25,000 urban party members were appointed as supervisors of the new collectives – with police backing – to ensure compliance with government directives. Their ignorance of farming and hostility towards the peasants caused much of the dislocation of the early 1930s. In addition, the promise of mechanisation was embodied in Machine Tractor Stations. In theory these were regional cooperatives providing services to several collectives, but in fact they added another level of state supervision of the peasants.

From the point of view of agricultural efficiency, collectivisation was a massively expensive failure. In addition to the direct losses resulting from peasant resistance, average yields of grain crops declined by some 5 per cent between 1928–32 and 1932–7. The state certainly succeeded in extracting resources from agriculture; procurements of grain rose 50 per cent from 1928–32 to 1933–7. Urban consumption of bread and potatoes actually rose slightly, and exports of wheat paid for some imports of capital equipment. Rural areas went hungry. Despite the cost, however, the peasantry was not eliminated and neither was private trade. In addition to working for the collective, each peasant member was permitted to farm a small plot privately and to raise limited numbers of animals which could be pastured on collective land. Already by 1938 the peasants owned three times as many cattle, twice as many pigs, and half again as many sheep as the state. The state farms and collectives specialised in basic foodstuffs, especially grains, while the small private sector provided a disproportionate share of higher-quality foods.

Soviet planning allocated resources on the basis of 'physical balances' or the quantity of inputs required to produce a given output with unchanged technology. The state imposed heavy taxes (especially a turnover tax assessed at each stage of production), forced workers to purchase government bonds and engineered a steady inflation (an indirect tax) to accumulate the capital which was invested in heavy industry. Prices were set by central authorities, and no role was allowed to consumer demand; therefore decisions among competing projects and types of output were essentially political. In fact, during the First Five-Year Plan, labour and raw materials were forced into designated 'shock areas' without regard for cost. The Party mobilised young enthusiasts who rejected the 'fetishism of figures' and threw themselves into the project at hand with abandon. The results in favoured areas were spectacular. Output of coal, pig iron and petroleum, for instance, doubled between 1927 and 1932. At the Seventeenth Party Congress, the 'congress of victors', S. M. Kirov enthused, 'our success was really immense. The devil take it, to speak frankly, one so wants to live and live! After all, look and see what is going on around us. It's a fact!'

During the Second Five-Year Plan, from 1932 to 1937, coal and pig iron output more than doubled again. However, petroleum output, though rising, did not keep pace and fell far short of the target figure. Further, yearly figures reveal a stagnation in output beginning in 1937. A number of large plants had come on line in early 1937, and no others were near completion; in addition, Stalin had ordered a shift of production towards military goods and a transfer of factories towards Russia's interior regions, expensive measures taken to defend against a possible war with Nazi Germany. Without question, however, the purges were affecting the performance of the economy. A year after the 'congress of victors' Kirov had fallen victim, and most of the other delegates eventually shared his fate. A large fraction of party members, civil servants, army officers, technicians, plant foremen – and virtually all statisticians and economists – suffered in the purges. Millions died; other millions entered the labour camps, which now grew to encompass a large fraction of total national output, though operated at low levels of efficiency under appalling conditions. When the war did come, in many districts the Germans were welcomed as saviours – at first.

7

EUROPE AND THE WORLD BETWEEN THE WARS

Through the interwar years European nations continued to be linked to each other by the international economy, and with the rest of the world by the twin bonds of economic exchange and political domination. However, the war had accelerated changes and aggravated the strains in the international economy already visible before 1914. Two new powers, the United States and Japan, had emerged into the world economy, and a new aggressive nationalism began to appear in the Middle East, Africa, Asia and Latin America. Together these factors undermined Europe's attempt to re-establish the prewar system. The resulting instability contributed to the collapse and depression of the 1930s – which led in turn to a further weakening of Europe's position. Europe's role in the world had already been considerably reduced – relatively in the economic sphere, absolutely in the harsher political arena – before the new and greater war.

THE ATTEMPT TO RESTORE THE PREWAR WORLD

International bankers, and especially the heads of the central banks of the major countries, enjoyed immense prestige between the wars. Their arcane knowledge and freedom from 'political influences' lent them an aura similar to that which surrounded business magnates and emergency cabinets of 'experts'. Many of the leading figures enjoyed personal reputations which added weight to their opinions. Hjalmar Schacht, head of the German Reichsbank, as the inventor of the Rentenmark and confidant of British and American financial leaders, was a formidable figure. He resigned

dramatically in 1929 in protest over the terms of the Young
Plan, was reappointed by Hitler and presided over the
extension of German economic power in eastern Europe. He
gradually lost influence, but as late as 1937 Berliner wits
were saying 'Germany is Hitler, and Hitler is Dr Schacht'.
Émile Moreau, head of the Bank of France, though a
government nominee, was far from being the French
government's hatchet man. He had been elected by the two
hundred largest shareholders of the bank, and in practice he
and the other 5 government regents acted in the interests of
the shareholders and in cooperation with the 12 private
regents. French governments contended with the bank at
their peril. Across the Atlantic, Benjamin Strong, the head of
the Federal Reserve Bank of New York and dominant
member of the committee which coordinated the activities of
the twelve regional reserve banks in the United States, also
enjoyed virtual autonomy. Regulations requiring him to
report to the Treasury and legislative interference from the
Congress might cause him occasional worry, but in general
his unparalleled experience and connections with European
leaders gave him unassailable authority.

The doyen of the international banking community was
Montagu Norman, governor of the Bank of England. Both
his grandfathers had served as directors of the Bank of
England, one of them for 50 years, and as a junior partner in
his maternal grandfather's London commercial firm it was
virtually inevitable that he would be selected as a director
himself at a relatively early age. He was, in 1907, when he
was 35. In the normal course of events, he would have served
on various committees, awaiting his turn to serve a year as
deputy governor and a year (perhaps two) as governor, and
then have moved to the senior committee which advised
incumbent governors. Throughout he would have maintained
his private interests, his part-time services to the Bank of
England taking a distinct and distant second place. During
the First World War, however, the unprecedented demands
on the Bank had led to the reappointment of the incumbent
governor to ensure continuity of policies; at the same time
Norman, who broke with his partners in 1915, had devoted
himself entirely to the affairs of the Bank. In 1920 his

experience and lack of private interests made him the obvious candidate to succeed as governor. The complexities of reconstruction made it seem wise to reappoint him the next year, and so it went – he served until illness forced his retirement in 1944.

Sporting a Vandyke beard and a hat worn at a rakish angle – affectations considered quite Bohemian in banking circles – Norman cultivated an air of mystery. Indeed he was compulsively secretive. When he finally married in the early 1930s, he and his bride fled their wedding reception, climbed over a wall and spent several hours riding round in the London underground, in order to escape a group of newspaper reporters. He had personally supervised and participated in the redecoration of his house in the style of William Morris, and he clearly regarded banking in the same light, as a traditional craft practised by those with the requisite artistic temperament, instinct and experience, and preferably practised in complete secrecy. Norman's long tenure as governor, the source of his power, resulted from a growing conviction that monetary management required the services of full-time professionals and therefore ironically paved the way for the eventual nationalisation of the Bank of England, the thing Norman wanted above all to avoid. In the meantime the Bank's increasing professionalisation worked to increase Norman's power. The full-time advisors and assistants gradually added to the Bank's staff were Norman's personal selections, and the introduction of a statistical service permitted him to control the Bank's operations more closely. His international connections reinforced his power. The new central banks established in South Africa, India and New Zealand not only took the Bank of England as their model, but also utilised senior personnel nominated by Norman. Norman and his close associates dominated the League of Nations' Financial Committee, through which stabilisation loans were arranged for central and eastern European countries. Norman was also a key force behind the establishment in the late 1920s of the Bank for International Settlements, which he hoped would if necessary defy governments in the pursuit of correct financial policies. Most important for Norman, and typical of the banking world, were his personal friendships. He was godfather to Schacht's grandchild and vacationed regularly with Strong in Maine or in southern France. Indeed some saw his failure to cultivate the friendship of Moreau as one of the crucial weaknesses in the interwar financial edifice.

These, then, were the men who controlled the interwar economy, and they shared Norman's conviction that their instincts, experience and personal connections provided an infallible foundation for policy. They devoted their efforts to an attempt to restore the prewar system; however, in relying on their instincts and prewar experience, they failed to recognise that the prewar system had not functioned as they thought, and that the fortuitous circumstances which had permitted it to operate so smoothly had changed drastically. The changes had been well advanced before the First World War, but the war had accelerated them and added new intractable problems to the old.

Most obviously and perhaps most crucially, the war accelerated the decline of Britain. Britain's trade deficit increased. At the same time, because overseas holdings had been liquidated to pay for wartime imports and because of increased competition in the shipping industry, Britain's 'invisible' earnings declined, and the overall balance of payments declined and became a deficit. Britain was therefore far less able to lend to foreign borrowers than before the war, and one of the crucial supports of the prewar international economy disappeared. Britain's decline was matched by that of sterling. Before the First World War, London had maintained its traditional position as the crucial international money market, relatively little money had moved among currencies and rates of exchange remained stable. Between the wars, several financial markets competed for pre-eminence, there were several 'key' currencies and relatively large amounts of money flowed from one currency to another. Rates of exchange, though officially fixed, were not stable, because economic conditions, speculation and indeed mere rumour could cause a 'run' on a currency and force a revaluation.

Britain's decline and the concomitant rise of new competitors were old problems, even if much more pressing than before. The problem of war debts and reparations, however, was new and unique in its complexity. Of the 28 countries involved, 5 were debtors only and 10 creditors only; the others all occupied some middle position, and a generation of economists laboured to determine exactly who owed what to whom. A settlement showing even a semblance of reason was unlikely enough in any case; the intransigence of all parties made it impossible. The policies of the United States and France posed particular problems. The Americans insisted that the loans made to their allies during the war now be repaid in full, and by the original debtors. They refused as well to admit any 'linkage' between war debts and reparations. Worse, the United States increased its tariffs, which made it even more difficult for the debtor countries to earn the gold and dollars in which the Americans insisted on being paid. The French, more understandably, demanded reparations to pay for reconstruction; some Frenchmen hoped in addition that heavy reparations payments would weaken Germany permanently and make France more secure.

Intransigence in part simply continued wartime habits. Britain's Lloyd George, for instance, having failed to 'hang the Kaiser', committed himself to squeezing the German lemon 'until the pips squeak'. For all politicians, open compromise with an enemy whom they had portrayed for four years as the embodiment of evil was impossible, because all feared the reaction of public opinion to any show of weakness. In addition, all were committed to re-establishing the prewar social status quo, and all therefore refused to consider tax increases as a way of financing reconstruction. In purely economic terms, Germany could have paid the reparations actually levied, France could have financed reconstruction without reparations, the United States could have forgiven the war debts and the United States and Britain could have financed reconstruction in central and eastern Europe. In political terms, such policies were impossible. Instead, all of the burden of international adjustment was thrown onto the exchange mechanism and therefore onto domestic unemployment. The interests of wealth holders were protected; the interests of wage earners were not.

The fruitless attempt to collect reparations and war debts poisoned the political atmosphere and hampered the operation of the international economy. The Franco-Belgian occupation of the Ruhr in 1923 resulted in the collapse of the German mark and the near destruction of the French franc as well. The Dawes Plan of 1924 reduced German reparations, but imposed a deflationary policy on Germany resulting in high unemployment and required heavy foreign borrowing which could come only from the United States. The resulting underlying instability of the German economy became evident in 1928 and 1929. The Young Plan of 1929 recognised the inability of the depressed German economy to meet the payments foreseen in the Dawes Plan. However, the reductions in reparations did not prevent the Nazis from vehemently denouncing the Young Plan, and the German government's deflationary policy was intended in part to prove – by worsening the depression – that Germany could not afford any reparations. There had been little likelihood in any event that Germany could earn enough through exports to pay reparations. Under the Dawes Plan Germany was forbidden to devalue its currency, and no conceivable German policy could have lowered prices of German exports enough to increase sales in foreign markets sufficiently – most of Germany's potential customers had no desire for German goods, as they were intent on protecting their own industries. Germany therefore had to borrow abroad to meet reparations payments, and German borrowing reduced the potential flow of funds to countries in central and eastern Europe and overseas. America's allies in turn required reparations if they were to repay the war loans, since most already had a negative trade balance with the United States, made worse by the increase in American tariffs. The reparations issue greatly weakened the Weimar Republic, and the unstable balance of reparations, war debts and short-term loans from the United States to Germany contributed to the financial collapse of 1931, the deepening depression, the triumph of the Nazis and ultimately the Second World War.

Next to reparations and war debts, the most discussed problem of the interwar economy was the restoration of the gold standard. No respectable authority doubted it should be restored; as Winston Churchill said in announcing Britain's return to gold in 1925, every expert conference, every expert committee, every party, every government and every chancellor of the exchequer had favoured the move. So overwhelming was the consensus that no one bothered to give an argument in its favour. Churchill asserted that most other countries were returning to gold, which was not the case. For Churchill, as for others, the commitment to gold was not one of reason but one of belief: 'I believe that the establishment of this great area of common arrangement will facilitate the revival of international trade and of inter-Imperial trade'.

In a world where its assumptions are met, there is no reason why a gold standard system would not bring the benefits for which interwar experts and political leaders hoped. However, the world of the 1920s and 1930s was not that world. First, the system which spread over most of the world in the later 1920s was not the gold standard. Only three countries adopted a full gold standard, with their currencies convertible on demand – the United States, Sweden and the Netherlands. Three more – Britain, Denmark and Norway – adopted a bullion standard under which paper currency could still not be converted into gold but gold would be used to meet international obligations. All other countries adhering to the 'gold' standard in fact adhered to an 'exchange' standard, under which they pegged their currencies to one of the gold or bullion standard currencies and used reserves of those 'key' currencies as if they were gold. They were not, of course, and a desire for real gold, feelings that one or another currency was unsound, or changes in interest rates could lead to pressure on a 'key' currency. The inherent instability of the system made speculation more attractive, and the existence of several major currency markets made it easier. The negative British balance of payments made sterling the weakest of the 'key' currencies. By 1928 foreign central banks held British currency equal to more than four times the Bank of England's gold reserves. Britain's negative trade balance resulted in part from overvaluation of the pound; yet to devalue the pound to a more reasonable level would have reduced the value of the reserves of those foreign central banks and possibly set off the financial crisis and 'run' on the pound which everyone feared.

Second and more important, though in theory virtually all observers and policy makers believed that government intervention in the economy should be held to a minimum, in fact every country engaged in extensive intervention designed to further national interests. These policies seriously hampered the operation of the new gold exchange standard. All countries wanted to protect their own producers, and no one wanted to pay for reconstruction or monetary stabilisation. Exchange rates were selected and maintained artificially. The British pound and the Italian lire were set too high for reasons of prestige, and the French and Belgian francs were set too low to stimulate exports. Both France and the United States had large surpluses in their balance of payments, but both attempted to 'neutralise' or 'sterilise' the resulting inflow of gold in order to prevent domestic inflation. Keeping domestic prices low helped keep American and French exports high, but the refusal to allow prices to take their natural course eliminated the major adjustment mechanism by which the gold standard ensures stability. High protective tariffs and the growth of cartels and monopolies, many of them either directly sponsored or encouraged by governments, worked in the same direction. Behind tariff walls, firms exercised their monopoly power by raising prices, lowering output, closing plants and throwing off workers. Economic resources were not permitted to move as they had before 1914. The United States drastically reduced the international flow of labour in 1924 by effectively forbidding immigration from southern and eastern Europe. International capital flows, though large, were tied up with reparations and war debts settlements among the industrialised nations. Insufficient capital flowed to eastern European countries, which British and American bankers considered poor credit risks, and to tropical countries suffering from excess capacity and low levels of demand for their primary exports.

IMPERIALISM UNDER ATTACK

The social and political structures of European imperialism were as profoundly affected by the First World War as the international economy, but again the war accelerated trends already in evidence. Outside of Europe aggressively nationalistic leaders were emerging who resented European domination of their countries. In China the Boxer Rebellion, the Manchu reforms and the revolution of 1911 all drew on anti-foreign sentiment. Similarly the Young Turk movement in the Ottoman Empire grew out of a combined desire for reform and resentment over great power interference. In India the spread of the nationalist movement was influenced by the success of the Japanese against the Russians and by the bitterness of Indian Muslims after British acquiescence to Ottoman losses in the First Balkan War in 1912. Within Europe itself a conception of imperialism was emerging which saw overseas territories not only as sources of wealth, but also as backward areas which it was Europe's duty to civilise. In 1895 Kipling had viewed 'the white man's burden' as the simple though arduous task of caring for the native races, described as 'half devil and half child'. By 1912 the preface to a French compendium of colonial legislation defined 'colonisation' as a programme 'to bring to the native peoples the intellectual, social, scientific, moral, cultural, literary, commercial and industrial benefits of which they are deprived . . . to establish an advanced form of civilisation in a new country'. The author still thought each colony's resources should be developed 'for the benefit of the national interest', and his programme had no timetable. Nevertheless, by implication some day the colonies would no longer require European tutelage.

Most obviously, the First World War saw the colonial powers fighting among themselves. Previously, though often disputing the possession of particular territories, the European powers were united in their conviction of their collective right to rule, and cooperated whenever non-Europeans resisted, for instance in suppressing the Boxer Rebellion. Now, in addition to denouncing each other as uncivilised barbarians, they began to use the desire for national independence itself as a weapon in their struggle. Germany established theoretically independent nations in occupied portions of Russia. Britain and France announced as one of their war aims the 'liberation of subject peoples' in Austria-Hungary and promised independence to subjects of the Ottoman Empire. The United States in turn was openly committed to the concept of self-determination for all nations and opposed to colonialism. To be sure, Britain and France occupied German colonies in Africa, and the commitment of the United States to self-determination did not extend to, say, the Philippines. Nevertheless, the general moral tone of wartime propaganda made it impossible for Britain and France simply to appropriate German and Ottoman possessions and therefore the colonies and dependencies of the defeated powers were taken over by the victors as 'mandates' granted by the League of Nations. The mandated territories were 'a sacred trust of civilisation' and were to remain under control of the occupying powers only until they should become able 'to stand on their own feet in the arduous conditions of the modern world'. Logically these principles had to apply to other colonies as well.

Though it rang hollow to the ears of many non-Europeans, during the 1920s European colonial authorities repeatedly announced their commitment to the economic and social development of their possessions, and to eventual self-government for the indigenous peoples. The vision took different forms. The British tended to speak in terms of allowing non-European peoples to 'develop on their own lines'. The British did not think very systematically about what those lines might be, though the existence of the self-governing 'white dominions' and the promise in 1917 that India would be allowed 'responsible' government marked out a possible line of development. Most ambitious were the Dutch, who claimed to be creating 'a new way of life which would be a synthesis between East and West'. The French, Belgians, Portuguese and Italians were more straightforward. They considered their non-European territories as extensions of the mother country, and therefore in theory as the native peoples developed they would gradually be assimilated into the extended mother country and take part in its life on the same basis as its European citizens.

European colonial policies were tinged with hypocrisy. All colonial administrations discriminated against natives and in favour of the minority of European settlers. Funds for economic development remained scarce. Colonies were supposed to support themselves and raise money for roads, railways, health and education from local taxes. Tax revenues depended on export earnings, and as the prices of many commodities declined during the 1920s and especially after 1929, revenues and spending declined as well. Private investment flowed only to those areas where immediate profit could be gained and ceased to flow to those areas producing products with declining prices.

Nonetheless, the European presence had the effect of moving non-Europeans toward national independence. The extension of direct European administration, though breaking the initial resistance to the colonial powers, also extended communication among larger fractions of the native populations and therefore created the conditions out of which a broader nationalism could grow. Education along European lines, despite being extremely limited in scope, created educated native elites whose indignation at discrimination led them to opposition and to leadership in the nationalist movements. The inability or unwillingness of Europeans to help primary producers as prices declined served as a further stimulus. Increasing numbers of native leaders began to work for independence, and in areas where political independence remained circumscribed by economic vulnerability, nationalism took on a much more assertive tone.

Non-European nationalist movements also drew on indigenous traditions, though often reshaping those traditions in attempting to create an effective ideology. They drew inspiration from successful movements elsewhere in the non-European world, particularly the Meiji Restoration in Japan and Atatürk's modernisation programme in Turkey. Also, in the Soviet Union they had a model of a European regime committed to freeing the masses of people from traditional forms of domination. The Comintern announced its opposition to colonialism, causing a fair bit of consternation among the colonial powers. Soviet support for specific nationalist movements was limited, however. The poverty and disorganisation in the Soviet Union limited Soviet willingness to offer aid. Nationalist leaders, though they might favour socialist ideals, had no desire to exchange one form of foreign control for another, and therefore tended to hold the Russians at arm's length when aid was offered.

The Near East

Turkey provided a paradigm for non-European nationalism. The campaigns of the First World War stretched Turkish forces past their breaking point, the Ottoman Empire collapsed and a nationalist government under Mustafa Kemal, or Atatürk, came to power. Kemal remained president until his death in 1938, and he and his followers forced through a series of changes intended to secularise and westernise Turkish society. Although Islam remained officially Turkey's national religion until 1928, in 1925 polygamy was outlawed and the old Muslim religious orders and schools were first placed under strict government control and then gradually eliminated. The government forbade men to wear the traditional fez and actively discouraged women's veils. New civil, criminal and commercial law codes were introduced. Women were granted the right to vote and sit in the national assembly. In theory all Turkish citizens under the age of 40 were required to learn the Latin alphabet after its introduction in 1928. Arabic and Persian words were eliminated from public usage and place names changed to Turkish forms: Istanbul for Constantinople, Ankara for Angora, Izmir for Smyrna. In 1935 all Turks were required to adopt western-style surnames.

Atatürk wanted to create an independent industrial economy, a foundation for military power to ensure political autonomy. Virtually all industrial investment was subsidised or undertaken directly by the government. The funds were almost exclusively Turkish. The government sought no new loans from western Europe and purchased old foreign concessions and factories as rapidly as possible. A new treaty with the Soviet Union signed in 1925 brought economic and military aid, but the government firmly suppressed the local communist movement in 1929. A new tariff protected the new industrial plants, and a five-year plan provided funds for agricultural development, transportation and new mining ventures.

On the negative side, Turkey also provided a paradigm of the problems encountered by non-European states attempting to establish their independence. Ethnic divisions, traditionalist opposition, shortage of economic expertise and capital, and continued dependence on the world economy hampered the Turkish government's efforts and limited their success. Turkey's refusal to recognise the right of Armenians and Kurds to their own national states led to brutal campaigns in 1915 and 1920, during which a substantial fraction of the Armenian population perished, and to uprisings of the Kurds in 1925 and 1930. The exchange of population with Greece deprived Turkey of large numbers of merchants, industrialists and skilled workers. Capital remained largely in the hands of traditionalist landlords, and peasant agricultural techniques changed little, if at all. The government was unable to reform either land tenures or the taxation system and could not raise capital from agriculture. In addition the government remained burdened with the debts of the old Ottoman government until 1947; in the late 1920s these payments absorbed perhaps ten per cent of government revenue.

From Turkey the revolt against the European powers spread to the former Ottoman possessions in the Middle East which the British and French had occupied as League of Nations 'mandates'. In the face of nationalist agitation the British ended their protectorate over Egypt, but they continued to occupy the country and to restrict Egyptian autonomy in various ways. In Iraq the British suppressed a nationalist revolt only with difficulty in 1920; a plebiscite produced a 96 per cent majority in favour of a monarchy, which the British accordingly proclaimed in 1921, although they maintained their mandate until 1932. Similarly, the French suppressed a nationalist revolt in Syria in 1920, but in 1925 faced a new uprising of the Muslims who accused the French of favouring the Maronite Christian community.

The French defeated the Muslims after an extended two-year campaign, in the meantime granting independence to Lebanon, the Christian population centre. Various experiments with limited autonomy failed to satisfy the Syrian nationalists, and a general strike in 1936 finally decided the French to give up their mandate, though with a three-year transition period. The newly independent states attempted to modernise and westernise along the lines marked out by Atatürk, but found themselves limited by traditionalist protests of their own people and the hostility of the European powers.

Africa

Following the First World War, Spain, France and Italy all resumed their efforts to establish their authority over the interiors of their north African possessions. As their operations extended, however, so did the scale of resistance. Moroccans destroyed a Spanish force of 21,000 at Anual in 1921, and by 1924 the Spaniards were once again confined to the coastal towns. The Moroccans then began to attack the French, who eventually mobilised 150,000 troops for the campaign in 1925 and 1926. In Libya an uprising against the Italians in 1914 had driven them out of the interior, and they remained confined to a few coastal strongpoints until the end of the war. In 1922 Mussolini ordered a new effort to conquer the interior, but this war dragged on until 1930.

In west Africa the British and French contented themselves with treating the region as a supplier of agricultural raw materials. No mineral bonanzas appeared, and the climate generally did not favour plantation crops or pasturage; consequently the numbers of European settlers remained relatively small. To hold costs down both the British and French relied heavily on local chiefs for routine administration, while reserving all important questions to themselves. When their interests required, they had no hesitation in exacting the necessary sacrifices from their African subjects. Between 1921 and 1932 a total of 127,500 'fit adult males' laboured to construct the French railway linking the Congo with the ocean, and by 1928 official figures had recorded 10,200 deaths. Belgium, seriously damaged during the First World War, sought to expand its own earnings from trade by increasing production of tropical crops and minerals in the Congo. However, by 1924 the economy threatened to collapse because of the massive dislocation of manpower resulting from forced labour on roads and railways, because manipulation of import duties reduced native income and because the increased demand for export crops reduced the supply of food for local consumption.

In southern and eastern Africa the situation differed because of the relatively large number of European settlers. Throughout the interwar years the settler communities pressed for greater autonomy. Southern Rhodesia became a British Crown Colony with a responsible government in 1923, in 1934 the South African Union declared itself 'a sovereign independent state' and in 1935 a 'parliament' of settlers in Kenya denounced British administration and demanded a closer union of east African territories. Autonomy was for whites only; in 1936 South Africa permitted 'natives' to vote, but only for 3 Europeans to represent them in the Union parliament and for 12 of the 22 members of a native advisory council. European settlement brought expropriation. Laws restricting the purchase or leasing of land by Africans effectively eliminated their rights of ownership over wide areas, while the requirement to pay taxes in money forced them to seek money wages and racial segregation of the job market ensured that they worked as labourers for the white settlers. In Kenya, for instance, by the mid-1920s white farmers had occupied most of the prime land, half of the able-bodied men of the indigenous communities worked for them, and the African workers in turn may have paid as much as three-quarters of their wages in taxes to the government. Railways extended the area open to commercial agricultural production and provided access to mineral deposits, and therefore their spread increased the area open to white penetration. As elsewhere in Africa, they were constructed by African labour recruited with varying degrees of force. Also as in other regions, the increased output they made possible came onto the world market just as prices for most commodities were declining.

The Dominions and India

The First World War disrupted established trade patterns and impelled the British dominions to expand their industrial sectors. Following the war all moved to protect their infant industries. During the 1920s the dominons also began to establish direct financial and political ties with the United States. Concern for the financial relationship between London and the dominions helped Churchill to decide to return to the gold standard in 1925, as the dominions had already effectively done so, and 'trade always follows the bank'. The creation of new central banks throughout the British Empire contributed to decentralisation of authority in economic matters. The flow of people, traditionally one of the strongest links between Britain and the dominions, also declined. British emigration to the 'white' dominions dropped to about 40 per cent of prewar levels during the 1920s and virtually ceased with the onset of the depression. For the 'white' dominions these economic developments created the conditions for significant changes in their political relationship with Britain. In 1926, in response to pressures within Canada and South Africa (as well as developments in Ireland), the Balfour Declaration allowed for a new autonomy of communities within the British Empire. In 1931 the Statute of Westminster granted the dominions statutory autonomy.

India posed the greatest challenge to the emerging humanitarian conception of imperialism and to the idea of a British Commonwealth embodied in the Statute of Westminster. Indian leaders expected that the Indian contribution to the war effort would be repaid with substantial political concessions – if not immediate independence, then dominion status within the empire. Fully 1 million Indian soldiers had served and they had suffered 100,000 battle casualties. India had paid the entire cost of supporting Indian troops overseas as well as making an immediate gift of 100 million pounds to the British government and contributing an additional 20 million pounds to the general war effort each year of the war. Within India the war had created boom conditions in urban industrial centres but had also led to inflation and acute distress in the countryside. The 51 million tonnes of wheat exported to Britain had reduced domestic food supplies. In 1918–19 widespread crop failures worsened the situation, and the worldwide influenza epidemic spread to India as well. The combination of starvation and disease may have resulted in five million deaths.

The expectations of the increasingly self-confident Indians were disappointed by the British. In 1917 the British government announced it would develop self-governing institutions in India, which eventually would lead to responsible Indian government. However, the reforms actually proposed in 1918 appeared hopelessly inadequate to Indian leaders. Protest was immediate. Work stoppages, demonstrations and rioting spread, particularly in the Punjab. Half of the soldiers who had served in the war were Punjabi, and for them the humiliation of once again being treated as mere 'natives' was especially galling. Whether the Punjab was in 'open revolt', as the local British authorities seemed to think, remains an open question; however, the demonstrators in Amritsar upon whom British troops opened fire on 13 April 1919 were peaceful and unarmed. Nearly 400 were killed and 1,200 wounded. The Amritsar Massacre crystallised Indian opinion; for moderates previously restrained by tradition and loyalty to Britain, the question was no longer whether, but when and how, India should become independent. The largely Hindu Congress Party, led by Gandhi, announced a policy of 'non-cooperation' with the British and a boycott of British goods. Through the 1920s and 1930s the figure of Gandhi, the Mahatma, grew into legend as he repeatedly instigated non-violent protests, was arrested, then began to starve himself while millions waited by their radios for word of his condition and disorder and violence spread through the country.

East and Southeast Asia

The First World War greatly reduced European influence on China. European exports to China declined, and Chinese industrial development greatly expanded the size of the politically conscious entrepreneurial class and created a larger and more concentrated industrial labour force, an audience for modern political appeals. However, China seemed to have escaped one sort of imperialism, only to fall victim to another. During the war the Japanese had occupied the German concessions and seized control of the entire Shantung peninsula. In 1915 Japan presented the 'Twenty-One Demands' to the Chinese government, under which the Japanese would have been guaranteed possession of Shantung and the way opened for them to expand into the northeast, while key Chinese government departments would have employed Japanese 'advisors' and Japanese police would have been employed 'where necessary'. The Chinese government – weak and with only nominal authority in some regions – agreed to most of the demands. A protest demonstration by some 5,000 students in Peking on 4 May 1919 was one of the crucial events in the emergence of modern nationalism in China and soon protest was directed against all foreign powers.

The colonial powers introduced limited self-government into their Southeast Asian possessions in the aftermath of the First World War. The Dutch established an assembly in Indonesia in 1917, the British created a partially elected legislative council in Burma in 1922 and the French increased the number of Vietnamese sitting in the Colonial Council of Cochin China. European investment increased; indeed, in Southeast Asia the 1920s appear the heyday of colonialism. The annual transfer of dividends from the Dutch East Indies to the Netherlands bulked large in the Dutch balance of payments. French enterprises in Vietnam grew rapidly. Earnings from Malayan rubber and tin permitted Britain to balance accounts outside the sterling area – Malaya, in fact, had replaced India as the cornerstone of the British imperial economy.

THE INTERNATIONAL ECONOMY AND THE DEPRESSION

Shifting trade patterns

The war had disrupted patterns of trade; in the interwar years, some of those disruptions proved permament. Russia's share of world trade declined from nearly 4 per cent in 1913 to 1.5 per cent in the late 1920s and barely 1 per cent in the 1930s. Soviet leaders wanted to trade with the west, but they wanted 'trade to end trade' – trade on their own terms which would make the Soviet Union independent of the capitalist powers. Having repudiated the tsarist government's debt and nationalised all foreign-owned firms, they demanded a share of reparations, payment for damage done by western armies during the civil war and extension of long-term trade credits on favourable terms. Without some settlement of their own claims, western governments refused to extend the credits without which trade was impossible; only Germany, the other 'outcast' power, engaged in any extensive trade with Russia, and some of this trade was a cloak for clandestine rearmament by both the Weimar and Hitler regimes. In the remainder of Europe, wartime shortages, embargoes and blockades had forced many countries to produce goods they had previously imported, notably in the chemical and machinery industries. Virtually all countries decided to protect these new industries when the war ended, and the industralisation programmes of eastern European countries continued this development through the entire interwar period. The industrialised countries of western Europe therefore could not resume their prewar role in intra-European trade.

Overseas, the United States and Japan both entered the interwar world with greatly enlarged industrial sectors and, having occupied markets vacated by Europeans during the war, showed little disposition to leave. The United States, its large population and high average income giving it a huge domestic market, expanded the scale of industrial production to unprecedented levels, the resulting increases in productivity being translated into lower export prices. Domestically, the boom in the United States rested on an expansion of consumer credit and advertising. Of the 26 million automobiles registered in 1929, half had been sold during the 1920s, and most of those on credit. The multiplier effects of the automobile were felt in ancillary branches of manufacturing as well as in highway and residential construction. Electric power consumption doubled, much of the increase going to power the domestic appliances in suburban households.

Japan, perhaps a generation behind the United States, with a smaller population, lower incomes, a smaller domestic market and lower productivity, relied on lower wages for competitive advantage in export markets, but the results were equally unpleasant for European producers. Japanese cotton textiles in particular displaced British goods in India and Southeast Asia. Yet the 1920s were years of hardship in Japan as well. The wartime boom had raised prices and wages in Japan, while the government's generally deflationary policies slowed new investment. Exports of cotton textiles required imports of raw cotton; meanwhile, exports of silk declined because of competition from rayon, and imports of other manufactured goods tended to increase. Japan's trade balance was therefore negative; in foreign exchange terms, Japan lived off the capital accumulated during the war. Employment in large-scale industry actually declined from 1920 to 1930; urban workers absorbed into small industry or service occupations were often in fact underemployed and enduring real hardship, and the situation in the countryside was worse. Japanese leaders, particularly younger army officers, began to see expansion as the only way to overcome the crisis.

In addition to competition in third markets from the United States and Japan, Europe discovered that other countries which had imported European goods before the war had begun to fill their own needs. For Britain the explosive growth of the Bombay textile industry was the most damaging, for India had traditionally been the most important market for British cotton textiles. Now Indian purchases from Britain declined sharply and never recovered. Textile and machinery production had also expanded in the 'white' dominions in response to wartime demand – and Austrialia, South Africa and Canada showed distressing nationalist and protectionist tendencies as well. Similar development had occurred in several countries in Latin America, where the wartime boom continued through the 1920s, stimulated by United States investment in primary production.

Not only European manufacturing faced new competition; potential agricultural output too had expanded during the war. Those regions of Europe which produced staple crops, already hard pressed before 1914, could therefore expect no improvement in their international position. For Europe, the products most crucial in terms of their political and social impact were wheat and sugar. Canada, Australia, Argentina and the United States all increased their wheat acreage during the war, and Cuba, Java and Mauritius had opened new sugar plantations. The newly ploughed land did not simply disappear when farmers in Europe began to produce again. Between 1924 and 1929 the price of wheat dropped by two-fifths and that of sugar by three-fifths. In many areas of Europe, the desperation of wheat and sugar farmers led them to support authoritarian governments promising greater control over the market.

The crisis in which European farmers found themselves was only one aspect of a more general crisis affecting primary producers throughout the world. A broad spectrum of agricultural and mineral products seemed to suffer from 'excess' capacity, and as in the case of the declining industries, calls for relief and schemes for restrictions and limitations on output and competition were widespread. The problem was real enough; in the late 1920s there were 49 countries in eastern Europe, Latin America, Africa, Asia and Oceania in which primary products made up half or more of the value of exports, and they accounted for 36 per cent of total world trade. Looked at from a slightly different angle, the non-industrialised countries shipped over half of all primary exports and purchased just under half of all manufactured imports; the bulk of their trade, both exports and imports, was with the industrialised countries of western Europe and the United States. Most of the primary producers depended on one or two products. For example, tin made up 71 per cent of Bolivia's exports, and coffee and cotton together 65 per cent of Brazil's exports. In addition, foreign trade made up a larger fraction of their incomes than of the incomes of the major industrialised countries. They were therefore highly vulnerable to fluctuations in export markets.

The problem for primary producers varied from commodity

to commodity. For some, the problem was a completely new competitor; rayon drastically reduced the market for Japanese silk, and synthetic nitrates cut into Chile's former world monopoly. Rayon had covered the wings of fighter planes, and nitrates had been required for explosives; now the plants constructed during the war needed peacetime outlets. For other primary products, technical advance led to more efficient production, higher yields, lower prices and to what producers saw as excess supply. The spread of mechanical sowing and harvesting lowered the costs of overseas wheat producers, for instance, and new sugar varieties doubled output per hectare in Java. Not all primary products suffered; high-quality foods, vegetable oils, timber products, copper and petroleum all found ready markets. However, stocks rose and prices dropped for a depressingly long list of products: wheat, sugar, tea, coffee, wool, cotton, rubber, silk, lead, tin, zinc and mineral oils.

Overall, according to League of Nations estimates, prices for primary products declined by fully one-half between 1924 and 1929. More important, they declined relative to industrial prices. By the late 1920s, a producer of primary products probably had to produce 10–30 per cent more to purchase a given amount of manufactured goods than in 1913. This translated into lower real incomes and hardship in those regions and countries which depended on primary production. In addition, it affected industrial regions and countries as well because the depressed incomes of primary producers left them less able to purchase manufactured products. Britain was particularly vulnerable, with three-fifths of its exports going to primary producing countries and foreign trade making up a relatively large share of national income, the United States less so as exports to primary producers made up a third of total exports which in turn were a much smaller fraction of national income. For the United States, France, Germany and the less developed countries of southern and eastern Europe these relations were apt to be internal, with the depression in specialised agricultural regions slowing the growth of industrial centres.

The world crisis

The various sources of instability in the international system began to act together in the late 1920s. The downturn began in different countries at different times and for different reasons. The mix between internal and external factors varied, as did the balance between autonomous economic forces and the effects of political decisions, but in virtually every case the policies of central banks and governments worsened the situation. Italy, largely in consequence of the overvaluation of the lira, stagnated after 1926. In Germany investment peaked in 1927 and began to turn downward. In Britain the return to gold caused unemployment, and housing investment declined in 1927 and 1928 as government subsidies were cut. In the United States the markets for housing and consumer durables were approaching saturation in 1927 – there were fewer young families because of the new restrictions on immigration – and investment therefore began to decline in 1928.

In late 1926 and early 1927 the stabilisation of the French franc led to the return of French capital which had fled the previous devaluations, and to a large inflow of foreign funds which speculators wanted to convert to francs because they believed the value of the franc would be raised. The Bank of France therefore accumulated large amounts of sterling, which it began to convert to gold. To maintain the Bank of England's gold reserves, Norman wanted Moreau to fix the franc definitively in terms of gold; Moreau wanted Norman to raise British interest rates; the British threatened to demand repayment of the entire debt owed them from the First World War; the French threatened to convert more sterling to gold. A complex compromise involving Strong and the Federal Reserve Bank of New York provided temporary relief. In mid-1927 the American, German, British and French bankers agreed to take a number of measures to reduce the flow of gold out of Britain, including moves by American authorities to reduce American interest rates.

Conscious that he had the power to drive Britain off the gold standard if he chose, Moreau continued to press for equality with the Bank of England. 'Would it not be useful', he asked his diary in February 1928, 'to have a serious conversation with M. Norman, with a view to dividing Europe into two zones of financial influence which could be attributed respectively to France and to Britain?' Moreau took the lead in a stabilisation programme for Rumania's currency; to Norman's intense displeasure, Strong agreed to participate in Moreau's plan. The negotiations over reparations which resulted in the Young Plan further widened the already considerable differences among the key financial leaders. Schacht insisted that the old German colonies and the Polish Corridor must be returned if Germany were to pay any reparations at all; the French were incensed, and Schacht later accused them of threatening to withdraw short-term credits from Germany. Later, a British negotiator demanded a larger share of the proposed payments for Britain, and insulted the French minister of finance during the debate; the British later accused the French of threatening to convert their sterling balances into gold in retaliation.

As the economic outlook darkened, the strain began to tell on the participants. Schacht's 'tantrums and exhibitionism' drew unfavourable comment. Norman descended into deep depression, flew into unpredictable rages – he threw a bottle of ink at one of his assistants – and finally was forced to take an extended vacation to recover his equilibrium. Strong, ill through most of 1928, died in October, aged only 54. His death greatly weakened the connection between American and European policy makers, and the absence of a clear successor left the decentralised American banking system adrift.

In the meantime the New York stock market boomed through 1928 and most of 1929, but then collapsed in the spectacular crash which has become the conventional starting point for the depression. At each stage, the boom, the crash and their consequences were closely connected to economic developments outside the United States and to the course of financial diplomacy. The decision to reduce American interest rates in 1927 reinforced a speculative tendency in the stock market by making money more easily available. Once begun, the boom absorbed money by increasing the amount of money being held to take advantage of speculative opportunities. In March 1929 the Federal Reserve Board turned down the recommendation of George Harrison, Strong's replacement as head of the Federal Reserve Bank of New York, that central bank interest rates be raised. When the Board finally permitted the increase in August, speculative enthusiasm and the rate at which stock prices were increasing made the move ineffective. The inability of German borrowers to renew their short-term loans in New York accelerated the decline of the German economy, undermined the central European banking system and threatened the new reparations agreements, but it was the general feeling of insecurity, rather than French government action, which probably resulted in the withdrawals of French short-term loans from Germany at this time. Similarly, it was probably not French conversions of sterling to gold which caused the sudden flow of gold out of London in August and September, but the increase in American interest rates. On the other hand, the positive French trade balance and French conversions of currency into gold placed almost as much strain on the system as the stock market boom. During the first half of 1929 the United States gained 210 million dollars' worth of gold, but France gained 182 million dollars in gold during the same 6 months.

The flow of funds to New York and Paris reduced the reserves of other central banks. To protect themselves and their currencies, they increased their interest rates. In raising their rates, they of course restricted domestic credit. Investment and production, already declining in all countries except France, dropped further as interest rates rose; the demand for cash caused by the general decline, combined with the direct effects of higher interest rates, finally burst the speculative bubble. In early October Europeans began to withdraw large amounts from the New York market, worsening the growing credit shortage in the United States. The market slipped after 3 October, and the panic selling of 'Black Thursday' on 24 October and 'Black Tuesday' on 29 October reduced the Dow-Jones index of share prices by nearly half. The boom was over.

Although in theory the stock market decline could have improved the economic situation by making credit more generally available, in fact the sudden collapse led to cuts in spending, output and imports as institutions, firms and individuals across the United States attempted to increase their cash holdings. Banks began to foreclose on home mortgages – which at that time were normally three-year unamortised loans – and housing construction declined further. Manufacturing firms cut production and began to run down inventories. Aggregate industrial production declined 10 per cent between October and December 1929; automobile production had already declined from a peak of 622,000 in March to 440,000 in August, but then shrank to 92,500 in December. Imports declined 20 per cent from September to October, and foreign lending dropped from 458 million dollars in the first half of 1929 to 213 million in the second half.

Because of its size, the United States played a crucial role in the collapse. The United States produced over 40 per cent of the world's manufactured goods and purchased 12 per cent of the world's imports, including a proportionately large share of primary products. The United States had become the world's most important foreign lender, investing nearly one billion dollars a year in other countries during the 1920s, about twice the amount raised in London. The decline in the United States therefore would in any case have had a severe impact elsewhere. American monetary policy continued to drift, probably further worsening the decline. During 1930 Harrison pressed for a rapid reduction in interest rates and more vigorous measures to increase the money supply but was voted down by the Federal Reserve Board. Widespread bank failures caused a large decline in the total supply of money in 1931, a further restriction on credit which acted with the very gloomy expectations of potential investors to worsen the downward spiral.

Personal negotiations among central bankers, the supposed cornerstone of the international system, failed to produce results. In late 1930 Norman and Moreau's successor Moret discussed a possible British loan in Paris. In early 1931 Hans Luther, the new head of the Reichsbank, enquired whether the United States might fund some of Germany's short-term debt. The so-called 'Norman Plan' proposed by Britain suggested a new subsidiary of the Bank for International

Settlements which would raise funds in Paris and lend them to 'agreed' borrowers – mainly countries having difficulty meeting payments on loans owed to Britain. None of the proposals succeeded. In May 1931 international aid for the ailing Creditanstalt, Austria's largest bank, was delayed by French attempts to extract a promise from the Austrians to abandon their plan to join a customs union with Germany. When the aid did arrive it was too little to prevent the bank's collapse. The fall of the Creditanstalt set off a chain reaction in central Europe and particularly Germany. Hoover's proposed 'moratorium' on reparations and war debts, by discriminating in favour of 'commercial obligations', disadvantaged France relative to the United States, which delayed French acceptance of the plan and greatly reduced its potential positive impact.

Hoover considered American loans to Europe impossible because of an impending deficit in the government budget; Norman asserted the Bank of England had 'already lent quite as much as is entirely convenient to Austria, Hungary and Germany to avoid financial collapse'. Accordingly, the collapse proceeded. An agreement to a 'standstill' on withdrawals of foreign credits from Germany was reached, but this had the effect of reducing the reserves of smaller countries, notably Belgium, the Netherlands, Switzerland and Sweden. They in turn sold sterling to increase their gold holdings, placing pressure on Britain. In addition reports of parliamentary committees on declining British gold reserves and an impending budget deficit undermined confidence in sterling. The new National Coalition government secured loans from Paris and New York and introduced a deflationary budget, but the drain continued, and Britain left the gold standard in September 1931.

International cooperation broke down entirely in the areas of exchange rates and tariffs, and governments began to impose direct controls on foreign exchange and trade in the hope of salvaging something from the wreckage. In the case of exchange rates, direct manipulation was still regarded as unethical, but to leave the gold standard and allow one's currency to sink to its 'natural' level permitted depreciation while maintaining at least the appearance of virtue. Sterling declined some 30 per cent in 2 months after Britain went off gold, but the government, acting under guidelines suggested by Norman, refused to intervene. Twenty-five countries abandoned the gold standard immediately after Britain, and those countries remaining on gold found it even more difficult to export than before.

After Britain left gold, fear that the United States might also suspend gold payments led countries which had lost as a result of Britain's move to begin to convert dollars to gold. France was the most important, but Belgium, the Netherlands and Switzerland also converted large amounts. Private investors followed, and altogether the United States lost some two billion dollars' worth of gold between mid-1931 and mid-1932. The response of American authorities, though on balance excessively restrictive, appears to have been confused rather than intentionally deflationary. President Hoover explicitly asked the Federal Reserve Board for policy suggestions, but received none. The new Roosevelt administration tried a number of expedients in quick succession; the decision to end gold payments in 1933 was taken not so much to improve the balance of payments, as in the hope that arbitrarily setting the price of gold well above market levels would raise other prices as well and thereby stimulate recovery. It did not, but the move increased the pressure on the 'gold bloc'. In 1936 the flight of capital forced France off the gold standard, and meanwhile the Low Countries, Switzerland and Italy had all carried out controlled devaluations to keep their export prices in line with those of their competitors. Competitive devaluations and 'managed' exchange rates had become the order of the day.

Tariffs remained the most important barrier to trade, and they increased. The American Smoot-Hawley bill passed in 1930 imposed large increases on the entire range of American imports. Some countries increased their duties on American goods in direct retaliation, while others raised the levels of existing tariffs or imposed new ones. Most strikingly, Britain abandoned free trade, raising existing tariffs in 1931, imposing a general ten per cent tariff on all imports in 1932, and substantially increasing the rates on particular items in subsequent years. Britain granted exemptions and preferences to imports from Empire countries; though their impact was small, they strongly affected certain foreign countries such as Denmark and Argentina, and the publicity given to the idea of 'imperial free trade' before the 1932 Imperial Conference in Ottawa contributed to the general sense of the world being divided up into self-contained autarkic empires.

Direct controls, quotas, prohibitions and bilateral agreements further restricted the flow of trade. After Britain left gold the French franc appreciated in value, lowering the price of imports to the point where even high tariffs became ineffective. In order to hold imports down while still remaining on the gold standard, the French government began to impose quotas and prohibitions on imported goods and had extended the system to cover most foreign trade by 1936. Other countries used quotas to discriminate against particular competitors, as in the case of quotas on Japanese textile imports into the British empire. Direct controls over the quantity of trade also figured in bilateral agreements, which often involved direct rationing of foreign exchange as well. In addition to the Ottawa Agreements, Britain signed bilateral agreements with a number of 'foreign' countries. Argentina relaxed foreign exchange restrictions on sterling transactions and agreed to purchase more British goods, in return for a British promise not to lower the Argentine meat quota or impose other new tariffs and quotas on Argentine products. The British began to violate the spirit of the agreement almost immediately by restricting Argentine meat shipments in favour of supposedly 'experimental' shipments from Australia. The agreements imposed on the northern European and Baltic countries were even less favourable. Britain retained the right to impose quotas while requiring that British products be given preferential treatment.

Germany developed a particularly extensive system of bilateral agreements with eastern European countries. Desperate for markets for their primary products, eastern European countries also wanted to avoid paying for imports with gold or 'hard' currencies, which they required to service their foreign debts. Germany wanted to exchange manufactured goods for primary products but, as a debtor country, also wanted to save foreign exchange. Under an agreement signed with Hungary in 1934 the German government provided a fund to pay the tariffs on imports of Hungarian agricultural imports into Germany. The Hungarian government used the fund to subsidise farmers and in return agreed to end embargoes and increase quotas on German manufactured goods. German importers paid for Hungarian goods into a special account opened for the National Bank of Hungary at the German Reichsbank, and German exporters were paid for their goods shipped to Hungary from the same account. Hungarian exports to Germany doubled in a year, and Hungarian farmers at least benefited. However, German exports to Hungary rose only a little, and a portion of the resulting positive Hungarian trade balance was effectively frozen in the Reichsbank. Germany also linked the tariff subsidy to the settlement of claims for German assets frozen in Hungary, and German exporters benefited by selling their goods at high prices inside the Hungarian tariff wall. The Hungarian scheme became the model for agreements with Bulgaria, Yugoslavia and Rumania, and Germany signed less ambitious clearing agreements with nearly every other European country and several Latin American nations as well.

Worsened by the new restrictions, the decline in trade spread the depression from one country to another. In addition, once they were in place, the restrictions hampered recovery. By 1933 the exports of most European countries had declined by at least a third, and in several important cases by as much as two-thirds from their 1929 levels. There was some recovery after 1934 or 1935, but only the Scandinavian countries exported as much in 1937–8 as they had in 1928–9; British and French exports were around three-fifths, and German exports less than half, the levels of the late 1920s. The countries of Europe, and especially the industrialised countries of northwestern Europe, had always been each others' best customers, and it was on this trade that the depression and the new restrictions had the greatest impact. Belgium's four most important trading partners, for instance, were France, Britain, Germany and the Netherlands. In 1929 they supplied 56 per cent of Belgian imports and purchased 55 per cent of Belgian exports; their purchases from Belgium declined from 17.6 billion francs in 1929 to 7.9 billion in 1933, while their sales to Belgium dropped from 19.9 billion francs to 8.2 billion. In 1937 their trade with Belgium still was only two-thirds its 1929 level, and they supplied only 40 per cent of Belgian imports.

The depression in the dependent economies

The effects of the decline in trade were even worse in those countries which depended on exports of primary products to the industrialised nations. Having already declined by a third from 1924 to 1929, primary product prices dropped a further 60 per cent between 1929 and 1932. Income from export earnings declined in China by nearly four-fifths, in Latin America by two-thirds, in eastern Europe and Africa by three-fifths and in Australia by over half. The collapse of export markets cut income and substantially increased the real costs of servicing existing foreign debt. At first the exporting countries attempted to cover the resulting deficits by deflationary policies intended to reduce their domestic price levels, but as their small reserves of foreign exchange and gold disappeared they were forced to abandon the gold standard. Several Latin American countries, Canada, Australia and New Zealand had already gone off gold by early 1930, and most other exporters followed after Britain abandoned gold in 1931. Many of those with recently developed manufacturing sectors introduced or increased tariffs, and some, such as Denmark and New Zealand, engaged in competitive devaluations in the hope of holding on to dwindling markets.

Declining commodity prices also reduced the attractiveness of investment in the exporting countries. In Britain the Treasury and the Bank of England together imposed informal controls over capital exports, both reducing them drastically and directing them towards Empire countries. The decline in direct investment reduced potential income in the exporting countries. In addition, the worldwide shortage of credit caused the failure of commodity control schemes intended to maintain prices by holding stocks off the market. Production of most commodities continued at high levels; despite dumping, at progressively lower prices, world stocks only began to decrease in 1934. Indeed in some cases output increased, as exporters attempted to compensate for declining prices by increasing production, which lowered prices further. Australia's 'Grow More Wheat Campaign' increased acreage by over one-fifth from 1929 to 1930, for example. The Soviet government had decided in 1928 to export wheat to finance imports of capital equipment, and raised exports from 100,000 tonnes in 1929 to 2.3 million in 1930 and 5.2 million in 1931. However, the rapid decline in prices meant that Australia gained virtually nothing from the increase in production, while Russia gained only a 10-fold increase in income from the initial 23-fold rise in exports and earned virtually the same amount in 1931 as in 1930 despite a further doubling of volume.

In north Africa the economic crisis led to severe hardship. Morocco and Tunisia had become two of the world's major suppliers of phosphate, and Morocco supplied coal, cobalt and nickel as well. Unemployment spread as commodity markets contracted, and a severe drought cut harvests. Unrest spread rapidly in Morocco, and the new outbreaks of violence were not suppressed until 1934. In the meantime, the social dislocation resulting from the wars of conquest and from economic development was creating the basis for a new, more widely based nationalist opposition. Models of organisation and ideology lay close at hand in the Middle East. A Young Tunisia movement was already active in the early 1920s, a Muslim nationalist organisation emerged in Algeria in 1931 and in 1934 a group of Moroccans founded a new nationalist movement. In response, European governments in north Africa suppressed insurrections, confiscated more native land and encouraged the migration of European settlers. Meanwhile the Italians conquered Ethiopia in 1935, and the failure of sanctions imposed by the League to deter Italy was an important mark on the trail leading to the Second World War.

The depression cut west African incomes drastically. In 1929 British and French west African possessions had exports of 86 million pounds, but in 1931 only 47 million. Taxes did not decline with income, however. In Nigeria the share of revenues coming from direct taxes, nearly all of which came from rural African agricultural producers, substantially increased during the 1930s. In the Belgian Congo the depression brought new investment to a halt, and jobs in the modern sector of the economy disappeared. Nonetheless the rigidly authoritarian and paternalistic Belgian administration proved able to maintain itself against occasional resistance, though one Belgian administrator later recalled that 'in those grim days I had to kill in order not to be killed myself'. In eastern and southern Africa the situation varied, depending on the product – the demand for gold remained high – but overall exports from British East Africa declined from 40 million pounds in 1929 to 21 million in 1931.

Southeast Asia demonstrated the difficulties and dangers entailed in the position of the colonial economies with a one-sided emphasis on production of raw materials and cash crops, which were not guaranteed favoured treatment by the 'mother' countries as the depression spread. Under the international rubber restriction scheme of 1933–8, native smallholders were usually underassessed for quotas and their production decreased by nearly half, compared with an average decline of 12 per cent for European-owned large estates. Similarly the distribution of quotas under the international tin agreement of 1931 had the effect of squeezing smaller Chinese-owned firms in Malaya out of business and granting a virtual monopoly to large European firms. Profits derived from the Dutch East Indies allowed Holland to remain on the gold standard and avoid devaluation until 1936. At the same time the Dutch beet sugar industry was protected from the competition of cane sugar grown in the Indies, which was forced onto the world market at whatever price it could find. Native producers of sugar and other products sold in dollar and sterling markets for low equivalents of guilders; in effect the Dutch government shifted much of the burden of adjustment to the Indies, where it was borne in the form of wage cuts and unemployment.

In Latin America the First World War boom continued so long as international demand for primary product exports remained high. The effects of the general crisis in commodity production varied from country to country, depending on the particular products on which each depended, but eventually the depression struck them all. In Cuba, for instance, where sugar and tobacco contributed four-fifths of export income, declining sugar prices had already led to protests and rioting in 1928, and by the early 1930s Cuba's foreign trade had sunk to ten per cent of its 1929 level. Argentina's exports in 1930-4 averaged 40 per cent less than in the previous five years. Unemployment rose in primary industries and in the service and manufacturing sectors which depended on them. Unemployment created discontent, and the military proved a particularly dangerous source of pressure on existing governments. Over 50 revolutions occurred in Latin America between the wars, and every country endured at least one coup staged or supported by the military. Internally a three and sometimes four-cornered struggle emerged. Leftists, some of them Marxist, and right-wing corporatists, some of them explicitly fascist, advocated social reforms to aid the agricultural and industrial proletarians. The great landholding families, the Catholic church (itself a major landholder) and the urban middle classes were less enthusiastic about social reforms which involved increased taxation or redistribution of land. By the end of the 1930s leftists ruled only in Chile, though the moderate liberal regime of Colombia had disestablished the Catholic church. Elsewhere right-wing regimes had established themselves, though not always securely. Left or right, however, all Latin American governments committed themselves to much more assertively nationalistic economic policies in response to the depression. 'Economic nationalism' aimed to reduce their dependence on unstable international markets and on single crops or minerals. Governments attempted to diversify their primary production, particularly agriculture, and to develop their manufacturing sectors, particularly heavy industry.

Throughout the world, Europe's role diminished. Independent nations attempted to regulate, limit or exclude foreign economic interests, as in the Middle East, Latin America and China. Profits from colonial areas decreased because of the depression and, as in India, because of rising nationalism. Where the old forms of imperialism were still being practised, Europe tended to be on the sidelines. In

China the expansion of Japanese power in the 1930s brought Japan into conflict with the United States, but Europe did not figure in the ensuing struggle. Similarly, the creation of the frankly exploitative regimes in Central America and the Caribbean during the 1930s owed much to United States influence and intervention, but did not involve Europe. Finally, even in Europe's own and apparently most secure colonies the weight of new competition increased. In 1927 the United States purchased 44 per cent of Malayan exports, while Britain took only 11 per cent, and in the late 1930s the United States purchased a third of exports from the Dutch East Indies. Even more ominously, in 1937 Japan supplied a quarter of the Dutch East Indies' imports and was only being held out of British colonial markets by the quota scheme adopted in 1934, and only over the protests of local interests. Once again war would intervene to accelerate change; once again, however, the transformation which later seemed so sudden had been a long time in preparation.

8

EUROPEAN SOCIETY 1918–39

THE AFTERMATH OF THE WAR

As in economic life, so too in the social realm the First World
War accelerated change and added new problems to the old.
Millions of Europeans – a generation of young people – had
died, and still more had become homeless refugees. Whole
areas of countryside were destroyed, and national boundaries
were changed. Women had assumed a new role in the
workforce and were now being given the vote. Old
occupational groups were no longer able to find work in the
postwar world, and the thousands of returned soldiers had to
be accommodated by the economy. Hardships did not end
with the armistice, and in fact war continued.

Throughout Europe, the aristocracy weakened. The upper
class had been numerically reduced by the war and lost
political power wherever the franchise was extended.
Aristocrats found it increasingly difficult to maintain their
old style of living with the economic and social changes of
the period, such as the agricultural depression and drastically
reduced numbers of servants. The unprecedented mingling of
classes in the trenches had somewhat narrowed the divide
separating the lords from the common people. Some of the
mixing had been picturesque, such as the episode of a British
titled lady giving a dinner party to celebrate her first month
of work in a munitions factory and inviting as her guests a
duchess, the wife of a cabinet minister and a working-class
colleague called Mabel. But there had been a real entry of the
aristocracy into the war effort in all countries, and the effects
were more than anecdotal. In central and eastern Europe, the
end of the German, Austro-Hungarian, Russian and Ottoman
empires disestablished the legal aristocracy, depriving it of

its titles and reducing its political and social influence. The killing of the tsar and his family ended not only the three centuries of Romanov rule in Russia but also the legal overlordship of the old elite. In Russia, the Soviet government confiscated noble estates, and land reform in eastern Europe worked in the same direction.

The death toll among the middle classes was also high, but the power consolidated by the bourgeoisie before the war remained largely intact after 1918. Businessmen profited from the war through the production of armaments and military supplies, by lending money to governments and by managing the war economy. The postwar inflation was not propitious for middle-class savings, but the release of pent-up demand was a spur to investment and production. The bourgeois refugees of war-torn territories in Europe suffered heavily; in Russia, many of the bourgeoisie suffered the same fate as the aristocracy. But elsewhere, the middle class emerged reasonably secure from the war. The war had even afforded the opportunity for upward mobility through government work and war work; thus, the lower middle class expanded.

Among the working classes, peasants and workers had become cannon fodder. They served as ordinary foot soldiers without the prestige or the remuneration of the officer corps, but they too could return home decorated with medals if they survived the fighting. The war gave new scope for the ordinary people of Europe to participate in public life, although many were aware that they were fighting their masters' wars. In eastern Europe, Lenin proclaimed that the war was an imperialist crusade, useful to the workers only if they could turn it into a working-class revolution. His slogan in 1917, 'Peace, Land, and Bread', responded to a dissatisfaction with the war, actual hunger and the peasant hunger for land. But everywhere in Europe, peasants and workers had rallied round the flag of their nations and reaped the consequences. At the end of the war workers could take pride in national victories, at least in the Allied countries, but many felt that they had missed out on the spoils of the war. In the defeated countries, the frustration was greater. The demobilised soldiers of Germany, for example, returned from the battlefront bewildered, angry at Germany's defeat and resentful of the new socialist government. Cries for a reversal of the defeat would be listened to attentively by such an audience, just as irredentist demands in the victorious countries (such as Italy) would also receive a warm hearing among many of the ordinary citizens. But others in the working classes adhered increasingly to the creeds of socialism, newly inspired by the triumphant Russian Revolution.

The war accelerated the changing role of women. During the war, many women had entered the labour force on the home front. They worked in factories, found increased employment as nurses and clerical workers and also entered 'male' occupations such as bus conductors. Inequalities still prevailed. By the end of 1915 the nationalised shell factories of Britain were employing three women to one man, but while the top weekly wage for men was about four and a half pounds, for women it was two and a half pounds. Nonetheless, women were out of the house and in the workforce in greater numbers than ever before, and this simple fact had important consequences. Many women would not want to give up their employment after the end of the fighting. The war proved to many men that women could work in a variety of tasks, and this economic development, paralleling the women's suffrage movement, heralded the beginning of a change in the composition of the workforce and the advent of women's emancipation. In societies where peasants remained the majority of the population – which included most of Europe – things changed less for women. But even here many of them had managed the farm while their husbands were at the front and so assumed a greater role in the household economy than previously.

THE 1920s

Britain

The 1920s in Britain marked a return to a semblance of normalcy. For the elite, these were the halcyon days of what

Robert Graves, the English poet, called 'the long weekend': the jazz age, the beginnings of the motor car age and the last decades of the empire. Young women wore bobbed hair and short skirts and dined in restaurants without chaperones; young men of the upper classes could ease into jobs in government, business or the colonial service, living comfortably in the houses of London or reigning like lords in imperial outposts.

The elite of Britain in the 1920s had changed little from that of Victorian times. The aristocracy and bourgeoisie had preserved their grip on the wealth of the country and continued to monopolise political power. Universal manhood suffrage had been achieved, and soon after the war women were given the right to vote. The working classes seemed in a better condition thanks to the round of social welfare legislation passed earlier in the century. The Anglican Church was still the official state religion, and the universities of Oxford and Cambridge exercised a near monopoly over the training of the nation's intellectual and cultural elite. Critics of the established order were numerous, but dissidents were not really troublemakers. Colonial independence movements did not yet pose a serious threat to the imperial system. Marxism had made few inroads in Britain life and the British version of socialism was a tame variety; the Labour Party would not form a government until 1924 and that government would last only a year.

Yet underneath the surface all was not so calm. Britain in the 1920s was faced with an unparalleled series of strikes, leading to a general strike in 1926. The most discontented group were the miners. Coal was Britain's most important product, employing the largest numbers of workers and accounting for the greatest volume and value of exports. Miners worked in desperate conditions in Lancashire, Yorkshire and southern Wales. Wages averaged 100–150 pounds yearly for miners, while the owners of the land on which coal was mined earned staggering royalties for the mineral rights; Lord Bute was paid 115,000 pounds a year, Lord Tredegar 84,000 and the Duke of Northumberland 83,000. Mining was one of the most dangerous of jobs; from 1922 to 1924, for example, 3,603 miners were killed and

597,198 sustained injuries which kept them away from work for at least seven days. Even in the absence of injury the work was so debilitating that miners were usually unfit for work after the age of 40. A government report issued in 1919 said that working conditions and housing were 'a reproach to our civilisation . . . . No judicial language is sufficiently strong or sufficiently severe to apply to their condemnation'.

Since the government had taken over control of the mines as a war measure during the First World War, the question of nationalisation of mines loomed large at the beginning of the 1920s. A government commission recommended that the mines be nationalised; the House of Commons, which had commissioned the report, found this unacceptable and shelved the inquiry. By 1921, the postwar boom had ended and there were two million unemployed. Coal exports declined and mine owners reduced wages. The outraged miners went out on strike. But the 'triple alliance' of miners, railwaymen and transport workers collapsed on 15 April 1921 – colloquially known as Black Friday – and the miners were defeated. Their dissatisfaction festered for the next few years. Britain's return to the gold standard in 1925 once again cut exports, and this time the mine owners demanded a 13 per cent cut in wages. The Trades Union Congress or TUC threatened further action, and the government agreed to subsidise the mines to preclude wage cuts. The miners claimed a victory, a 'Red Friday' to redress the 'Black Friday'.

Then again in 1926, mine owners asked for a 13 per cent wage cut along with an increase in hours. The miners refused, and on 30 April mine owners locked out one million coal miners. The TUC had been negotiating with the government, but then the government pulled out. Thereupon the TUC called for a 'national strike'. This 'general strike', as the press called it, began at midnight on 3 May 1926 and the next morning 3.5 million workers refused to show up for their jobs in solidarity with the miners. The general strike lasted until 12 May; during the 'nine days that shook Britain', Britain came to a virtual standstill. Only a small number of non-unionised blue collar workers continued to work; there was no transport, no factory work, no mining.

The general strike was a confrontation between the

government and the unions and between the social classes which they represented. In the disputes earlier in the 1920s, one politician had said: 'Is England to be governed by Parliament and by the Cabinet or by a handful of trade union leaders?' and the prime minister had said that miners' actions were 'practical, and not theoretical, Bolshevism and must be dealt with with a firm hand'. Now Prime Minister Baldwin proclaimed: 'The Constitution is in danger'. The Catholic primate of Britain said that the General Strike was 'a sin against the obedience which we owe to God'. The government commandeered a printing press and put out a propaganda sheet called the *British Gazette*, edited by Winston Churchill – although even Churchill's wife Clementine remarked: 'He knows nothing of the life of ordinary people. He's never been on a bus, and only once on the Underground'. The BBC refused to broadcast a conciliatory speech by the Archbishop of Canterbury, while the government-controlled media trumpeted the judgement of the Catholic cardinal. The government recruited volunteers to staff essential services, and upper-class Oxford and Cambridge undergraduates cheerily drove trains and buses. Only a few intellectuals, such as the socialist historian G. D. H. Cole, supported the miners, while the rest of Britain saw the strike as an all-out attack on king and country.

On 12 May, faced with threats of arrest and overwhelming opposition from the elite and middle classes, the TUC called off the national strike. Only the miners fought on, and they were forced to return to work in November at substantially lower wages. The General Strike had thus been a total defeat for the workers. It showed that the government was strong enough to enforce its will and that much of the country cared little about the plight of the working people of Britain. But it also presaged further industrial disputes in Britain, often spearheaded by the miners' union, even after the nationalisation of the mines following the Second World War. Finally, the strike showed that the 'roaring twenties' was restricted to only a few Britons. The year 1926 was not a revolution; unlike in Russia in 1917, in Britain the capitalist system and the establishment had plucked victory from the jaws of rebellion.

France

In France the elite could also live much as they did before the war. Profiting from the economic boom, they enjoyed the benefits of the nascent consumer society and delighted in the culture of Paris. The economic elite of major landowners, financiers and businessmen and those in positions of state authority – the 'two hundred families' – still controlled the country. The French bourgeoisie was a conservative force, both socially and economically; its spokesmen argued strongly against the devaluation of the franc and against the sort of deficit financing and public works used elsewhere to combat the depression. The bourgeoisie largely monopolised entry to the universities and elite training schools and thus enjoyed easy access to political and cultural power. The French workforce was fairly evenly divided, with 36 per cent in agriculture, 30 per cent in industry and 34 per cent in the service sector by 1936. Increasing industrialisation had enlarged the working classes, but the peasantry's position was largely unchanged; despite an economy that was certainly capitalistic in its industry and trade, rural France continued to be an area of peasant farms and relative poverty. Not until the census of 1932 did more Frenchmen live in urban areas than in rural areas.

The problem which seemed to cut across class lines was the low birth rate in France, a question which preoccupied analysts and officials, worried about a 'depopulation' of France. The French population in 1936 was only one per cent higher than before the First World War, while the populations of Britain and Germany had increased by approximately one-third. The massive loss of life in the First World War had created a population trough in the group of men who would have married and fathered children in the 1920s and 1930s; consequently, both the marriage and the birth rates dropped. Furthermore, the French had smaller families than other nationalities, which was blamed on both voluntary limitations (though widespread use of contraception, despite the position of the Catholic church) and on landholding patterns (since the division of property among heirs limited the inheritance of profitable properties). Rural crises and the 'depopulation of the countryside' meant a stagnation of rural population, a phenomenon which had been apparent since the end of the nineteenth century. The lack of population growth and the resulting lack of a reservoir of manpower would later be cited as a cause of France's defeat by the Germans in 1940; ironically during the depression of the 1930s, however, the demographic contraction benefited France.

Germany

Germany was devastated by the human and economic costs of the First World War and the collapse of the Hohenzollern monarchy. The socialist government established in 1918 pleased few; right and left-wing uprisings demonstrated the hatred many felt for the new regime. The problems returned soldiers faced remaking their lives in the new society proved particularly intractable and dangerous to the republic. From 1919 until 1933, when it was overthrown by Hitler, Weimar had to deal with disaffected citizens, economic problems and political pressures. Tracing the decline and fall of the Weimar Republic is partly a question of understanding these social grievances, which created groups fertile for the demagoguery of men like Hitler. Many believed defeat had not come on the battlefield; rather, they thought that Germany had been betrayed. Some said Germany had been 'stabbed in the back' by the socialist politicians, while others singled out the Jews, whom they blamed for 'poisoning' Germany. Soldiers were often from lower middle-class or rural backgrounds, already imbued with conservative or anti-Semitic beliefs, and immediately on returning from the front began to manifest their discontent by forming illegitimate armed bands ready to subvert the republic. But the workers of Germany were also aggrieved. For many, the establishment of a socialist republic seemed a dream come true; yet they quickly found that the Weimar government would not be a revolutionary one. Many were further radicalised and supported the Communist Party, which preached class warfare; following Lenin's philosophy, they hoped to turn the imperialist war that was the First World War into a class war. In 1919 and

1923 they were brutally suppressed by the government, creating another marginalised social group.

Then in the early 1920s, much of the middle class was threatened by economic crisis and thereby alienated from the parliamentary government of Weimar. Particularly affected during the hyperinflation of 1923 were the middle-class individuals and families who lived on rent, interest dividends and fixed incomes such as pensions. Bank accounts became worthless within a few weeks in Germany in 1923; since the middle classes were precisely those with a propensity and the ability to put aside part of their earnings in savings, they were the ones whose nest eggs were wiped out. A ditty from the inflation period sums it up: 'We are drinking away our grandma's/Little capital/And her first and second mortgage, too'. Thousands of middle-class and lower middle-class savers were left penniless, disenchanted and open to the arguments of those who preached a restoration of Germany's fortunes.

It was the poor, however, who suffered worst from inflation and speculation. In 1923, 23 per cent of trade unionists in Germany were out of work and 47 per cent worked only part-time, while a quarter of the schoolchildren in Berlin, according to a government official, suffered from malnutrition. Photographs from the time show the poor trying to scrounge for food in wastepaper barrels and carving up the carcasses of dead horses. It was reported that letterboxes were plundered for the sake of stamps, that door handles and brass ornaments were stolen and that lead was removed from roofs. An English writer living in Germany reported that he bought a box of matches with a ten-mark note on which someone had scribbled: 'For these ten marks, I sold my virtue'. (The writer, the Englishman Malcolm Cowley, wrote a short story about the event, for which he earned ten million marks, which he used to buy his mistress a pair of synthetic stockings.)

Other Germans profited from the hyperinflation. One of them was Hugo Stinnes. Already the owner of the German-Luxemburg Mining Company and the Rhenish-Westphalian Electric Company before the war, he was a wealthy man. During the inflation, he bought up huge forests to supply pit props for his mines; he also acquired the largest coal mine in

Europe, and invested in iron and steel plants in Hungary and chemical, aluminium and timber factories in Rumania. Stinnes also bought up 150 newspapers and periodicals. By his death in 1925, he had a large share in 69 construction companies, 66 chemical, paper and sugar works, 59 mines, 57 banks and insurance companies, 56 steel and iron works, 49 brown coal works, 37 oil fields and petroleum factories, 100 metallurgical works, 389 commercial and transport concerns, 83 railway and shipping companies and over 100 other businesses. In 1923, seeing the misery of his fellow Germans, Hugo Stinnes magnanimously decided to double his tipping rate.

During 1923 the rich became richer, foreigners lived cheaply, the poor became poorer and those on the borderline between working-class poverty and lower middle-class security were either ruined or found their position more precarious. This dislocation, added to the unsure fortunes of the Weimar Republic, the inheritance of the defeat of 1918 and the aborted revolution of 1919, created grave social problems for Germany which were not resolved during the prosperous years after 1925. Largely because of this, Weimar society in retrospect seems schizophrenic: the avant-garde of Berlin versus the struggles of the masses, the wealth of businessmen versus the poverty of workers, the increasing appeal of both the far right and the far left.

Nordic Europe

At the end of the First World War, all of the Nordic countries retained elements of their pre-industrial ascriptive and rank-ordered societies, where prestige and status remained largely conditional on birth. Membership in the upper classes continued to provide certain privileges for education, status and political power; for instance, only three per cent of the entrants to the Swedish military officer training college came from working-class backgrounds in the mid-1920s, and the nobility still dominated the higher echelons of Sweden's bureaucracy. The hardships of the war's final years exacerbated social conflict; the strikes and riots in Sweden and Norway appeared genuinely revolutionary, and in

Finland the conflict between left and right escalated into full-scale civil war. However, the war also accelerated political and social change. The right to vote was extended to virtually all adults; in Denmark, for example, domestic servants who lived in their employers' households were enfranchised in 1915. With economic growth, industrialisation and some war profiteering throughout the region, a new upper class of bank directors, industrialists and wholesale merchants was emerging. The role of agriculture declined; the share of the population depending on farming and forestry declined in Sweden from 49 per cent in 1910 to 39 per cent in 1930.

Social and cultural cleavages existed along lines similar to the rest of Europe. Tensions between urban and rural residents – reflected in Norway by the different dialects spoken in the towns and countryside – were heightened by larger currents of migration to cities. The chronic agricultural crises of the 1920s and 1930s drove many from the land, and the bitterness of those remaining found expression in the rise of agrarian parties. Tensions existed as well between the members of the established Lutheran church and both Catholics and members of the free churches. Life for the common folk was perhaps better than in other regions of Europe, but much misery remained. Housing in both town and country in Sweden was especially inadequate and overcrowded. If increasing numbers of farmers' children entered university (the gateway to the bureaucracy), upward mobility was less common in the working-class milieu.

Nevertheless, despite several instances of confrontation, Nordic societies achieved a greater social harmony than other regions of Europe in the interwar period and avoided the political polarisation common elsewhere. An important source of stability was the role played by the bureaucracy. The wealth of the industrial and commercial elite still gave them less prestige than membership in the bureaucracy, the acknowledged apex of northern society. However, though socially exclusive, the bureaucracy did not act exclusively in the class interests of its members. The prewar tradition of centrally-administered reform legislation continued. Nordic bureaucrats proved willing to work with socialist ministers, in sharp contrast to other western European countries. They also proved more receptive to new ideas emerging from the universities, especially those of the 'Stockholm school' of economists regarding the active role government could play in managing the economy. In addition, the dispersed pattern of industrial development, the 'self-help' movement within the labour unions and the widespread net of cooperative associations of both producers and consumers all worked to reduce social tension and make communication between the government and interest groups easier.

The exception was Finland. The civil war in 1918 left deep and bitter divisions between classes, as well as nationality problems between Finns and the Russian and Swedish minorities. A protest movement which emerged in 1929 combined rural, clerical and anti-communist elements and led to an attempted coup in 1932. Finnish manufacturing still supported only 16 per cent of the population in 1930, and the 70 per cent still dependent on agriculture and forestry suffered from the decline in world markets. In the absence of a firm national consensus, threatening disputes with neighbouring great powers and a tendency towards authoritarian militarism, Finland between the wars more nearly resembled the Baltic and eastern European states than the other Nordic nations.

The Soviet Union

While the western European societies were trying to 'recast bourgeois Europe' or to reconcile experimentation with conservatism, the Soviet Union was making a concerted effort to change society. Russia had suffered through almost seven years of war, civil war and foreign intervention, and the Bolshevik government had to change course several times to keep the economy going, consolidate its power and try to put its theories into practice. The aristocracy was abolished, land distributed to the peasantry and most businesses and industries nationalised. Yet the government had found it was impossible to implement all of its programmes immediately and had made some major concessions; the New Economic Policy allowed a certain amount of private trade and industry, and the government had stopped the forced grain requisitions which had alienated the peasants. During the 1920s the government attempted to satisfy some of the peasants' and workers' desires and at the same time move towards a fully socialist society. The difficulty lay in the conflict between old structures and habits, such as the desire of the peasants to own land, and new groups, such as the communist elite, with their own demands and theories.

A broad range of legislation profoundly affected Russian institutions. The influence of the Russian Orthodox Church, a pillar of tsarist society, was reduced by the avowedly atheist regime. State and church were separated and the land of the church and monasteries was confiscated; the church's influence on education was eliminated, and only civil marriages were recognised. The Soviet government aimed not only to reduce the church's corporate power but also to lessen the importance of religion for the individual and so create a secular society. Such a development was unprecedented in Europe and substantially altered the focal points for many in the population. The new government also reorganised education; a 1917 decree mandated an immediate effort to wipe out illiteracy. Henceforth education was to be uniform, free and mandatory for both males and females up to the age of 17 years. In a related development, concessions to the national minorities in the Soviet Union included the teaching of the many non-Russian languages. The new Family Code of 1918 greatly reduced the power of fathers over their families and guaranteed the independence of each family member. Divorce was made available to both husbands and wives on demand, at a time when it was illegal in most European nations, and even abortion was legalised. Deeply shocked, the regime's detractors elsewhere in Europe claimed that the government encouraged 'free love' among its citizens.

Mediterranean Europe

Italy under Fascism was quite a different matter from France, Germany or Russia. The arrival of Mussolini to power in 1922 brought to the fore a group of conservative, largely rural property owners, suspicious of cultural experimentation and terrified of 'Bolshevism'. They imprinted the country with their nationalist fervour, which meant a subordination of social differences to the ideals of their messianic leader. Mussolini's economic policies favoured the elite, and they in turn provided him with much support. In the name of economic self-sufficiency, Mussolini levied high import duties and granted subsidies to businesses, which protected the interests of the industrial and agrarian elites. The establishment of state-controlled firms permitted the concentration of capital in the hands of those who ran the economy and benefited from government policies.

If Fascism was good for landowners and industrialists, at least initially, it was less good for labour. Workers had to surrender their hard-earned eight-hour day. Real wages plummeted; farm labourers, for example, lost 50–70 per cent of their purchasing power from 1926 to 1932. The official wage index, in fact, showed such a terrible downturn that Mussolini suspended publication of the document. The peasants waited for land reform. Mussolini had promised to break up the large estates but never did so. In 1930, some 3,500 large estates of over 500 hectares comprised a fifth of the land under cultivation. The large landowners grew wealthier because of the rising price of wheat, thanks to government tariffs and subsidies, but the peasants' condition deteriorated. Many of the Italian peasants, particularly in the south, were still sharecroppers with little security of tenure, inefficient farming methods and low standards of living. These conditions had obtained before 1922, but then the possibility of emigration to America had provided some alternative. Now, however, the United States drastically restricted immigration. In 1920, some 350,000 Italians entered the United States but in 1924 only 4,000 were admitted. Mussolini was also opposed to emigration and restricted the movement of the population; along with his encouragement of large families (through premiums to married couples and parents), this aggravated the problem of overpopulation in the countryside.

Mussolini tried to pacify Italians with his quest to recreate a Roman empire and to regenerate Italy. Some public works projects such as highway construction had a positive effect on the economy but others such as the Fascist monuments were window-dressing. The Fascist regime placed much emphasis on ceremonies, but Mussolini's Fascism never established a totalitarian stranglehold over Italy. Opposition newspapers continued to appear throughout the 1920s; in fact, their circulation was higher than that of the official Fascist newspaper. Professors were forced to take an oath of loyalty to the government, but strict allegiance was never entirely enforced. Researchers sometimes tailored their works to reflect positively on the regime – the historian Gioacchino Volpe wrote a new introduction to his book on medieval heresies to make it more politically relevant – but a certain freedom did exist for those not directly condemning the regime. Debate was allowed on such questions as educational policy; some theorists advocated all-out propagandising, while others argued for a critical training. New courses were instituted to teach Fascist doctrines and to emphasise the role of great men in history, and textbooks were required to conform to the aims of the regime. Youth associations for 'young Fascists' attained great popularity but not so much for their Fascist ideals as for their sponsoring of sports competitions. Similarly, Mussolini earned and maintained much of his popularity (at least until the invasion of Ethiopia) not because of his policies but because of his posing as a national redeemer.

Social conditions elsewhere in southern Europe changed little during the interwar years. Political disputes, the international agricultural depression and the entrenchment of the elites all worked against substantial social evolution. The masses were peasants, and agriculture remained the most important economic activity. Illiteracy remained high – three-quarters of the population in Portugal, for example – and the manifestations of consumer society, such as motor cars, were not much visible in southern Europe. Low levels of industrialisation meant the absence of a significant factory proletariat, and the workers' ideology was more often anarchism than orthodox Marxism. The ruling classes continued to debate the questions of monarchism versus republicanism, the relations between church and state and national regeneration as they had before the war. The peasants, with a standard of living that barely rose during the interwar years, tried to make the best of their poor situation and supported any political movement which promised to improve their lot.

The result was increasing discontent in all groups. Strikes, bombings, assassinations and coups marked public life. Violence reflected underlying social dissatisfaction and stagnation, yet none of the changes proposed seemed to satisfy a majority. The most important initiative, considering the role of agriculture, concerned land reform. In Greece, the government did carry out land redistribution. The Greek government had passed a major piece of land reform legislation in 1917 which had the result of establishing 130,000–140,000 families as landowners through the expropriation of large estates. A total of 1,684 estates were broken up and land provided to families numbering about a million persons in Greece during the 1920s, proportionately one of the largest redistributions of land ever made. In Spain, the new republican government passed an agrarian statute in 1932 which allowed the expropriation of grandees' property without compensation and that of other large holders with compensation but the programme had not been completely implemented before the beginning of the civil war in 1936. In Portugal, a proposal for rural reorganisation and the parcelling of private property in 1924–5 died with the fall of the left-wing government.

The upper classes' position remained secure. In Spain, the republicans instituted various reforms, but none was incompatible with capitalism or the power of the elite; income taxes were raised but at the top of the scale took only 7.7 per cent of income. The army, always in a privileged position, retained its power, as shown by the coups engineered by army officers in Spain in 1923, Portugal in 1926 and Greece in 1936, and by the victory of Franco in Spain in 1939. The church, another pillar of the establishment, suffered several reverses, notably with the separation of church and state in Portugal before the First World War and in Spain with the 1931 constitution. But the authoritarian rulers of the 1920s and 1930s enjoyed the support of the church, and the Vatican made friends with the strongmen with the 1929 Lateran Treaty and a 1940 concordat with Portugal; Franco posed as a defender of the faith, and the non-religious Mussolini largely left the church in peace. In Greece, Orthodoxy remained unchallenged. Thus, throughout the Mediterranean, the church retained both its influence on governments and its social and cultural role at the local level. Finally, a pro-government intellectual elite maintained its role, if only because dissidents were silenced through censorship, exile or imprisonment.

Eastern Europe

The states of eastern Europe between the wars, burdened by economic underdevelopment, political insecurity and unresolved questions of nationalism, were forced to cater simultaneously to the often contradictory demands of a large peasant population, a nascent industrial labour force and a powerful entrenched elite. The states were overwhelmingly rural and agricultural. Peasants made up 34 per cent of the population in Czechoslovakia and 55 per cent in Hungary, but in other countries the proportion was much higher: 68 per cent in Poland, 75 per cent in Yugoslavia, 78 per cent in Rumania and 80 per cent in Bulgaria. Productivity was low. In Bulgaria, Hungary, Yugoslavia and Rumania, the average production of wheat per hectare in the 1930s was about a third that of Denmark. Technology was minimal; in Rumania, for example, there was only 1 plough for every 2.1 holdings. Living conditions were also substandard. The mortality rate for infants was as much as four times higher in eastern than in western Europe, and such diseases as tuberculosis, which had almost disappeared in the west, were widespread. Housing was overcrowded, and peasants suffered from malnutrition. Illiteracy was commonplace. Few alternatives to peasant life existed, because of the slow development of an industrial sector and the choking off of immigration into the United States. During the 1920s migration to more industrialised western European countries provided an alternative, but with the depression, many eastern Europeans were forced to leave their host countries.

At the end of the First World War several of the governments of eastern Europe undertook programmes of land redistribution similar to those of southern Europe. Theoretically, this was evidence of their modern outlook and desire to improve the life of the masses; but the project also testified to the governments' fear of 'Bolshevism' and desire to win peasants over to the support of the regimes. The government of Rumania voted a land reform in 1918 and by 1930 over four million hectares of land had been redistributed. More modest programmes came into force in Czechoslovakia and Yugoslavia. Poland's rulers were less interested in the idea, but from 1921 to 1937, a total of 2.5 million hectares were redistributed. In Hungary, a land distribution scheme was discussed but little actual change took place. The result was that large estates remained numerous in Poland and Hungary, but elsewhere in eastern Europe, small properties became the norm. The disparities in landholdings, even after the reforms, were obvious; in Czechoslovakia, while holdings of under 5 hectares (71 per cent in all properties) accounted for 23 per cent of the total land, estates of over 100 hectares (only 0.5 per cent of all properties) accounted for 16 per cent of land, and in Hungary properties of over 1,000 hectares, 0.1 per cent of the landholdings, comprised 30 per cent of the land. These disparities kept the peasantry in a state of economic submission to large landowners, who could also exercise inordinate political and cultural influence. The division of properties had partially satisfied peasants' land hunger, but it had created holdings too small to farm profitably. The opposition to cooperatives, another manifestation of anti-Bolshevism, meant that many peasants continued to live at subsistence level in the interwar years just as before the First World War.

The land reforms did not affect the peasantry alone. The dispossessed landowners looked for other sources of income and took jobs in the state bureaucracy or moved into such fields as finance. Such changes did away with the traditional pattern of rural dominance by a landed elite. But the upper classes in eastern Europe were far from homogeneous; in Hungary, the upper class was largely German or Jewish, not Magyar, while in the Balkan peninsula, the upper class was very little developed because of the predominance of subsistence farming. In Poland, the old aristocracy, the *szlachta,* had for long been impoverished and without real authority. And in areas of greater industrialisation – western Poland, Silesia and Bohemia – a class of capitalist entrepreneurs already existed and consolidated its authority in the interwar period. Almost everywhere in eastern Europe, the lower middle classes expanded with the recruitment of new members, largely from the peasantry. Peasants became schoolteachers, public servants or clergymen in larger numbers, achieving a certain social mobility for themselves and expanding the national bourgeoisies of their countries. Clientelism and patronage continued to play a greater role in advancement than in the west, and the connection between the state and the economy was strong.

The industrial workforce was still small in eastern Europe. The most industrialised labour force was in Czechoslovakia, where 37 per cent of the population worked in industry, followed by Austria with 33 per cent. In Hungary, the figure was 20 per cent and in Greece 16 per cent, but elsewhere in eastern Europe, less than 10 per cent of the population worked in industry. Such workers as there were existed in poor conditions and were badly paid; political organisations were not well developed, and rural interests maintained a predominance in government. The small number of workers largely accounts for the development of populist movements during the interwar years and the relative failure of socialism in eastern Europe, notwithstanding the successful Bolshevik revolution in rural Russia.

A continuing problem for eastern European societies, in addition to economic difficulties, was the mixture of nationalities. The establishment of independent nation-states after the dissolution of the Austro-Hungarian empire had been an effort to resolve questions of nationalism, but many of the states remained ethnically diverse. The census of 1921 indicated a population in Poland which was 69 per cent Polish, 14 per cent Ukranian and 8 per cent Jewish. Czechoslovakia was 62 per cent Czech and 23 per cent German; Bulgaria had over 600,000 Turks and Tatars in a population of 6 million; Yugoslavia had approximately 9 million Serbs and Croats, over 1 million Slovenes, 506,000 Germans, 468,000 Magyars and 440,000 Albanians. Tensions existed among many of the national groups, the irredentist aspirations of outsiders further aggravated ethnic disputes, and a rising tide of anti-Semitism threatened the large Jewish groups of eastern Europe and the Balkans.

THE DEPRESSION AND THE 1930s

The 1920s came to an end with the depression. The depression's origin and impact varied, but eventually the crisis engulfed all of Europe except the Soviet Union. Socially, unemployment and its repercussions posed a fundamental challenge to the existing order. In Britain and Germany the numbers of unemployed peaked, at 2.3 and 6 million respectively, in 1933. In countries with larger agricultural sectors, recorded unemployment was lower; just under a million in Italy in 1933 and 454,000 in France in 1936. Figures in all countries understate the actual numbers of unemployed, since many more were temporarily without jobs or underemployed. The amount of concealed unemployment was larger in agricultural regions, as unemployed industrial workers went 'home' to their villages and rural artisans and shopkeepers went bankrupt without being recorded. Agricultural markets collapsed as well, and throughout central, southern and eastern Europe those farmers who managed to retain their land retreated into a subsistence level of living.

For the unemployed, the first task was to survive. Malnutrition was widespread, and lack of food caused a higher incidence of certain diseases. In Durham, a medical officer for a charitable organisation reported in 1933: 'Most of our children are suffering not so much from tuberculosis as from starvation. Seventy-five per cent of the cases admitted to the society's sanatorium were suffering from under-nourishment'. Tuberculosis, scarlet fever and rickets became more common, particularly among children, whose resistance was worn down by the lack of adequate nourishment. The poor suffered the worst; in Newcastle, only 16 per cent of middle-class children were anaemic, but 81 per cent of the children of the poor were, and the incidence of pneumonia was 8 times as high and cases of bronchitis were 10 times more common among poor children in 1933.

The depression aggravated social tensions. In some areas, observers remarked on an increase in crime. An English electrician-turned-burglar admitted: 'Some of the people I meet have been criminal almost from birth, but I estimate that fifty per cent have drifted into burglary through bad economic conditions'. Family relations became tenser. An unemployed engineer in Britain said: 'Eventually, after the most heartbreaking period of my life, both my wife and son, who had just commenced to earn a few shillings, told me *to get out*, as I was living on them and taking the food they needed'. Psychologists pointed out that 'unemployment tends to make people more emotionally unstable'. Workers came to resemble mental patients 'suffering from anxiety neurosis'. They were given to fits of irrational spending or desperate attempts to win a fortune. Outside Brussels a group of workers spent their income buying and keeping pigeons in the hope that some day the pigeons might win a race. Observers described the progression in attitudes from optimism through pessimism to fatalism, 'the increase of inferiority feeling, the destruction of family relationships, and the weakening of interest in politics and organization with an increasing length of unemployment'. One writer summed up much of the disenchantment:

> Morning after morning, all over the immense, damp, dreary town and the packing case colonies of huts in the suburb allotments, young men were waking up to another, workless empty day to be spent as they could best contrive; selling boot laces, begging, playing draughts in the hall of the Labour Exchange, hanging about urinals, opening the doors of cars, helping with crates in the market, gossiping, lounging, stealing, overhearing racing tips, sharing stumps of cigarette ends picked up in the gutter.

Britain

Such personal accounts of the depression confirm the statistical evidence of unemployment, falling wages and human misery. In *I Was One of the Unemployed*, Max Cohen tells of being dismissed from his work as a cabinetmaker on one hour's notice. The next weeks were spent looking for a job, any job, living in squalid housing, reporting daily to the Labour Exchange and spending his waking hours trying to find food. In the Labour Exchange, he saw the armies of those out of work:

> I had never before seen faces so gaunt and white as these; not white – grey. And I came to recognise this gaunt grey pallor as the true hallmark of the chronically unemployed: the hallmark of those who have undergone years of underfeeding, of feeding on cheap imitations of food, of never knowing what it is to have a full stomach. Many of the faces were covered with angry-red blotches. This, too, was because the food they ate lacked vitamins and nourishment, was without the power to stave off rust and decay .... I lived in dread of those empty, boring, monotonous days of walking about searching for a job that was never there, and returning to a lodging bereft of warmth and stimulating food. The emptiness of the belly, and the accompanying tension and worry, produced an emptiness of the brain and the spirit.

A worker without a job for a month fell under the rule of the means test: if he had any income or lived with relatives whom the government thought capable of supporting him, he was not allowed to receive the dole. 'The result', says Cohen, 'was that he was debarred from living with those whom it was most economical and natural to live with, and whom it was possible to repay with all or most of his dole'. Families were thus split apart, and overcrowding in tenements increased. Time was wasted applying for jobs that did not eventuate, and days were spent queuing up for the dole.

Another observer of the depression – and author of a classic document on the crisis, *The Road to Wigan Pier* – was George Orwell. In 1937 Orwell journeyed to Yorkshire to visit the collieries:

> On a Sunday, for instance, a mine seems almost peaceful.

The time to go there is when the machines are roaring and the air is black with coal dust, and when you can actually see what the miners have to do. At those times the place is like hell, or at any rate like my own mental picture of hell. Most of the things one imagines in hell are there – heat, noise, confusion, darkness, foul air, and, above all, unbearably cramped space. Everything except the fire, for there is no fire down there except the feeble beams of Davy lamps and electric torches which scarcely penetrate the clouds of coal dust.

He experienced the heat and dust of the mine faces, saw that miners had to walk as much as three miles underground before arriving at their work site, and that they returned home black with coal dust since most pitheads lacked facilities for bathing. Orwell also noted the difficulties of the out of work, when 'keeping warm – is almost the sole preoccupation of a single unemployed man in winter' and men took refuge in cinemas because they were at least heated buildings. He found little political consciousness among the working class, only resignation: 'They have neither turned revolutionary nor lost their self-respect; merely they have kept their tempers and settled down to make the best of things on a fish-and-chip standard'.

The depression did not do away with class differences in England; rather, it increased the gap between the rich and the poor. In 1929, 110,000 Englishmen had incomes of at least 2,000 pounds a year and 15.5 million survived on incomes less than 250 pounds; in 1938, 105,000 still earned top incomes, while 20.3 million were in the bottom category. The rigidities of the class system, both quantitative and qualitative, remained impervious.

France

France did not feel the effects of the depression until later than Britain and Germany. The effects of the depression were less severe in France, partly because of the somewhat lesser importance of industry and because of France's greater self-sufficiency in foodstuffs (about 80 per cent of French food was produced in France). But if the crisis did not reach France until 1932, grave difficulties persisted until the end of the 1930s, and France had not fully recovered by the beginning of the Second World War. The major manifestation in the social arena was unemployment; the figure of over 400,000 Frenchmen who received government assistance at the height of the depression disguises a much larger amount of underemployment and partial unemployment, especially among women, older workers and unskilled men. The labour force probably contracted by two million jobs. Most immediately affected were the foreign workers. In the 1920s, France had imported hundreds of thousands of workers for both agriculture and industry, largely from eastern Europe. The largest number came from Poland, where government bureaux recruited migrant labour. With the depression, an estimated 600,000 were laid off and returned home. The departure of these migrants cushioned the native French workforce against higher levels of unemployment, although, conversely, it worsened the situation in the home countries of the migrants.

Social tensions grew markedly during the 1930s, both because of the depression and because of international developments. The peasants were becoming increasingly politicised, often supporting conservative populist leaders; right-wing organisations such as the Action Française enjoyed wider support. A major demonstration in Paris in February 1934 by the right-wing forces was seen by some as a failed attempt to seize power; then the victory in the elections of 1936 of the Popular Front, a group led by the Radicals and socialists but with the support of the communists, implied that the pendulum had swung in the other direction. The new government of Léon Blum undertook a programme to satisfy some worker demands with paid vacations, a shorter working week and other concessions. But in the end the experiment satisfied neither workers nor employers, and the end of the decade saw France still divided into different ideological camps.

Germany

The depression plunged Weimar Germany into turmoil once again. The crisis in Germany paralleled conditions existing elsewhere in Europe: workers without jobs, families trying to scrape together enough money to put food on the table, demands for some solution to the problems and increasingly vocal and active extremist groups. The remnants of Weimar were now in tatters, and Berlin's reputation for licentiousness became a symptom of economic desperation. Violence was endemic, and demagogues looked for scapegoats to blame for Germany's plight. Economic difficulties aggravated social discontent and political recriminations, leaving both government and society in a shambles. In January 1933 Adolf Hitler stepped into the breach. The depression did not bring Hitler to power, but economic conditions did help to create the context in which the Nazis could assume office. Nazism was a motley creed which promised to restore order and economic prosperity and to make Germany great once again. Hitler's appeals found an avid audience among out-of-work Germans, businessmen who felt threatened, farmers, the middle class, bitter soldiers and opportunists; the regimentation of his party contrasted with the anarchy of Berlin, and his racism promised to purify the German body politic of 'foreign' (primarily, Jewish) influences.

Hitler spent his first year in office consolidating his authority and creating the terrorist instruments of his regime. Police agencies extended their grasp into previously private spheres. Nazi storm troopers attacked Jewish businesses, and legislation began the process of stripping Jews of their civil rights. Nazis closed down the cabarets and brothels of Berlin. They attacked Magnus Hirschfeld's institute of sexual research, destroying archives pertaining to sexuality in general and homosexuality in particular. They conducted book-burnings, destroying works that did not conform to Nazism. Intellectuals were forced to leave the country or were put under arrest. Resistance to the new regime seemed hopeless, and few dared attempt it. By the late 1930s the Nazi government had expelled most of the dissidents and stifled the innovation that was a hallmark of Weimar. The innovative architecture of the Bauhaus had been replaced by a sort of Nazi neoclassicism, gigantic edifices planned so their ruins would still be impressive milennia hence. The paintings of the avant-garde artists were banned in favour of an official art glorifying German strength. The movies which had made Germany a cinematographic pioneer were now replaced on the screen by propaganda. Having destroyed Weimar society, the Nazis were now attempting to build a new society. The new society was a society in uniform, characterised by regimentation and militarisation, puritanism and sexual repression (girls were to become wives and mothers exclusively) and a cult of the party and the *Führer*.

One of the main interests of the Hitler government was labour. The Nazi creed claimed to surmount the class struggle and the party and government fought against any notion of class warfare; trade unions were eliminated, and the workforce was reduced to docility. One of the few benefits of the regime was the creation of greater employment through public works programmes and, later, by rearmament. From 1933 to 1939, employment in the metal industries increased by over 150 per cent and in the building trades by over 210 per cent; since Hitler favoured heavy industry, employment in this sector expanded considerably more rapidly than jobs in consumer goods. By the late 1930s, Germany enjoyed something resembling full employment. Wages had also risen by approximately 50 per cent in the 4 years after Hitler's accession to power. Recovery from the depression meant that the standard of living was also moving upwards; for example, the calorie deficiency in diets evident in 1933 had been reversed by the middle of the decade. Fixed rents and a decline in the cost of certain household commodities meant that the worker could live in more comfortable conditions under the Nazi regime than under the Weimar government. These gains for the workforce were accomplished at the price of severe restrictions on labour movement and the suppression of dissent. The eight-hour day remained the theoretical ideal of Nazism, but workers were often encouraged or coerced to work overtime. From 1934 onwards, a series of laws restricting labour mobility prevented migration to the larger cities of

Germany, and ultimately introduced compulsory registration of workers and a sort of internal passport.

Nazism instituted a cult of work. Slogans such as 'Work Ennobles' and 'Labour Liberates' – 'Arbeit Macht Frei', the cruelly ironic slogan carved on the entrance to the death camp at Auschwitz – testified to the regime's consecration of controlled labour. Competitions were held for workers, and the winners of this annual Reich Vocational Competition were brought to Berlin to meet the *Führer*. The motto of 'worker of the head and hand' supposedly symbolised the union of blue and white-collar labourers, and the slogan was personified in a parade in which the head of the University of Heidelberg and a manual labourer rode through the streets together.

The 'Strength Through Joy' organisation, a government establishment, organised holidays and cultural activities for workers as a way to propagandise the proletariat and reward servants of the regime. An official proudly claimed: 'The demands for liberty, equality, and fraternity, with which the German worker was betrayed by liberal-Marxist demagogues, have become reality, thanks to National Socialism'. A certain Nazi fraternity there might well have been, but liberty was missing and equality was a myth. Although Nazism claimed to have created a classless society, wage differentials were still very much in evidence. Furthermore, the National Socialist Party favoured the career advancement of its stalwarts, and the major bankers and financiers earned incomes much in excess of those of simple workers. Social mobility did exist for many Germans, but statistically the division of the labour force changed little during the first years of Nazi rule. Employment in agriculture declined from 29 to 27 per cent from 1933 to 1939, while the industrial workforce remained stable at 41 per cent of the active population.

The Soviet Union

The 1930s marked a substantial change from the experimentation of the 1920s in the Soviet Union. Stalin's rise to power signalled a regimentation of society and alterations in the philosophy of the state. Stalin's effort to build 'socialism in one country' required a continuation of the revolution in Russian society but narrowed its focus onto the problem of industrial development. Bad harvests and the refusal of the peasants to sell their grain to the government at low prices prompted Stalin to undertake a collectivisation of agriculture in 1929. Resistance was widespread, though disorganised and ultimately hopeless. Peasants fought against officials, killed and ate the animals which were to be taken from them anyway, planted as little as they could and attempted to hoard enough food to survive. The government retaliated with deportations, summary executions, systematic confiscation of all food supplies and embargoes on shipments of food into 'offending' areas. The famines in those areas therefore represented deliberate policy, intended to eliminate resistance. Taking the average for the entire Soviet Union, consumption of bread and potatoes in rural areas dropped one-fifth and consumption of animal products by half.

In the early 1930s, some engineers and foreigners had been arrested and executed for sabotaging or 'wrecking' the industrialisation programme. In December 1934 the purges began to become a mass phenomenon after a group of about a hundred alleged accomplices in the assassination of the powerful party leader in Leningrad, Sergei Kirov, were shot. Now the purges spread in widening circles, the family and associates of each person arrested themselves being arrested, then their families and associates, and then theirs. The terror reached its peak from late 1937 to mid-1938. At one point orders were issued simply to arrest given percentages of the population. Three spectacular 'show trials' in 1936, 1937 and 1938 paraded famous Bolshevik leaders before the world, all of whom confessed to fantastic charges of treason, conspiracy and sabotage. The confessions shocked world opinion; explanations ranged from torture and an effort to win a reprieve, to devotion so complete that even public confession to imaginary crimes could be justified if it served the cause. Estimates of the total number of victims range from 5 to 30 million; the higher figures lump the purges, famine and collectivisation together. Millions died from hunger or because they resisted collectivisation. However, the victims of the purges, perhaps eight million arrested, were not masses of ordinary citizens, but predominantly the new elite of Soviet society; administrative and managerial personnel, intellectuals, army officers and especially members of the Communist Party. Millions of undernourished men and women slaved in mines and forests and in constructing canals, dams and railways in the Soviet Union's subarctic regions; the fate of those millions in the labour camps cast a pall over the remainder of Soviet society.

An effort to tighten state control of culture and personal life also marked the 1930s. Decrees in 1935 and 1936 increased parental control over children, made divorce more difficult to obtain and prohibited abortion except for medical reasons. Marriage and large families were encouraged – women who bore ten children were given the title of 'Mother Hero' – and behaviour regarded as bourgeois decadence (such as homosexuality) was outlawed. The experimentation which marked Soviet education during the 1920s was ended, and schools began to teach communist doctrine and technical subjects in a traditional and disciplinarian fashion, emphasising rote memorisation. History books were altered to follow the approved interpretation of Russian and Soviet history. Elements of nationalism were resurrected with Ivan the Terrible and Peter the Great now being seen as national heroes rather than exploiters, and Stalin's own history of the Communist Party was written to underline his personal role in the 1917 revolution. Experimental literature, abstract painting, contemporary music and modern architecture all fell into disfavour. 'Socialist realism' ruled the novel and painting – stories recounting the saga of building a new steel plant to fulfil a quota assigned in the Five-Year Plan and pictures of earnest young workers and farmers struggling forward to the distant goal of socialism.

The new cult of hard work was embodied in the new hero, a worker named Stakhanov, a coalminer who hewed 102 tons of coal in one shift, and exceeded his quota by 1,400 per cent. (Stakhanov actually had discovered ways of rationalising his work by dividing tasks and attacking each systematically, though his 'method' also involved the cooperation of his fellow workers, who did not receive credit for their efforts.) 'Stakhanovites' soon appeared in all industries, held a conference and became the subject for stories, paintings and music in the style of socialist realism. The government used the accomplishments of these 'worker heroes' as justification for raising quotas for all other workers, in some cases by 50 per cent, and for introducing piecework payment and a system of bonuses to force increases in productivity. Women had their role to play as well, as a letter published in *The Woman Worker* in 1936 showed:

> We must help our husbands, fathers, sons and daughters to become Stakhanovites. We must live for their interests and help them to put into effect the suggestions of the great Stalin ... peace at home, comfort, sensible entertainment, cleanliness and tidiness everywhere .... The Stakhanovites' wives cannot remain uneducated, undeveloped: we, too, must learn .... Some may ask: When? Here we must approach the matter in Stakhanovite fashion. We must arrange our work in such a way that we have time for everything – for housework, for study and for rest.

The Stalinist system largely succeeded in cutting off the Soviet Union from the outside world and forcibly creating a homogeneous and docile population. A broader social process was at work in these developments. Party enrolments in 1929 had been 81 per cent workers, 17 per cent peasants and 2 per cent 'intelligentsia and white collar workers', but enrolments from late 1936 to early 1939 included only 41 per cent workers, 15 per cent peasants, and 44 per cent 'intelligentsia' – scientists, teachers, engineers and technicians, doctors, students and office workers. In the final burst of recruitment in 1939 and 1940, the share of workers dropped below 20 per cent. The new elite certainly constituted a class in the sense of having an identifiable relation to the means of production, as well as in its acceptance of the emerging Soviet ideology. The new Party members were young, recently graduated from the newly-expanded educational institutions. The purges and rapid industrial development both opened paths of advancement, and many were promoted well beyond the level indicated by their age and experience. This young, untried elite had to withstand the onslaught of Nazi Germany; having triumphed, they remained in power, and their values dominated Soviet society and culture for another generation.

9

POLITICS AND IDEOLOGY
1918–39

The First World War led to the fall of the emperors of Germany, Austria-Hungary, Russia and Turkey; the Bolshevik Revolution of 1917 and aborted revolutions in eastern Europe in the years immediately following the war enlarged the spectrum of political choice and confronted Europe with leftist theory put into practice. The establishment of a social democratic republic in Germany heralded a third path between Bolshevik Marxism and the nineteenth-century liberal-conservative ideology, and the exigencies of the depression mandated new approaches to solve economic and social problems. The strong-arm authoritarian rulers of the 1920s were succeeded by the era of the totalitarian state in Germany and the Soviet Union in the 1930s, new governments which tried to establish a total control over society. Then, the end of that decade witnessed a violent confrontation among the old and new ideologies in the civil war in Spain. Extra-parliamentary and formal politics mingled, as movements considering themselves outside the normal configuration of politics emerged and used tactics ranging from general strikes to street brawls and coups d'état to achieve their ends. The institution of universal manhood suffrage – and the opening of the franchise to women in some countries – enlarged the number of participants in politics; even the peasantry, a relatively quiescent mass before the First World War, displayed a new degree of politicisation.

Social and economic developments played a major role in these political metamorphoses. After all, Lenin's revolution posited a state and society based on totally different rules of politics; a socialised economy, the dictatorship of the proletariat and the Communist Party as the 'vanguard' of the working class. The hyperinflation in Germany in 1923 alienated the middle classes from liberal-conservatism, while the depression radicalised substantial segments of the working class. The corporatist state of Mussolini's Italy attempted unsuccessfully to reconcile management and labour, and the 1926 general strike in Britain was 'class war, in polite form'. The rising lower middle class found in reactionary demagoguery the hope of upward social mobility, and many of its members supported such movements as Nazism. Technological innovations – foremost among them the radio – made possible new sorts of propaganda useful for recruiting political support and enforcing the regimentation of society. Questions of nationality and ethnicity occupied important places in politics and the anti-Semitism of the prewar years metamorphosed into Hitler's genocidal 'final solution'.

Interwar international politics was moulded by the Versailles Treaties, the set of documents which formally ended the war. The leaders of the United States, France and Britain were each intent on gaining the maximum of spoils for their country, and the defeated powers, particularly Germany, provided their foraging ground. First, they forced Germany to acknowledge responsibility for the war. Article 231 of the settlement read: 'The Allied and Associated Governments affirm and Germany accepts the responsibility of Germany and her allies for causing all the loss and damage to which the Allied and Associated Governments and their nations have been subjected as a consequence of the war imposed upon them by the aggression of Germany and her allies'. The Allies thereby absolved themselves from, and Germany's new republican leaders were forced to shoulder, a moral burden. Throughout the interwar years, the socialists and republicans of Weimar would be excoriated for having accepted the 'war guilt clause', although their alternatives were uncertain. Furthermore, the Germans were ordered to pay reparations to the Allies for damages caused in the war – although the actual sum was only to be determined after the signature of the treaty. Even some of the Versailles negotiators baulked at this financial burden placed on Germany. John Maynard Keynes resigned from the British delegation and wrote *The Economic Consequences of the Peace*, in which he argued that the reparations payments would bankrupt the new Germany and lessen chances for international reconstruction. Finally, Germany was forced to give up large amounts of territory: Alsace and Lorraine to France, parts of Posen and West Prussia to Poland, Danzig a free city, some border areas to Belgium and Germany's colonies to the Allies.

Paradoxically, the settlement which sought to punish Germany also tried to ensure future European harmony by setting up the League of Nations for conciliation and arbitration of disputes. However, the United States Congress refused to recognise the treaty establishing the League, Germany was not allowed to join until 1926, and the Soviet Union was not a member until 1934. By that date, Germany had already withdrawn and Japan, Italy and Russia were soon to do so as well, leaving the League a shambles.

SUCCESSFUL AND FAILED REVOLUTIONS

The Soviet Union

'The Union of Soviet Socialist Republics is a socialist state of workers and peasants', stated the Soviet constitution. The state established by Lenin and his Bolshevik revolutionaries in the wake of the October Revolution of 1917 was a socialist society based on the common ownership of the means of production and government by the working class. In theory the new state was ruled by the masses of the people in a non-exploitative relationship, with a common dedication to the principles of Marxism-Leninism and the goal of an international proletarian revolution. The class struggle had reached the stage of the overthrow of the aristocracy and bourgeoisie and of the capitalist economy, and the new society was to be one of the workers marching towards the classless society of communism, where the state would in time wither away. In the context of the international situation, this meant a defence of the revolution and the establishment of a 'dictatorship of the proletariat'; more especially, it meant the dominance of the Communist Party.

Lenin was the recognised and unchallenged master of the Party and the nation from 1917 until his death in 1924. Debate within the Party continued, and changes of programme did occur; the switch from War Communism to the New Economic Policy is the prime example. But Lenin insisted all counter-revolutionary groups and ideologies had to be eliminated to secure the gains of October 1917. This was the rationale behind numerous policies – the lack of democracy in government, the establishment of the secret police and the foundation of the Communist (or Third) International as the spearhead of an international Marxist revolution. Lenin intended the Soviet Union to foster international proletarian solidarity and encourage the uprising of the working class; without this, the revolution in Russia would be unsuccessful, and without domestic allegiance to the revolution, that international rebellion could not be achieved.

If the ideology of the new Soviet state differed from that of the rest of Europe, so did its structure. The real innovation was the parallel structure of the state and the Communist Party. Legal government was reserved for the state, manifested in the Supreme Soviet, the national parliament, and exercised through a president, prime minister and cabinet. In practice, the Communist Party was the real ruler of the country on the basis of 'democratic centralism', that is, with power concentrated at the apex of the party. Troubles arose on the death of Lenin, since the Party structure was unclear about the inheritance of control. Lenin's testament said that Trotsky and Stalin were those most suitable to take over his position; the years 1924–8 were consequently marked by rivalry between the two heirs and changing alliances with other top Party leaders. The eventual result was the victory of Stalin and the exile (and later murder) of Trotsky. During the 1930s, both the state and the Party weakened with the creation of a personality cult around Stalin, who posed as the father of the people, the sole interpreter of Marxism and absolute ruler. Along with the industrialisation drive, collectivisation and the end to experimentation in the arts, the purges rid the Soviet Union of all real or imagined opponents to Stalin. He became the first European ruler to create a totalitarian dictatorship, one in which each individual and each institution not only had to conform to his wishes but to champion his ideas and personal merit. Works of scholarship customarily began with an epigraph from Stalin's writings, no matter his expertise (or lack of it) on the subject at hand.

Marxist-Leninist theory and Stalin's personality coloured the Soviet Union's international relations. The Third International, the Comintern, enforced ideological and political allegiance in communist parties outside the USSR just as Stalin demanded total loyalty in his own party. Different creeds, whether social democracy, liberal-conservatism or fascism, were considered part and parcel of bourgeois imperialism, at least until the mid-1930s. As late as 1939, Stalin could still sign a non-aggression pact with Hitler in an effort to keep peace between the countries and with the idea that Hitler's politics were no worse than those of other bourgeois rulers. The Soviet political achievement fell short of its goals; democratic centralism did not mean democracy, and the state did not wither away. Stalin's autocracy did not resolve the question of succession to the leadership of the Party and state. However, some of those dissatisfied with their own governments saw in the USSR the hope for civilisation.

Attempts at revolution

In the aftermath of the war and the collapse of the empires, the time for revolution seemed propitious, and the victory of the Bolsheviks gave hope to Marxists in other countries. In Germany, in November 1918, socialists proclaimed a republic, and in the elections held in January four-fifths of the votes were cast for socialist and democratic parties. For the Social Democratic Party (SPD), this was indeed a revolution; for those further left, however, it was not. The new government not only did not proceed to implement socialist theory – there was no nationalisation of property – but seemed incapable of solving other problems. Unemployment stood at one million during the first six months of the Weimar Republic, a quarter of the total in Berlin alone. Political dissatisfaction was particularly prevalent in the left wing of the Socialist Party. On 30 December 1918, a group of left socialists, the most prominent of whom was Rosa Luxemburg, established the Communist Party of Germany. Luxemburg was a committed revolutionary, as opposed to the 'revisionists' who controlled the SPD. She objected to the ideology of the new government and also to its dismissal of left socialists from their government positions. On 4 January 1919, the Prussian Minister of the Interior dismissed the left socialist chief of police in Berlin, but he refused to leave his post. The following day the communists and other leftists issued a call for action in his support. For the next week, the uprising against the SPD government gripped Berlin. The government used all its forces to put down the insurrection. These included the *Freikorps*, troops recruited from the old imperial army. In the aftermath the police and *Freikorps* murdered Luxemburg and several of her colleagues. So ended the Spartacist Revolution – so called because of the name of the proto-communist group headed by Luxemburg. In the eyes of the government, this was a legitimate victory over a destabilising element in the fragile new republic; for the communists, it was the defeat of a true proletarian revolution. And for many in the general population, the use of the *Freikorps* to suppress workers was a slap in the face, a mistaken tactic which alienated many proletarians from the SPD.

A postscript to the aborted German communist revolution occurred in Bavaria. A separate government had been set up in Munich at the end of 1918 by a moderate socialist. In February 1919, he was assassinated and the workers' councils took over the government under SPD leadership. In April, however, leftist socialists gained the upper hand and a Soviet republic was proclaimed. By the beginning of May, federal troops had defeated the radical Bavarian government and installed their own supporters in power. The incident left many tensions in Bavaria – traditionally a conservative, Catholic area of Germany – and again in 1923, Munich would be the site of an attempted coup, this one a right-wing bid to take power led by General Ludendorff and Adolf Hitler.

In Hungary, the prime minister dissolved the union

between his country and Austria just before the end of the war; within weeks, Hungary was proclaimed a republic under the leadership of a liberal aristocrat. The new government enlarged the suffrage and began to put together a programme for land reform; the prime minister himself set the tone by giving his own estate of 20,000 hectares to the peasants. Yet the question of nationalities and the continued Allied blockade of Hungary posed problems. A change in government brought to power Béla Kun, a socialist who had been a prisoner of war before going to Russia, where he participated in the Bolshevik Revolution. Kun set out to establish a more radical society in Hungary; he nationalised all businesses with 25 or more employees, confiscated church property, seized some one million hectares of land, and put the control of the state in the hands of peasants', soldiers' and workers' councils. Soon the Rumanian army was attacking Hungary. Meanwhile, Kun quarrelled with the trade unions; strikes broke out, and in the countryside, peasant uprisings began, which the government combated with executions. With little support from abroad – since the Soviet Union was preoccupied with its own affairs – and domestic opposition, coupled with the invasion by the Rumanian forces, Kun's position was untenable. On 1 August 1919, after less than five months in office, Kun resigned and left Hungary, bringing to an end the Hungarian Soviet Republic.

A third radical revolution, this one agrarian populist rather than communist, lasted longer, but it, too, was ultimately defeated. At the end of the war in Bulgaria a republic was organised and by the summer of 1919 was dominated by a peasant leader, Alexander Stamboliski. Like Kun, Stamboliski dissolved the large estates – although there were far fewer of them in Bulgaria than in Hungary – and reorganised the legal and taxation systems. He was not a Marxist, and the Communist Party organised strikes against the new government, but Stamboliski made no real attempt to repress them. The main opposition he faced came from the bourgeois politicians, the army and the Internal Macedonian Revolutionary Organisation (IMRO). The Macedonians in Bulgaria objected to Stamboliski's peaceful attitude towards the new state of Yugoslavia, which had inherited the portion of Macedonia formerly belonging to Serbia. The Macedonians murdered Stamboliski's war minister in 1921. Although elections in 1923 brought victory for Stamboliski, in June 1923 a coup organised by the Macedonians, the army and bourgeois participants – and perhaps with the aid of the former king – overthrew the government in Sofia. Stamboliski was turned over to the IMRO terrorists, who tortured and then killed him.

The overthrow of both Kun and Stamboliski was followed by repression of the left. The terror was particularly severe in Bulgaria, where between 10,000 and 30,000 supporters of the progressive regime were executed. In both Hungary and Bulgaria, government reverted to the conservatives and eventually to those further on the right. In Germany, the socialists maintained a strong position in the government during the 1920s, but there too the conservative forces had defeated the SPD by the end of the 1920s, and democracy in Germany, for all practical purposes, was dead several years before the accession of Hitler to power.

PARLIAMENTARY POLITICS IN WESTERN AND NORTHERN EUROPE

Britain

The General Strike of 1926 in Great Britain revealed the social tensions masked by the façade of parliamentary democracy. Yet it was one of the few overt manifestations of these conflicts during the interwar period; politically, Britain muddled through without revolution, a radical change in government or dictatorship. This can be credited to the real alternatives presented by Britain's electoral system and political liberties and also to the capacity of the state to adapt to changing circumstances. New ministries – labour, pensions, health, transport – responded to economic and social needs, while the government managed to keep a subtle control of the broadcasting media through the formation of the British Broadcasting Company (which enjoyed a monopoly) in 1922. The government also pursued public works programmes, although its ideology downplayed government intervention in the economy. Action to increase the supply of housing was necessitated by a real shortage but also by the desire to build 'homes fit for heroes', the returned soldiers. The Unemployment Insurance Acts of 1920–2 set up the system of the 'dole' for those out of work. Such legislation continued prewar developments and laid the foundations for the postwar welfare state in Britain.

The spanner in the works was still Ireland. The British had suppressed the Easter Rebellion of April 1916, but they had failed to stem the independence movement. In 1917 the independence party, the Sinn Fein, declared a republic in Ireland, adopted a constitution and elected a president, but in 1918 the British arrested the new president. A repeat performance occurred in 1919, when the Sinn Fein again declared independence, and the British again suppressed it. In 1920 the British attempted a compromise with legislation setting up separate parliaments for the predominantly Protestant six counties of Northern Ireland, or Ulster, and for the Catholic south, while allowing Irish deputies to sit in Westminster as well. Sinn Fein won all but four of the seats in the south and proceeded to boycott the British-sponsored legislature. Civil war broke out, with fighting in both the south and in Ulster, even though Britain had agreed to give Ireland dominion status as the Irish Free State. In December 1922, the Irish Free State was officially declared, but not until 1938 was an agreement signed which normalised relations between southern Ireland, or Eire as it now styled itself, and Great Britain. Ulster, however, remained part of the United Kingdom, a status which continued to be the main point of contention (and source of frequent violence) between Britain and the Sinn Fein.

A new force emerged in British domestic politics in the 1920s, the Labour Party. It was social democratic rather than socialist and wary of platforms unacceptable to the majority of the electorate. Although many of its members were sympathetic to the Bolshevik revolution, it refused to join the Third International. In 1924 Labour won a majority of the vote. Realising that it lacked a mandate for great changes, however, the labour government moved hesitantly although it did sign a commercial treaty with the Soviet Union. Yet it was brought down after less than a year in office because of fear of communism. A telegram from the head of the Comintern, the Zinoviev telegram, allegedly incited the British to revolution; although the document was almost certainly forged, the suspect Labour Party lost the next elections. The depression brought to power a coalition government in 1931, although participation in it split the Labour Party. A shifting coalition, the National Government, lasted through the decade. The National Governments of the 1930s proved unimaginative in fighting the depression, but Britain did avoid the political extremism which plagued the Continent. Communism counted for little except among a small elite of workers and intellectuals and those who supported the Republicans in the Spanish Civil War. On the right, a British Union of Fascists was organised in 1932; they sported black shirts, organised street demonstrations and resorted to violence, but never constituted a real threat to the British system.

Britain produced the most comprehensive diagnosis of the ills of the interwar economic system and the most effective prescription for their cure, those of John Maynard Keynes. Before the *General Theory of Employment, Interest and Money* appeared in 1936, Keynes immodestly predicted that it would revolutionise professional economics. Keynes incorporated not only the entire analytical apparatus constructed by his teacher Marshall, but all of the criticism and improvements suggested since the publication of Marshall's *Principles* in 1890, especially those of economists in the Nordic countries. Keynes rejected Marshall's assumption of simple rational behaviour and argued instead that because knowledge is not perfect, everyone will attempt to hedge against the future. Hedging leads to hoarding of money, which however affects not the price level but the rate of interest. Adjustment comes through changes in the prices of capital assets. If interest rates decline to the point where the prices of existing capital assets are higher than the cost of producing new ones, an increase in investment will lead to a boom, while an increase in interest rates which lowers the prices of existing assets below the cost of production will choke off investment and create a depression. Therefore Keynes concluded that capital investment is much more volatile than Marshall had thought. Further, spending on investment also affects consumption; the increase in income caused by new investment will raise consumption, but by a lesser amount, with the difference being saved and invested. An increase in investment therefore results in a more than proportional increase in income (the 'multiplier' developed by Keynes' colleague R. F. Kahn). The reverse situation, with declining investment resulting in large declines in income, was the key to understanding the problems of the 1930s. Further, unless output of consumer and investment goods balance, there will be under and over-shooting; the resulting cycles carry the possibility of growth, but also of depression. Keynes thought depression rather more likely because of the role of uncertainty, and noted that if expectations became very pessimistic the economy could fall into stagnation because of insufficient investment.

Insufficient aggregate demand and excessive pessimism had combined to produce the situation of the 1930s. However, once the situation was properly understood, Keynes argued that governments could intervene, adjusting interest rates and their spending to compensate for instability in the system or to make up for deficient aggregate demand. Keynes himself had been giving the same advice since 1924. However, he and others who recommended that governments lower interest rates and increase their own spending to overcome depressions had done so without a convincing theoretical justification, and made no headway against the orthodox argument that only increased interest rates and decreased government budgets would lower prices and wages far enough to restore profitability, raise investment and lead to recovery. Now Keynes could demonstrate that such politics would not only worsen the depression but would actually delay recovery, and his demonstration made converts rapidly. Many of those converts moved into positions of influence during the Second World War and the reconstruction period, and exercised a pervasive influence on the postwar world.

France

The old Radicals never regained their importance in France, although many of the interwar governments pivoted around their participation. Their standard issue of anticlericalism had been somewhat defused by the separation of church and state, although a resurgence of Catholic feeling, often linked to right-wing political activities, continued to keep religion in the news. The socialists split at the 1920 Tours conference on the question of affiliation with the Third International; the Communist Party took control of much of the party apparatus and the party newspaper, and the socialists were left in a quandry over whether to cooperate with the communists or with the centre and radicals. The conservatives were left to put together coalitions which ruled France during much of the 1920s and early 1930s. They were concerned with liquidating problems associated with the war: the destruction of large amounts of French territory, the loss of 1.4 million lives, the reintegration of the regained provinces of Alsace and Lorraine, reparations and an attempt to build a system of alliances to protect France against an eventual German revival.

Governments during the early 1930s were marked by a shifting set of alliances and rapid turnover in the cabinet, which helped to reinforce the reputation of the Third Republic as lacking political stability. The rise of right-wing extra-parliamentary groups troubled public order. In 1934, the confrontation between parliamentary and extra-parliamentary groups came to a head in the streets of Paris. The prime minister dismissed the powerful Paris police prefect for his laxity in controlling rightist demonstrations. On 6 February, the right marshalled their forces in the Place de la Concorde in the centre of Paris; for six hours, a battle raged between the right and the government, resulting in the deaths of fourteen demonstrators and one policeman and leading to the fall of the government. The socialist leader, Léon Blum, referred to the demonstration as the 'attempted murder of the Republic'.

Election of the Popular Front in 1936 brought to power a coalition of Radicals, socialists and communists. The new government was formed by the Radicals and the socialists under the leadership of Blum; although the communists did not enter the cabinet, they agreed to support the government in the Assembly. The first achievement of Blum was the Matignon Accords with the trade unions: the establishment of a 40-hour week, compulsory arbitration and paid vacations for workers. The government also reorganised and then nationalised the Bank of France and devalued the franc. Such measures delighted the left but outraged the right; within the coalition, the communists were dissatisfied that the reformist measures had not gone further. The Popular Front was short lived, and an indecisive conservative coalition confronted Hitler's resurgent Germany.

The Low Countries, Switzerland and Scandinavia

Following the First World War Belgium faced a massive task of reconstruction, and the Netherlands and Switzerland, though both had remained neutral, had been quite severely affected by the conflict. In all three countries demands for radical political change arose, especially in the aftermath of the revolution in Russia, yet the old elites managed to retain power with programmes of moderate reform. Both Belgium and the Netherlands extended the franchise to women in 1919. In Switzerland, following the defeat of a general strike in 1918, the federal government promised political and social reform and instituted proportional representation for parliamentary elections in 1919; this allowed a significant rise in the number of socialist deputies, and a number of new political groups emerged including a communist party, a peasant party and several right-wing extremist factions.

Broader participation and greater power for the parliaments did not lead automatically to political stability, however. In Belgium the split between the Flemings and the French-speaking Walloons deepened. The introduction of proportional representation in the Netherlands and Switzerland led to an increase in the number of parties – fully 54 contested the Dutch elections in 1933. Despite the increase in the number of socialist deputies in Switzerland, the Federal Council continued to be dominated by conservative interests.

Governments in the Netherlands were dominated by parties with religious affiliations and the socialists only entered the cabinet in 1939. In Belgium the socialist party, perhaps more reform-minded, participated in coalition governments during the entire interwar period. The apparent instability of shifting government majorities was offset in the Low Countries by the fact that ministers often stayed in the same posts from one government to another, and in Switzerland by the continued increase in the power of the federal government over the cantonal governments.

Political reform in the aftermath of the First World War resulted partly from a fear of more radical change and was accompanied when necessary by active repression, as in the case of the Swiss general strike of 1918. As unemployment increased after 1929 radicals re-emerged on both the right and left. In Geneva in 1932, 12 persons were killed when police opened fire on a socialist demonstration. Nazi sympathisers and local Fascists won widespread support, and the Belgian far right Rexists secured 21 seats in the 1936 parliamentary elections. In dealing with the crisis all three governments chose authoritarian methods. Belgium had already suspended parliamentary government once before, to deal with a financial crisis in 1926, and now did so again. By 1935 all three governments were issuing legislation by decree, including the Belgian government's programme of unemployment allowances, minimum wage, shortened work-week and free holidays intended to lessen working-class discontent. In 1934 the Dutch government disqualified members of both right and left-wing parties from holding office. The Belgian government forbade the wearing of party uniforms and in 1936 declared martial law and arrested the leader of the Rexists. In Switzerland some cantons prohibited radical parties entirely. The federal government pressured industry and labour to sign an agreement to resolve industrial disputes in 1937, and in 1940 outlawed both communist and pro-Nazi organisations.

Sweden, Norway and Denmark had remained neutral during the First World War, but felt the reverberations from it. War profiteering at one end of the social scale and food scarcities at the other heightened class tensions. In both

Sweden and Norway troops were used against strikers, with considerable loss of life in Sweden. Denmark and Sweden introduced female suffrage in 1918 and 1919. At first liberal and agrarian interests dominated the governments, but the socialist parties increased in size and first came to power in Sweden in 1920, in Denmark in 1924 and in Norway in 1927. A broad consensus emerged embracing all the major parties; changes in government did not bring fundamental shifts in the direction of policy. These governments engineered agreements between management and labour intended to reduce social tension; Scandinavia was already pursuing its 'middle way' between orthodox capitalism and socialism. In Denmark, social legislation was passed which was among the most progressive in Europe; for example, social security benefits were extended to unmarried women and illegitimate children. In Sweden, new schemes for old age pensions and unemployment benefits were adopted, and later the government extended housing loan provisions and undertook countercyclical investments to combat the depression. Such measures helped to establish the welfare state which characterised northern Europe in later years and, in the interwar period, reduced political support for both left and right-wing extremists.

AUTHORITARIAN POLITICS IN SOUTHERN AND EASTERN EUROPE

The nations of western Europe and Scandinavia maintained a parliamentary system throughout the interwar period, though with some difficulty. Politics generally abided by the accepted rules of elections, parliamentary debates and the organisation of articulated political parties. In southern and eastern Europe, however, the situation was different. In these regions, there was less of a tradition of democratic government. The high levels of illiteracy and lack of political integration of the population meant that a democratic system could only function imperfectly. Political parties were not so well organised as in the west and were often interest groups tied together by particular concerns or individual leaders. Political patronage and clientelism loomed large in the resolution of issues and the division of spoils. The churches and the military continued to play a large role. Another feature of political life was widespread violence, including riots and assassinations.

The First World War had aggravated difficulties in the south and east, leaving nations like Italy disappointed with the peace and new nations, the successor states to Austria-Hungary, without a political or economic tradition of independence. The split in the workers' movement resulting from the revolution in Russia fractured left-wing politics, while on the right, increasing radicalism in the form of irredentism, moral regeneration or anti-Bolshevism made the achievement of parliamentary order difficult. In eastern Europe, the clash of nationalities had not been resolved by Woodrow Wilson's Fourteen Points or by the half-hearted attempt of the Versailles peace conference to make political and ethnic boundaries coincide. Political and social ferment encouraged a drift towards authoritarian government in all of the nations of southern and eastern Europe except Czechoslovakia.

Mediterranean Europe

The predominance of a politics based on interest groups with changing coalitions, characteristic of prewar Italy, seemed to be in store for postwar Italy as well. The small, closely-knit groups of industrialists, bankers and bureaucrats had become more powerful as the already considerable influence of the state in the economy had grown. The landowners who had controlled local government in rural areas remained powerful as well, though wartime controls over agricultural production pointed to the increasing effectiveness of central government power. The Pope lifted the prohibition on Catholic participation in Italian politics in 1919 and in 1921 elections under universal manhood suffrage gave victory to a coalition of Liberals and Democrats.

On the extremes, however, real challenges were posed to the parliamentary government. In 1919, the socialists voted for adherence to the Third International, splitting the workers' movement. Also in 1919 Benito Mussolini established the Fascio di Combattimento, the Fascist movement. He was partly inspired by the actions of Gabriele d'Annunzio, a poet turned conquistador, who in 1919 marched a band of volunteer soldiers onto the Adriatic city of Fiume – Italian-speaking but claimed by Yugoslavia – and temporarily established a government there. The Italian government also had to contend with a series of labour disputes. Landless agricultural labourers, many of them returning soldiers, began to occupy the land of absentee owners, especially in the south. In 1920, a strike movement began to spread through the countryside as well. Landlords began once again to recruit 'squads' of men as they had before the war, to end the land seizures and repress the strikes. At the same time the employers in the metal and machinery industry locked out their workers, who responded by seizing factories in Milan and Turin. Riots pitting Fascists against communists broke out in Florence in early 1921, and in the following year Fascists engineered coups to take over the city governments of Fiume, Bologna and Milan.

During these events, a series of coalition cabinets had passed into and out of office with little strength to combat the deteriorating situation. A Fascist conference in Naples in October 1922 demanded the appointment of a Fascist prime minister, and on 28 October Mussolini's black shirts marched on Rome. The king refused to declare martial law, the prime minister resigned, and on 31 October the king summoned Mussolini to form a government. Certainly, Mussolini's accession to power was technically legal, but the Fascists could have taken over the government by force if it had been necessary; Mussolini subsequently used his legitimate power to subvert the parliamentary system and install Fascism in power.

Mussolini was a schoolteacher from a modest background who had become editor of the socialist newspaper *Avanti*. In 1914 he broke with the socialist party to favour Italian intervention in the First World War. Influenced by Marxism, even when he rejected Marx's theories, Mussolini felt that in Fascism he had created the doctrine that would move beyond the class struggle; since capitalism was not withering away, some new organisation must be planned to bring together the owners of capital and the workers. This he felt he could achieve with a corporatist society, creating new organic institutions in all fields – manufacturing, mining, agriculture, and so on – for joint management of sectors of the economy under state tutelage. Mussolini was also an ardent nationalist who aimed to reverse Italy's defeat in the peace settlement, to avenge Italy's imperialistic embarrassments (particularly the defeat at Adowa in 1896) and to achieve greater Italian influence in the Balkans. To do all this, what Italy needed was a strong government, free from the dangers of socialism, weak-kneed liberalism and the spectre of Bolshevism, guided by a visionary leader. Italian society must be revivified, and the obvious model was the Roman empire. Thus, Mussolini's Fascists adopted the outstretched hand salute of Roman soldiers, and Mussolini took the title of *Duce* (*Dux*). More significant, perhaps, was his attempt to recreate the Roman empire with imperial and European conquests.

Such arguments dressed up Fascism as a political philosophy. It was not. Mussolini himself said that Fascism was 'action', and his programme was that he would *do* something for Italy rather than idly theorising or wasting time with the delicacies of constitutionalism. Fascism had little coherent philosophy. The Fascist party itself was an ad hoc movement of various discontented elements in Italian society, including peasants, soldiers and former socialists, held together by the charismatic personality of Mussolini. Mussolini realised the value of propaganda, including the use of the radio, and created the myth of himself as leader and father, a myth to which many Italians were attracted even if they did not approve of his policies. Mussolini made the trains run on time, as the cliché had it, and such proofs of action were enough to keep him in power for two decades.

Underneath a veneer of legitimacy Mussolini's rule was a dictatorship. Before the expiration of the emergency dictatorial powers he had been given in 1922, he passed a law giving the political party with the largest number of votes two-thirds of the seats in the Chamber of Deputies, effectively turning Italy into a one-party state. Through patronage and bullying by the Fascist squads, Fascist victories in subsequent elections were assured. In 1924, however, Mussolini faced a crisis when his supporters murdered Giacomo Matteotti, a socialist deputy and author of a book providing evidence of numerous cases of violence perpetrated by the Fascists. The left, which had not yet been entirely silenced, demanded an investigation and the dissolution of the Fascist squads. In response, Mussolini imposed press censorship and made strikes illegal; in 1928, a new electoral law abolished universal suffrage and reduced the voting population from ten million to three million.

Now secure in his power, Mussolini could move elsewhere. In 1929, he signed an agreement with the Vatican, the Lateran Treaty, which reconciled the Italian government and the Holy See. In 1933, he signed a four-power treaty with Britain, France and Germany, hoping thereby to maintain Italy's standing as a European power and take a middle road between the west and Hitler. Libyan resistance to Italian rule was gradually suppressed. Then, in 1935 Italian troops began invading Ethiopia, the scene of the defeat of 1896; the following year, Italy formally annexed Ethiopia and the Italian king took the title Emperor of Ethiopia. In April 1939, the rapid conquest of Albania permitted the king of Italy to assume the crown of Albania as well. In May Mussolini concluded a military alliance with Nazi Germany. Such conquests, however, could not obscure the economic failures of Italy or the repressive society of Fascist Italy.

In Spain, the deterioration of the government was also partly caused by extra-parliamentary forces. Anarchism, the dominant ideology of the workers' movement, opposed the parliamentary system. Bitter strikes marked the postwar years. Regional interests also opposed the central government, particularly among the Catalans and Basques. Army leaders, dissatisfied with the alternating liberal and conservative governments, demanded a larger role in politics. But a particular problem for the legitimate government was Morocco; the defeat inflicted by the Moroccans on the Spanish at Anual in July 1921 led to bitter recriminations in Spain, and the controversy further undermined the government. Finally, in September 1923, General Miguel

Primo de Rivera orchestrated a coup d'état in Madrid and became the new ruler of the country. Primo de Rivera promised to recoup Spain's losses in Morocco and to regenerate the country: 'Our aim is to open a brief parenthesis in the constitutional life of Spain and to reestablish it as soon as the country offers us men uncontaminated with the vice of political organisation'. His formal dictatorship ended in 1925 but he remained as prime minister until 1930; less than a year later, a republic was proclaimed.

A longer-lived military takeover occurred in Portugal. In 1917 a pro-German general led a coup and named himself president-dictator, but he was assassinated a year later. However, the military retained its dominant position in the government; from 1918 to 1926, 12 out of 26 cabinets were presided over by officers. The democratic forces were fragmented and unable to put together enough seats to form a stable government. Governments were compromised by corruption – one prime minister was convicted of embezzlement – and widespread political violence included the assassination of several prominent politicians. A royalist uprising in 1919 and an attempted coup in 1925 both failed, but the right was marshalling its forces in opposition to democrats. In 1926, a military-led uprising took over the government. A leftist uprising in 1927 was suppressed. By 1928, the dominant figure in the new authoritarian government was Antonio de Oliveira Salazar, a pro-Catholic and nationalist professor of economics. First as minister of finance, then as prime minister after 1932, Salazar established a dictatorial regime which lasted until the 1970s.

Greece displayed many of the characteristics of the other Mediterranean countries, including controversy over the actual form of government – monarchy or republic – and a fragile parliamentary structure. During the First World War, Eleutherios Venizelos had set up a government in Thessaloniki favouring Greek intervention on behalf of the Allies and in opposition to the vaguely pro-German government in Athens. By the end of the war, Venizelos' government was recognised as the legitimate one in Greece, and the peace settlement gave Greece the right to occupy Smyrna and the surrounding area of Asia Minor. A region which had been ethnically

Greek for centuries, Smyrna was a prosperous commercial centre. The Greeks saw their position in Asia Minor threatened by the newly renascent Turks under Kemal Atatürk, and in February 1921 Venizelos launched a military offensive in Turkey; the ultimate aim, at least in the eyes of extreme nationalists, was a reconquest of Constantinople, the old Byzantine capital. The effort was a fiasco, and a Turkish counteroffensive led to the total defeat of the Greeks in 1922. The episode put an end to the nationalist 'Great Idea' of a new Greek empire. Domestic politics remained chaotic during the next 15 years with first the abdication and then the restoration of the king, a coup d'état and inconclusive elections. In 1936, General Ioannis Metaxas staged a coup and formed an authoritarian government under martial law; censorship, persecution of the opposition and talk of a national revival characterised his regime, like those of the other Mediterranean strongmen. Metaxas remained in office until his death in 1941, by which time Greece was fighting in the Second World War.

Eastern Europe

In the Baltic states conditions were unstable throughout the interwar years. The Russian Provisional Government had granted Finland autonomy within a new federation, but the Finns declared their complete independence. The Russian Bolshevik government supported the Finnish communists in the ensuing civil war, but the Finnish 'Whites' defeated them with German support and then outlawed the Communist Party. Estonia, Latvia and Lithuania all had been occupied by the Germans and ruled through puppet governments during the First World War. All were invaded by the Bolsheviks and all successfully defended themselves. Agrarian reform dispossessed Swedish landlords in Finland and the largely German landholding class in the three Baltic states. In these latter three, land reform therefore created a dissatisfied national minority to which Nazi Germany could appeal. Government instability was common and the growing threat from Germany pushed all three towards authoritarianism. Estonia had 21 cabinets between independence in 1919 and the advent of a dictatorship in 1934. Elections in Latvia were contested by as many as 44 political parties until the parliamentary system was overthrown by a right-wing coup, also in 1934, following a socialist electoral victory. Lithuania had less political fragmentation, but its government was taken over by a coup even earlier, in 1926, and in 1936 all parties except the fascist National Union were outlawed.

Poland achieved independence in 1918 for the first time in more than a century but immediately had to contend with rival governments set up in exile. The victor was Josef Pilsudski, a former socialist now become a conservative nationalist. He left office in 1922, partly from dissatisfaction with the new constitution which limited the president's powers, but returned in 1926 in a military coup. The Polish parliament was dissolved and opposition outlawed. Pilsudski continued to dominate national politics until his death in 1935; during the remaining years before Hitler's invasion, Poland was ruled by an inept cohort of colonels.

Czechoslovakia was the most promising of the new countries at the end of the First World War. With significant natural resources, an economy balanced among the agricultural, industrial and commercial sectors, and close ties with western nations, Czechoslovakia managed to maintain a parliamentary system despite quarrels between Czechs and Slovaks. The leading force in politics was Edvard Benes, perhaps the most outstanding figure in eastern Europe in the interwar years, who was Czechoslovakia's foreign minister for 17 years. This, along with the 19-year presidency of Thomas Masaryk, was a force for stability, although actual governments were usually coalitions among the large number of political parties in the nation.

After the suppression of Béla Kun's revolution, Hungary went through ten years of conservative rule from 1921 to 1931. The government reduced the suffrage by a quarter, restricted opposition, and allowed landowning interests the upper hand in government. In 1932 a rabid nationalist and anti-Semite, Julius Gömbös, took office; in the next few years, he allied Hungary with Fascist Italy and Nazi Germany. His successors became less friendly with their allies. Fearing the influence of Nazism on the 400,000 ethnic Germans in Hungary, the government repressed fascists and Nazi groups and finally introduced a moderate land reform in 1938, but remained authoritarian and anti-Semitic.

Austria was the rump of the old Habsburg empire, a nation in which desire for union with Germany was strong. In 1919, the new Assembly, in which the socialists held the largest number of seats, voted to make Austria a part of Germany, but the Allies forbade union with Germany. The new state suffered from the schizophrenic split between Vienna, a cosmopolitan city ruled by the socialists, and the conservative, Catholic countryside. In Vienna, the leftist government pursued an imaginative programme of public works, symbolised by the building of the modernist housing complex called the Karl-Marx-Hof. Elsewhere, however, monarchists demanded a restoration of the Habsburgs, while conservatives wanted a revision of the peace settlement. During the 1920s, divisions deepened. In 1927 a general strike and grave riots in Vienna followed the acquittal of nationalist agitators of the murder of two prominent socialists; both the conservatives and the leftists formed private armies. The collapse of the Viennese Creditanstalt in 1931 was one of the sparks for the European depression and plunged Austria into greater uncertainty about its future. In 1933 the government of Engelbert Dollfuss suspended parliament and muzzled the press in an effort to contain pro-Nazi disturbances. Early in 1934 Dollfuss established authoritarian one-party rule by his Fatherland Front, dissolved the socialist party and did away with the autonomy of the Vienna government and repressed the ensuing leftist uprising. Dollfuss was murdered during the attempted Nazi coup in July 1934; his successor proved even less able to resist German pressure, and Austria was absorbed by Germany in 1938.

The Balkan countries, the least developed area of Europe, faced even greater problems. In Rumania, peasant and nationalist parties contended for dominance in the government, but the real ruler was the king. His government became more and more reactionary – in 1937 Jews were forbidden to own land and barred from the professions – and fanatical right-wing groups emerged. So radical were they, however, that the government suppressed them and their leader was killed while being moved from one prison to another. Meanwhile, the Rumanians signed alliances and treaties with almost every other country, but these efforts to guarantee its independence proved vain once the Second World War began. The Kingdom of the Serbs, Croats and Slovenes, or Yugoslavia, was proclaimed in 1918 with a Serbian prince as king. He proclaimed a temporary dictatorship in 1929 and ruled with a heavy hand that was particularly offensive to the large Croat minority. In 1934, he was assassinated; the remainder of the decade saw a confused political situation in the country with the official restoration of democratic government only in 1939. Albania was the poorest of the poor. Political power was contested between a Muslim leader and an Orthodox bishop; the former eventually made himself king and embarked on a programme of economic development with Italian assistance, which paved the way for Mussolini's invasion in 1939.

AUTHORITARIANISM, FASCISM AND NAZISM

The regimes which emerged in eastern and southern Europe in the 1920s and 1930s displayed similar characteristics. Several came to power by coups or with the threat of violence; they suspended parliaments and outlawed opposition parties, censored the press, limited assemblies, muffled intellectuals and used torture, imprisonment and execution to enforce their rule. They allied with the military and tried to remake their states in a regimented, militaristic fashion. They spoke about restoring order, regenerating the nation and defending the homeland against Bolshevism. Their leaders posed as saviours of their people. But did these authoritarian regimes really share some essential quality in common? Were they 'fascist'? The nature of fascism has preoccupied historians and political scientists since the interwar years. The men who took over the subverted parliamentary governments – from Franco in Spain to Mussolini in Italy and Metaxas in Greece, from the dictators of the Baltic states to Dollfuss in Austria - can be considered part and parcel of the same international phenomenon of fascism. However, it can also be argued that these rulers came to power for different reasons and that their takeovers were much more responses to local conditions than to the international climate. Those seeing an international connection point to the similarities in ideologies, such as anti-Marxism, extreme nationalism, dislike of parliamentary rule and militarism. They show that dissatisfaction with the First World War settlement was a factor in the rise of many of the right-wing movements and that the economic crisis of the 1930s was of importance in radicalising populations throughout Europe. Those who dispute the internationalism of Fascism point out the different chronologies of the takeover; if Italy became Fascist in 1922, then Germany did not succumb to a non-democratic government until a decade later. Some of the fascist governments entered power by legislative victories while others were naked coups. The social and economic structures of the 'fascist' countries differed considerably – from Italy with its dual economy and highly industrialised Germany to the peasant societies of Iberia and the almost tribal organisation of Albania. Though Fascism has frequently been identified as a movement of the lower middle class, the social groups supporting these authoritarian regimes varied from country to country. If imperialism marked Nazism, then irredentism was more characteristic of the governments of eastern Europe, while Spain and Portugal were, at least in Europe, isolationist.

At the time, however, many observers saw an international fascist movement, which they linked with economics and politics. The Comintern, in a 1933 pronouncement, stated: 'Fascism is the unconcealed, terroristic dictatorship of the most reactionary, chauvinistic and imperialistic elements of finance capital'. Communist theory linked the authoritarian regimes through the Marxist theory of history and saw in them the products of the contradictions of the capitalist system. However, the statement also mirrors the context in which it was written – the effort of Stalin to build a socialist society in one country, surrounded by its enemies. Later judgements also mirror the views of their advocates; for example, a work published during the Cold War between the United States and the Soviet Union asserted that communism and fascism were really only two sides of the same coin, dictatorship carried to the extreme in opposition to democratic society. Different methodologies also inspire different theories; the psychologist Erich Fromm, writing in 1944, concluded that the basis for acceptance of the new regimes was an emotional desire to 'escape from freedom', in which modern man, unable to cope with the crises of the modern world, capitulates to a system which promises protection and regeneration and satisfies a need for submission and obedience.

John Weiss – who does use the general term Fascism to describe the various governments – has isolated several features which they held in common. First, in contrast to the individualism of the modern world, these regimes indirectly or explicitly espoused a society based on corporatism, a union of producers and employees under the direction of the state or the party. Thus, society was viewed as organic; the perfect community can be achieved only by a cooperation of its constituent parts which must be made to work together. That precept implies a cleansing of the body politic through heightened nationalism or even racism, a belief in the nation, ethnic group or people who have set up the new state. For Mussolini, this was the revival of Roman greatness; for Hitler, it was the conquest of living space for the German *Volk*; for others, it was simply a rabid nationalism mixed with irredentism and xenophobia. Almost everywhere, it was tinged with anti-Semitism. To create the new society, the nation needs a leader capable of overcoming political factionalism and inspiring the nation with his regenerative vision – a messiah. Mussolini was the *Duce*, Hitler the *Führer*, Franco the *Caudillo*; Metaxas in Greece styled himself the First Peasant and First Worker, while Räts, the Estonian leader, called himself the National Guide. The leader was military commander (and, in fact, many of the new despots were military men), ideologue and father figure – Primo de Rivera worried that the Spanish ate too much. To assist the leader, an elite corps of loyalists was needed to carry out the 'revolution': the black shirts of Mussolini, the storm-troopers of Hitler, the members of the national parties in eastern Europe. The elite in its mission could use all means at its disposal, which implied the suppression of 'counter-revolutionary' elements by force if necessary; everywhere in the authoritarian countries (although not only there) the tactics of the police state were introduced, from the White Terror after the overthrow of Stamboliski in Bulgaria to the later concentration camps of Germany. Finally, according to Weiss, there is an element of expansionism, which reached its ultimate manifestation in a desire for world power.

From Iberia to the Balkans, the new despots thought something had gone amiss in the process of modernisation, and that the way to put it right was to do away with decadent parliamentary government and to regenerate the nation through their own leadership, to restore order and to create a 'New State' (a term used by Salazar, for example, from 1930 onwards). Ironically, such leaders' creeds were actually backward-looking: an attempt to restore something that had never been, to ignore the conflicts of industrial society, to create economic autarkies, to control the development of the nation economically, politically and morally through autocratic rule and regimentation of the population.

Such calls received a sympathetic hearing. Some of the dictators were hated, but many of them, at least initially, enjoyed widespread support. The problems arising from economic development, the effects of the First World War, the continuing chaos of the 1920s and the depression combined to create an audience for the siren song of the dictators. Right-wing movements were able to pose as both conservative and as reformist (even Hitler's party was officially labelled 'socialist'). Marginal and displaced populations hoped new leaders would restore their fortunes; others were merely opportunistic. Those living on the borderline between the lower middle class and the working class, in an economically precarious position and afraid of the rising working class and their socialist and communist leaders, found solace in the new ideologies. Small shopkeepers, eager to blame Jewish businessmen for their difficulties, found an opening for their anti-Semitism. Returned soldiers heeded the nationalistic rhetoric. Aristocrats displaced from their traditional position by the upheavals of the First World War responded to the elitism of the new authoritarianism. Some men of letters were seduced by the leaders who promised a crusade of action. Youth saw a means of rejecting the outmoded beliefs of their parents in the virile new cults. Peasants, who formed majorities in most of the new dictatorships, saw a possibility for land reform and redress of their grievances against landlords and socialists both. Hooligans could enlist in the terrorist brigades of the new leaders. Certain industrialists and bankers saw potential profits in the dictators' economic programmes. And the middle class might see the return of order after the upheavals of the immediate postwar period. Disillusion would set in only after the dictators came to power.

GERMANY FROM WEIMAR TO HITLER

The Weimar Republic had to deal with several attempted rebellions, even after the defeat of the Spartacists. In 1920, Wolfgang Kapp, a politicians from conservative East Prussia, led a group of *Freikorps* soldiers in a bid to take over the government in Berlin; the legitimate government took refuge in Stuttgart, and a general strike by workers brought the Kapp Putsch to an end after several days. Another attempt by the right was the Beer Hall Putsch of 8 November 1923, in the midst of the hyperinflation crisis. This uprising was led by the wartime commander Erich Ludendorff and a little-known political agitator, Adolf Hitler. The attempted revolution was put down with relative ease and Hitler was put under arrest – he used his months of confinement to write *Mein Kampf*, the gospel of Nazism. Although neither of these attempted coups was successful, they indicated that the government's main enemy lay to the right and not the left; ironically, the communists, so much an enemy in the eyes of many Germans, were unable to mobilise for an insurrection either in the crisis of 1923 or in the depression after 1930.

Meanwhile, the parliamentary parties were weakening. Most represented specific interest groups – workers, Catholics or agrarian interests – and were unable to come to a consensus. The more moderate parties were outflanked by radicals of both extremes. All suffered from a dearth of leaders and programmes to respond to the economic and social turmoil of the 1920s and 1930s. This crisis of party politics was reflected in the government: in the 15 years of its existence, Weimar had 15 separate cabinets lasting 3–18 months. After the fall of the socialist government in 1920, the cabinets were dominated by centrists and moderate conservatives until the end of the decade, but then the right increased its authority.

The depression wreaked political havoc on the country and the accession to office of Henrich Brüning in 1930 marks the actual end of the Weimar system. Faced with the economic situation and continuous street violence by the extremists, Brüning began to rule by decree. This was within his legal power but paved the way for an even more dictatorial regime. By the beginning of the 1930s, the Nazis had entered the Reichstag. Their strength grew, and the other parties and politicians seemed incapable of dealing with Germany's problems of unemployment, instability and international grievances. By 1933, for many Hitler seemed a real alternative, even if an unpalatable one. When Hitler became chancellor in January 1933, other politicians considered his government a temporary expedient; yet once in power, he stifled opposition and, to the extent that parliamentary democracy was still alive, Hitler quickly destroyed it.

National Socialism, or Nazism, was the most virulent of the interwar ideologies both in theory and practice. Hitler's imperial ambitions did not stop at irredentist demands for absorption of German-speaking populations or the conquest of an overseas empire, but aimed at world domination. His totalitarianism did not mean just the silencing of the opposition, but the extermination of such groups as Jews, Slavs, gypsies, homosexuals and any others he thought stood in the way of the triumph of his master race. Whereas Mussolini and the other dictators exiled or imprisoned their opponents, Hitler herded them into concentration camps and gas chambers.

Adolf Hitler was an unlikely leader of the movement which would take over Germany. The son of an Austrian customs official, he did not obtain German citizenship until 1932. Hitler had been a mediocre student and then tried, without success, to become an artist in the Vienna of the Belle Epoque. He fled to Germany at the outbreak of the First World War to avoid conscription, but once there he enlisted in the kaiser's forces. Wounded in action, he finished the war with few prospects for the future. Hitler then lived on the fringes of society, mingling with right-wing groups and joining the National Socialist Party. In 1923, after the failed Beer Hall Putsch, he spent time under arrest. Yet ten years later Hitler was called by the president to form a government. Hitler played on the Germans' desire for a reversal of the 1918 defeat, for the restoration of order in the chaos of the interwar years, for a government that would combat the communists (who were gaining ever-increasing numbers of votes), for a moral regeneration of Germany and the Aryan race and for a restoration of economic prosperity. In the Jews he found a convenient scapegoat for Germany's ills which fed on the anti-Semitism growing stronger in Europe since the late 1800s. Hitler spoke in a hypnotic fashion, using his rhetorical talents and mass propaganda to whip his audiences into a frenzy of passion. He cleverly highlighted or downplayed his ideas to suit the time and the audience.

The highly efficient Nazi Party organisation identified popular local issues, arranged meetings and mobilised voters, while the storm-troopers disrupted the opposition. Hitler's ultimate aim was clear – the conquest of *Lebensraum*, living space for the expanding German population, area which in the first instance must be taken from eastern Europe to form the greater German nation – and once in office, he moved to ensure that he would not lose power until his aims had either been accomplished or defeated. Less than a month after he took office in January 1933, a fire destroyed the German Reichstag. Claiming the arson was a communist plot, he suspended constitutional liberties and banned the Communist Party. In March the Reichstag passed the Enabling Act, giving him dictatorial powers. Soon the campaign against the Jews began; in March 1933, a law permitted dismissal of

Jewish government officials, and in August the Nazis instituted a national boycott of Jewish businesses. In 1934 Hitler eliminated opposition to his personal rule inside the Nazi Party; 77 members of the party were executed for an alleged conspiracy.

The foundations of Hitler's regime had been set, and Hitler now extended them. The Nürnberg Laws of 1935 deprived Jews of German citizenship and forbade intermarriage between Jews and Gentiles. Three years later, in the 'night of crystal' (*Kristallnacht*), well-organised Nazi gangs attacked Jewish businesses and synagogues, breaking windows (the 'crystal') and looting property. Concentration camps had already been set up for Hitler's opponents; although the Nazis provisionally contented themselves with driving Jews from the country, ultimately they would be shipped to their deaths in the extermination camps. The instruments of terror were also active, the Gestapo and SS only two among several 'security' agencies. The huge Nürnberg party meeting in 1936 consecrated Hitler's role and the absolute rule of the Nazi Party. Nazism incorporated all the backward-looking responses to the problems of the modern world and carried them to their logical extremes. After a series of encounters beginning in Spain, the other nations of Europe began to brace themselves for the inevitable conflict this implied.

EPILOGUE

During the 1930s, all the ideologies then current in Europe seemed to be battling in Spain. Just as the Dreyfus case summed up many of the social, political and ideological questions of the prewar period, so the Spanish Civil War brought together the themes of interwar society. In 1931, elections gave victory to the republicans, and the king left the country although he did not abdicate; the republicans established a 'provisional government' and another election gave a majority to a coalition of moderate republicans and socialists. The new constitution adopted in December 1931 provided for the election of the legislature and an electoral college on the basis of universal suffrage; the president was to be elected for a six-year term by the legislature and college; members of the army and the clergy were barred as candidates. Furthermore, the constitution made all property 'the object of expropriation for social utility'. The new government separated church and state, nationalised church property, laicised education and dissolved the powerful Jesuit order of priests. Workers were given an eight-hour day and social services were enlarged. The province of Catalonia, where opposition to the central government in Madrid was of long standing, was granted a large measure of autonomy.

Although the constitution was a compromise between the socialists – who wanted more thorough reforms – and their moderate allies, it provoked opposition everywhere. In August 1932, a rightist general captured Seville, a leftist revolt led by anarchists in January 1933 spread from Barcelona to other large cities and in October 1934 the regional government of Catalonia declared the province independent. Though

297

suppressed, these uprisings demonstrated the dissatisfaction of conservatives, radicals and regional interests with the new government. The government weathered its first internal crisis when the provisional president, Alcala Zamora, resigned in October 1931 in opposition to the anticlerical measures; he was then elected as the first president under the new constitution in December, but his successor, Manuel Azaña, became prime minister and pursued the anticlerical programme with an Associations Law in May 1933, which further reduced the power of the church. Elections in November 1933 gave victory to the parties of the right. In October 1933 the son of Primo de Rivera, José, founded a right-wing proclerical movement, the Falange; in October 1934 a conservative cabinet with strong clerical tendencies and monarchist sympathies was inaugurated. The pendulum reversed in 1936, and an election brought to power the Popular Front, an alliance of republicans, socialists, syndicalists and communists. Azaña became prime minister once again (and then president later in the year when the left-wing majority voted to remove Zamora) and resumed the reformist programme. The government decided to transfer several right-wing generals whom it mistrusted and feared were plotting against the government. The generals revolted, and their rebellion spread from Melilla in Spanish Morocco to engulf the entire nation in civil war.

The leaders of the uprising were the officer who had been behind the 1932 rebellion, Sanjurjo, General Emilio Mola and the Falangist General Francisco Franco; Sanjurjo was killed in an airplane crash soon thereafter, and Mola was later captured and executed. Leadership of the uprising therefore fell to Franco, who in October of 1936 took the title of Generalissimo and declared himself Chief of the Spanish State. The legitimate government and the Francoists fought for three years. At stake was control of Spain, but the civil war also pitted two ideologies against each other: the secular, reformist republican programme of the Popular Front versus the authoritarian, proclerical and nationalist Falange creed. The civil war also involved foreign countries. Hitler and Mussolini recognised Franco's government and contributed both arms and soldiers to the Falangist rebels. The German army used Spain as a proving ground for new mechanised weapons such as dive bombers and tanks; some 10,000 German and 75,000 Italian soldiers fought beside Franco's troops. The Soviet Union supported the republicans, sending arms to the government and fostering the formation of the International Brigade of volunteers for the republican cause. England and France attempted without success to prevent foreign aid to either side, fearing that the war would spread; their failure to intervene ensured Franco's victory.

The war was marked by fierce fighting and great dedication. Volunteer soldiers poured into Spain from other countries in Europe and even from as far away as the United States and Australia. Prominent intellectuals, such as the English writers W. H. Auden and George Orwell, enlisted on the republican side. The republican side seemed to express the hopes of an entire generation of reformers in Europe; for the European right wing, Franco embodied the ideas of Catholicism, order and the defeat of Bolshevism. The brutality of the fighting shocked Europe. The Falangist bombarding of Guernica was the inspiration for one of Picasso's major paintings, a testimony to the horrors of war and to Picasso's own republican and communist convictions. In their turn, republican forces bombed Falangist villages in Morocco and were guilty of atrocities against priests, nuns and other civilians.

The war ended in April 1939 with the defeat of the republicans. Franco, now styling himself the *Caudillo*, set up an authoritarian government, a personal dictatorship in alliance with the Catholic church, that would last until his death in 1975. The war had left 700,000 Spaniards dead in battle, and further tens of thousands murdered, summarily executed or killed in air raids. Nearly 200 towns had been totally destroyed, 250,000 houses were left uninhabitable, the railways lost over 60 per cent of their passenger cars, and over 5,000 churches were damaged or destroyed. Many of Spain's leading cultural figures perished in the war, foremost among them the brilliant dramatist Frederico Garcia Lorca, almost certainly put to death by the Francoists. Franco used terror tactics to punish his opponents – even the Italian foreign minister, who visited Spain in July 1939, estimated

that there were 200,000 prisoners and several hundred
executions a day in Madrid; in 1942, there were close to a
quarter of a million republicans in prison, and thousands
more had escaped to refugee camps in the south of France.

THE SECOND WORLD WAR

The Spanish Civil War was the symbolic focus of the
problems, tensions and conflicts which Europe had not yet
resolved, but it was only one of several places where the
fragile social and political order was being torn apart. In the
Far East, Japanese incursions into China grew from the
seizure of three towns in Manchuria in 1931 to a full-scale
invasion in 1937. In 1935 Italy invaded Ethiopia, a long-
deferred attempt to gain revenge for the humiliating defeat of
1896, and in 1939 invaded and annexed Albania. Germany
reoccupied the demilitarised portions of the Rhineland in
1936 and absorbed Austria in March 1938. In September
1938 Czechoslovakia was forced to cede the Sudentenland
(perhaps four-fifths German) to Germany, Ruthenia and part
of southern Slovakia (three-fifths Hungarian) to Hungary,
and Teschen (two fifths Polish) to Poland. In March 1939
Germany seized the remainder of Czechoslovakia, and then
on 1 September 1939 Germany invaded Poland, and the
world was again at war.

In retrospect, the moral repugnance of the Nazi regime
makes the Second World War seem unavoidable, for Hitler's
goals, announced in *Mein Kampf* in 1924, clearly required
war for their attainment. Yet to the leaders of the 1930s
things did not seem so simple, and the reasons for their
hesitation in combating the Nazi threat lie in the failure to
solve the problems arising from economic and social change
which had beset Europe since the 1890s. Nationalist demands
for new territory – even in violation of international law and
treaty obligations – could be used to overcome internal
divisions arising from economic problems, as could the
scapegoating and repression of ethnic minorities. Even in
countries where parliamentary institutions remained in
place, such as Belgium, the Netherlands and Switzerland,

governments employed authoritarian tactics to defend themselves. Until 1939 Hitler could present himself as a reasonable man, seeking only to redress the injustices perpetrated by the Treaty of Versailles, unite all ethnic Germans and combat the depression. Indeed he seemed more reasonable than the leaders of some other authoritarian regimes; even Nazi anti-Semitism seemed no more extreme than the pogroms in Poland or the anti-Jewish laws of Rumania and Hungary. Those who opposed Hitler were themselves divided; Britain, France and the Soviet Union all signed separate pacts with Hitler to protect their most important individual interests. In addition, while Germany boomed, the other economies of western Europe were only beginning to emerge from the depression; recovery in all countries was closely connected with rearmament, but so long as neither was complete, effective opposition to international aggression remained impossible.

The early days of the war confirmed the worst fears of those who had urged caution; German armies swept across Europe, and Japanese forces conquered European possessions in the Far East. Then in 1941 Hitler attacked the Soviet Union, the Japanese attacked the United States, and finally Hitler declared war on the United States as well. The reality of Nazi tyranny began to reveal itself. Across Europe Jews were rounded up and deported in sealed trains; although their appalling fate was not fully known until after the war, the atrocious conditions imposed on millions of forced labourers, the systematic brutality of the occupying German troops, the thousands of summary executions, and the terrible retribution exacted for any show of opposition, created an opposition so profound that it submerged the issues which had divided Europeans before. Capitalist Britain and the United States found themselves allied with the socialist Soviet Union. Within the occupied countries, resistance movements united all who opposed the Nazi regime, from devout Christian conservatives to committed communist radicals, from whatever social class.

The technologies of the second industrial revolution – in the form of chemicals, bombs, missiles, rockets, tanks, airplanes – were put to use in warfare. The rearmament programmes of the late 1930s had helped bring Europe out of the depression, and now the exigencies of another 'total war' fuelled the factories. Countries conquered by Germany saw their economies taken over by the Nazi war effort. The Germans exacted huge monetary payments and supplies of raw materials and manufactures in addition to forced labour; however, the Germans also created new industrial centres, laying a base for the rapid growth of industry after the war. Governments raced to develop and introduce new weapons, and Europeans became accustomed to solving problems by seeking out new technologies. All governments imposed strict controls over agriculture, industry and labour, allocating and managing resources to maximise output in ways which foreshadowed the increased government involvement in the economy which became one of the distinguishing features of the postwar world. The survival and eventual victory of the Soviet Union in eastern Europe, and the role of United States aid in the Allied victory in western Europe, laid the foundation for the domination of the postwar world by the two new 'superpowers'. The war loosened Europe's grip on overseas colonial empires, opening the way for 'decolonisation' and the creation of a new relationship between Europe and an emerging 'Third World'. The two atomic bombs which ended the war in Japan opened a new age of another kind, one which both promised unparalleled affluence and threatened unprecedented destruction.

The war therefore created many of the conditions which typified the postwar world and separated it from the half-century that had gone before. During the war, well before the outcome was certain, Allied leaders met repeatedly to discuss the mistakes that had been made during the previous two generations, and to analyse the possibilities of restructuring the postwar world. They divided Europe into spheres of influence, planned new organisations for arbitration of disputes and issued reports on the necessity for new systems of economic planning and social security. They did not always succeed; the movements of armies sometimes pre-empted their decisions regarding spheres of influence, the new United Nations, International Monetary Fund, World Bank and other international agencies sometimes failed to fulfil their intended roles, and the new systems of economic planning and social security sometimes became objects of bitter contention. Nevertheless, the war ended one epoch of European history and decisively influenced the shape of the next. The Second World War was not only the conflagration of the unsolved problems of the previous half-century but the crucible for the contemporary world.

MAPS

EUROPEAN SOCIAL AND ECONOMIC FEATURES: KEY TO REGIONS

1. Midlands
2. Ulster
3. Rhineland
4. Ruhr
5. Alsace-Lorraine
6. Basque country
7. Catalonia
8. Bavaria
9. Corsica
10. Sardinia
11. Sicily
12. Milan-Turin-Genoa triangle
13. Mezzogiorno
14. Bohemia
15. Silesia
16. Galicia
17. Transylvania
18. Macedonia
19. Ukraine
20. Donetz Basin

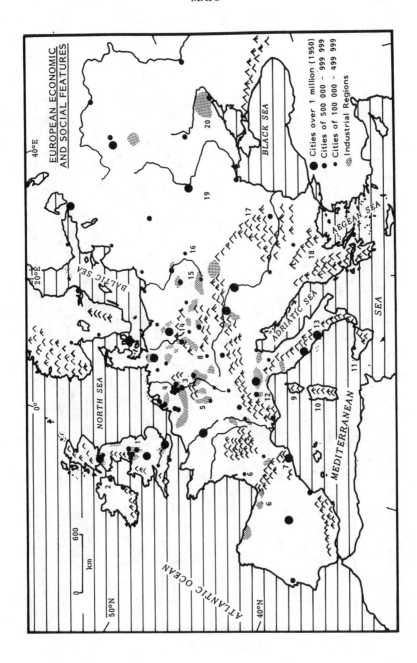

EUROPEAN ECONOMIC
AND SOCIAL FEATURES

• Cities over 1 million (1950)
● Cities of 500 000 – 999 999
● Cities of 100 000 – 499 999
▨ Industrial Regions

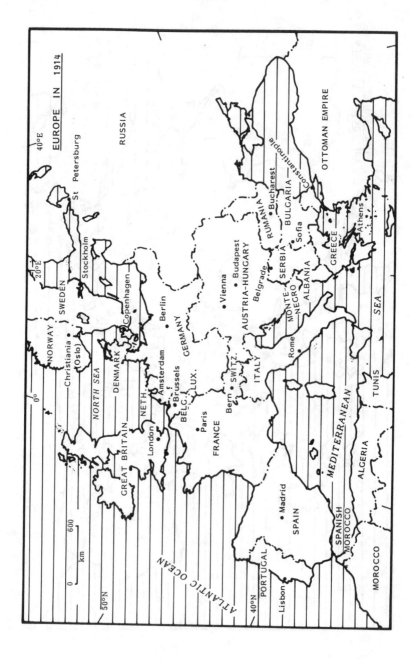

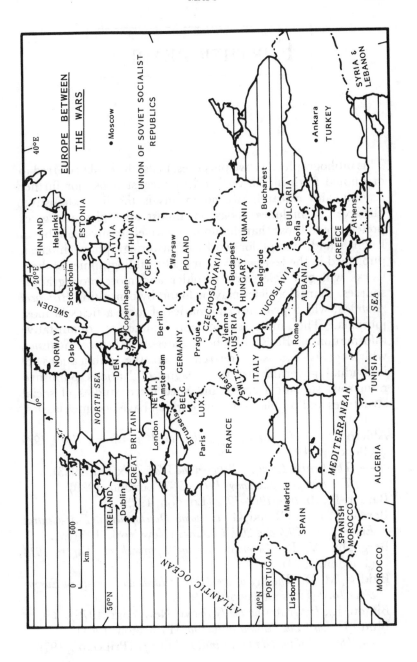

EUROPE BETWEEN THE WARS

FURTHER READING

This bibliography has two purposes: to list the books referred to or quoted from in the text and to suggest books for further reading and research. By no means is the list exhaustive. However, it includes books on almost all topics and gives preference to those that should be relatively easily available in English and, except for works of historiographical interest, published in the last twenty years. The bibliographies of these works will give references to older and more monographic sources. Journal articles may be found by consulting *Historical Abstracts*, which provides summaries of most articles in most journals. The most convenient source of quantitative information is B. R. Mitchell, *European Historical Statistics*, which gives extensive references to the publications of individual governments; the League of Nations published numerous statistical series and specialised studies of social structures and problems, many of which have become classics.

Aldcroft, D. H., *From Versailles to Wall Street, 1919–1929* (Berkeley, 1977).
——, *The British Economy Between the Wars* (Oxford, 1983).
——, *The European Economy, 1914–1980* (London, 1980).
Barker, E., *Austria, 1918–1972* (London, 1973).
Berend, I. T. and Rànki, G., *Economic Development in East-Central Europe in the 19th and 20th Centuries* (New York, 1974).
Berghahn, V. R., *Germany and the Approach of War in 1914* (London, 1973).
Biddiss, M. D., *The Age of the Masses: Ideas and Society in Europe Since 1870* (Harmondsworth, 1977).
Binion, R., *Hitler Among the Germans* (New York, 1976).
Blum, J., *Lord and Peasant in Russia*, (Princeton, 1961).
——, *The End of the Old Order in Rural Europe* (Princeton, 1978).

Bond, B., *War and Society in Europe, 1870–1970* (Leicester, 1983).

Bracher, K. D., *The German Dictatorship* (Harmondsworth, 1970).

Cardoza, A., *Agrarian Elites and the Origins of Italian Fascism: The Province of Bologna, 1901–1926* (Princeton, 1982).

Caron, F., *An Economic History of Modern France* (New York, 1979).

Carr, E. H., *The Bolshevik Revolution, 1917–1923*, 3 vols (London, 1950–53).

Carr, R., *Spain, 1808–1975* (Oxford, 1982).

Cipolla, C. (ed.), *The Fontana Economic History of Europe*, vols 4–6 (London, 1972–76).

Clark, M., *Modern Italy, 1871–1982* (London, 1984).

Clogg, R., *A Short History of Modern Greece* (Cambridge, 1979).

Clough, S., *The Economic History of Modern Italy* (New York, 1964).

Cohen, M., *I Was One of the Unemployed* (London, 1945).

Craig, G., *Germany, 1866–1945* (Oxford, 1978).

Davidson, B., *Let Freedom Come: Africa in Modern History* (Boston, 1978).

Davis, J. S., *The World between the Wars, 1919–39: An Economist's View* (London, 1975).

Delzell, C. F., *Mediterranean Fascism, 1919–1945* (1970).

Derry, T. K., *A History of Scandinavia* (London, 1979).

Deutscher, I., *Stalin: A Political Biography* (New York, 1979).

Dmytryshyn, B., *USSR: A Concise History* (New York, 1971).

Dobb, M. H., *Soviet Economic Development since 1917* (London, 1966).

Duus, P., *The Rise of Modern Japan* (Boston, 1976).

Erickson, C. (ed.), *Emigration from Europe, 1815–1914* (London, 1976).

Ferro, M., *The Great War, 1914–1918* (London, 1973).

Fitzpatrick, S., *The Russian Revolution, 1917–1932* (Oxford, 1984).

Foreman-Peck, J., *A History of the World Economy: International Economic Relations since 1850* (Brighton, 1983).

French, D., *British Economic and Strategic Planning, 1905–1915* (London, 1982).

Graves, R., *The Long Week-End: A Social History of Great Britain 1918–1939* (London, 1941).

Gulick, C. A., *Austria from Habsburg to Hitler*, 2 vols (Berkeley, 1948).

Habakkuk, H. J. and Postan, M. (eds) *Cambridge Economic History of Europe*, vol. VI: *The Industrial Revolutions and After* (Cambridge, 1965).

Hardach, G., *The First World War, 1914–1918* (Berkeley, 1977).

Hardach, K., *The Political Economy of Germany in the Twentieth Century* (Berkeley, 1976).

Headrick, D. R., *The Tools of Empire: Technology and European Imperialism in the Nineteenth Century* (New York, 1981).

Hertz, F., *The Economic Problems of the Danubian States: A Study in Economic Nationalism* (London, 1947).

Hilberg, R., *The Destruction of the European Jews* (Chicago, 1961).

Hughes, C., *Switzerland* (London, 1975).

Hughes, T. P., *Networks of Power: Electrification in Western Society, 1880–1930* (Baltimore, 1983).

Jelavich, B., *History of the Balkans*, vol. 2: *Twentieth Century* (Cambridge, 1983).

Kaiser, D. E., *Economic Diplomacy and the Origins of the Second World War: Germany, Britain, France and Eastern Europe, 1930–39* (Princeton, 1980).

Kaser, M. C. and Rodice, E. D. (eds), *The Economic History of Eastern Europe, 1919–1975* (Oxford, 1984).

Kemp, T., *The French Economy, 1919–39: The History of a Decline* (London, 1972).

Kenwood, A. G. and Lougheed, A. L., *The Growth of the International Economy 1820–1980* (London, 1983).

Keynes, J. M., *The General Theory of Employment, Interest and Money* (London, 1935 and various editions).

Keynes, M. (ed.), *Essays on John Maynard Keynes* (London, 1975).

Kiernan, V. G., *European Empires from Conquest to Collapse, 1815–1960* (Leicester, 1982).

Kindleberger, C. P., *The World in Depression, 1929–1939* (Berkeley, 1973).

Kossmann, E. H., *The Low Countries, 1780–1940* (Oxford, 1978).

Lampe, J. R. and Jackson, M. R., *Balkan Economic History, 1550–1950* (Bloomington, 1982).

Landes, D. S., *The Unbound Prometheus: Technological Change and Industrial Development in Europe from 1750 to the Present* (London, 1970).

Laqueur, W. (ed.), *Fascism: A Reader's Guide* (London, 1976).

Laue, T. H. von, *Sergei Witte and the Industrialization of Russia* (New York, 1963).

Lee W. R., *European Demography and Economic Growth* (London, 1978).

Lewis, J., *The Social History of Women: The Female Experience, 1870–1945* (Brighton, 1983).

Lewis, W. A., *Economic Survey, 1919–1939* (London, 1949).

——, *Growth and Fluctuations, 1870–1913* (London, 1978).

Lindert, P. H., *Key Currencies and Gold, 1900–1913* (Princeton, 1969).

Lotham, A. J. H., *The Depression and the Developing World, 1914–1939* (London, 1983).

Lyttelton, A., *The Seizure of Power: Fascism in Italy, 1919–1929* (London, 1973).

Macartney, C. A., *The Habsburg Empire, 1790–1918* (London, 1971).

Mack Smith, D., *Italy* (Ann Arbor, 1969).

——, *Mussolini: A Biography* (New York, 1982).

Maier, C. S., *Recasting Bourgeois Europe: Stabilisation in France, Germany and Italy in the Decade after World War I* (Princeton, 1975.

McCauley, M., *The Soviet Union since 1917* (New York, 1981).

McKay, J. P., *Pioneers for Profit: Foreign Entrepreneurship and Russian Industrialisation, 1885–1913* (Chicago, 1970).

Marques, A. H. de Oliveira, *History of Portugal*, vol. 2: *From Empire to Corporate State* (New York, 1976).

Marwick, A., *The Deluge: British Society and the First World War* (London, 1973).

May, A. J., *The Passing of the Hapsburg Monarchy, 1914–1918* (Philadelphia, 1966).

Mayer, A. J., *The Persistance of the Old Regime: Europe to the Great War* (London, 1981).

Mendelsohn, E., *Jews of East Central Europe between the World Wars* (Bloomington, 1983).

Milward, A. S., *War, Economy and Society, 1939–1945* (Berkeley, 1977).

Milward, A. S. and Saul, S. B., *The Development of the Economies of Continental Europe, 1850–1914* (Cambridge, Mass., 1977).

Nolte, E., *Three Faces of Fascism* (New York, 1963).

Nove, A., *An Economic History of the U.S.S.R.* (Harmondsworth, 1982).

Orwell, G., *The Road to Wigan Pier* (London, 1937).

Pendle, G., *A History of Latin America* (Harmondsworth, 1976).

Platt, D. C. M. (ed.), *Business Imperialism, 1840–1930* (Oxford, 1977).

Pluvier, J., *South-East Asia from Colonialism to Independence* (Kuala Lumpur, 1974).

Pollard, S., *The Development of the British Economy, 1914–1980* (London, 1983).

——, (ed.), *The Gold Standard and Employment Policies between the Wars* (London, 1970).

Pulzer, P. G. J., *The Rise of Political Anti-Semitism in Germany and Austria* (New York, 1964).

Renshaw, P., *Nine Days that Shook Britain: The 1926 General Strike* (London, 1975).

Riemen, E. S. and Fait, J. C., *European Woman: A Documentary History, 1789–1945* (New York, 1980).

Rogger, H., *Russia in the Age of Modernisation and Revolution, 1881–1917* (London, 1983).

Rothschild, J., *East Central Europe between the Two World Wars* (Seattle, 1974).

Sayers, R. S., *Monetary Policy in the 1920s* (London, 1970).

Singer, C. J. *et al.* (ed.), *A History of Technology* (Oxford, 1954–78).

Speer, A., *Inside the Third Reich* (London, 1970).

Spulber, N., *The State and Economic Development in Eastern Europe* (New York, 1966).

Stavrianos, L. S., *The Balkans since 1453* (New York, 1959).

Stearns, P., *European Society in Upheaval: Social History since 1750* (New York, 1975).

Sugar, P., *Native Fascism in the Successor States* (Santa Barbara, 1971).

Sylvère, A., *Toinou: Le Cri d'un Enfant Auvergnat* (Paris, 1980).

Taylor, A. J. P., *The Origins of the Second World War* (London, 1969).

Teichova, A., *International Business and Central Europe, 1918–39* (Leicester, 1983).

Thomas, H., *The Spanish Civil War* (Harmondsworth, 1977).

Vicens Vives, J., *Approaches to the History of Spain* (Berkeley, 1972).

Webb, R. K., *Modern England: From the Eighteenth Century to the Present* (London, 1980).

Webster, R. A., *Industrial Imperialism in Italy, 1908–1915* (Berkeley, 1975).

Wee, H. van der (ed.), *The Great Depression Revisited: Essays on the Economics of the Thirties* (The Hague, 1972).

Weiner, M. J., *English Culture and the Decline of the Industrial Spirit* (Cambridge, 1981).

Weiss, J., *The Fascist Tradition: Radical Right Wing Extremism in Modern Europe* (New York, 1981).

Woodruff, W., *The Impact of Western Man: A Study of Europe's Role in the World Economy, 1750–1960* (London, 1966).

Wright, G., *France in Modern Times* (Chicago, 1974).

——, *The Ordeal of Total War, 1939–1945* (New York, 1968).

Zeldin, T., *France, 1848–1945* (Oxford, 1979).

INDEX